# Developing Theatre in the Global South

# Developing Theatre in the Global South

*Institutions, networks, experts*

Edited by Nic Leonhardt and
Christopher B. Balme

First published in 2024 by
UCL Press
University College London
Gower Street
London WC1E 6BT

Available to download free: www.uclpress.co.uk

ISBN: 978-1-80008-576-3 (Hbk)
ISBN: 978-1-80008-575-6 (Pbk)
ISBN: 978-1-80008-574-9 (PDF)
ISBN: 978-1-80008-577-0 (epub)
DOI: https://doi.org/10.14324/111.9781800085749

# Contents

**Part I: (Un)sustainable Institutions: building a theatrical epistemic community**

**Part II: Technopolitics**

# List of figures and tables

## Figures

## Table

# List of contributors

**Nic Leonhardt** is a theatre scholar and a writer. Her scholarly activities focus on global theatre history at the turn of the twentieth century, inter arts, and the history of theatre in nineteenth- and twentieth-century Iran. Her latest monograph, *Theatre Across Oceans: Mediators of transatlantic exchange, 1890–1925*, was published in 2021 by Palgrave Macmillan. She is joint president of the International Association of Libraries, Museums, Archives and Documentation Centres of the Performing Arts (SIBMAS), and is currently a fellow at the Käte Hamburger Research Centre global dis:connect in Munich.

**Christopher B. Balme** is professor of theatre studies at the University of Munich. His publications include *Decolonizing the Stage: Theatrical syncretism and post-colonial drama* (1999), *Pacific Performances: Theatricality and cross-cultural encounter in the South Seas* (2007), *The Cambridge Introduction to Theatre Studies* (2008), *The Theatrical Public Sphere* (2014) and *The Globalization of Theatre 1870–1930: The theatrical networks of Maurice E. Bandmann* (2020). He was principal investigator of the European Research Council advanced grant project 'Developing theatre: building expert networks for theatre in emerging countries after 1945', and is currently codirector of the Käte Hamburger Research Centre, global dis:connect (globaldisconnect.org).

**Ziad Adwan** is a theatre maker and academic with a PhD in theatre studies from Royal Holloway, University of London. Ziad's work comprises playwriting, directing, teaching and writing for academic journals. He is currently based in Germany and was affiliated with the German Research Foundation-funded project 'Global theatre histories' and the European Research Council-funded project 'Developing theatre: building expert networks for theatre in emerging countries after 1945' at the University of Munich. Ziad cofounded the Tanween Theatre Company, and has produced theatre and other performance projects. He is also a consultant at Mamdouh Adwan Publishing House.

**Clara de Andrade** is an actor, teacher and researcher in theatre arts. Her main field of research is Augusto Boal and the transnationality of the

Theatre of the Oppressed. In 2020 she was a visiting fellow at the Centre for Global Theatre History as part of the 'Developing theatre' project at the University of Munich. She is currently conducting postdoctoral research at the Federal University of the State of Rio de Janeiro in the postgraduate programme in performing arts, funded by the FAPERJ foundation. She is also an international consultant for the University of Exeter project 'Performing resistance: theatre and performance in 21st-century workers' movements'.

**Bernardo Fonseca Machado** holds a PhD in social anthropology from the University of São Paulo, and studied as a visiting student at Princeton University. Between 2019 and 2023 he conducted postdoctoral research at the department of anthropology at the State University of Campinas (Unicamp) investigating notions of truth in theatre regarding gender, sexuality, race and the arts. He is the author of the book *Discourses on American Musical Theatre Between São Paulo and New York* and a member of the research groups APSA (Unicamp), and NUMAS and Etnohistoria (both University of São Paulo).

**Gustavo Guenzburger** is an artist, activist, teacher and researcher in theatre arts. His main fields of interest are transnationality and modes of production in theatre. In 2020 he was a visiting fellow at the Centre for Global Theatre History as part of the 'Developing theatre' research project at the University of Munich. He is currently conducting postdoctoral research at the Federal University of the State of Rio de Janeiro in the postgraduate programme in performing arts, funded by the FAPERJ foundation. He is also an international consultant for the University of Exeter project 'Performing resistance: theatre and performance in 21st-century workers' movements'.

**Abdul Karim Hakib** is a lecturer at the department of theatre arts at the University of Ghana. He received his PhD from the University of Munich. He is an artist, director, and a theatre for development and applied theatre practitioner and researcher, specialising in the use of culture and the creative arts for sustainable development. His research interests are theatre for development, applied theatre, performance and new media, institutions, decoloniality, organisational development, and sustainable development. With Christopher B. Balme he coedited *Theatre for Development in Africa: Historical and institutional perspectives* (2023).

**Viviana Iacob** is an independent researcher. Her work was supported through the years by prestigious fellowships programmes, including the Käte Hamburger Research Centre global dis:connect and the Humboldt Foundation. Her research interests centre on Eastern European theatre history after 1945, Cold War internationalism and the role of international organisations in the cultural diplomacy of state socialist regimes.

**Hasibe Kalkan** teaches at the department of theatre criticism and dramaturgy at Istanbul University, where she heads the department. Her research interests include documentary theatre, intercultural theatre, and theatre and migration. Kalkan has worked as a dramaturge at the Istanbul State Theater, and writes theatre reviews for various daily newspapers and magazines.

**Gideon Ime Morison** is an independent researcher, scholar, creative artist and cultural critic. He completed his PhD in the European Research Council project 'Developing theatre: building expert networks for the theatre in emerging countries after 1945' at the University of Munich's Institute of Theatre Studies. His thesis 'From Renaissance to Festivalisation: Festival networks and the institutional legacies of selected Pan-African cultural productions, 1977–2019' investigated the intersection of global history and expert networks in the development of African postcolonial festivals such as FESTAC '77 and PANAFEST. Formerly the acting head of theatre arts at the Federal College of Education (Technical), Omoku, Morison's research straddles media and theatre history, criticism, development communication, festivals, and comparative cultural studies, and has been published in the *Journal of Global Theatre History*, the *Nigerian Theatre Journal*, the *Parnassus* and *Banchi*.

**Rashna Darius Nicholson** is assistant professor of theatre studies at the University of Warwick. Her first monograph, *The Colonial Public and the Parsi Stage: The making of the theatre of empire (1853–1893)*, won the Theatre Library Association's George Freedley Memorial Award, and was shortlisted for both the TaPRA David Bradby Monograph Prize and the ASTR Barnard Hewitt Award. Her recent work has featured in *Theatre Research International*, *Theatre Survey*, *TDR: The Drama Review*, *The Routledge Companion to Theatre and Performance Historiography* and *The Methuen Drama Handbook of Theatre History and Historiography*.

**Judith Rottenburg** is an art historian with a focus on modern and contemporary art. She completed her PhD dissertation on the entangled art history of post-independence Senegal at the University of Munich in 2017. Following a fellowship at the German Center for Art History in Paris, she worked as a research associate on the European Research Council-funded project 'Developing theatre: building expert networks for theatre in emerging countries after 1945' at the University of Munich, conducting research on postcolonial Pan-African festivals. At present she is a member of the research group 'Bilderfahrzeuge: Aby Warburg's legacy and the future of iconology' at the Humboldt University of Berlin.

**Rebecca Sturm** is a theatre scholar focusing on German theatre history and its international relations in the postwar period. She was a doctoral researcher on the European Research Council project 'Developing theatre: building expert networks for theatre in emerging countries after 1945' at the University of Munich. In 2022 she successfully defended her dissertation, 'Theatre Experts for the Third World: East Germany's ITI and the globalization of theatre in the Cold War'. She is currently part of the research department at the German Literature Archive in Marbach.

# Preface

This volume contains a cross-section of papers and results arising from the research project 'Developing theatre: building expert networks for theatre in emerging countries after 1945' funded by the European Research Council (ERC) from 2016 to 2021 (grant number 694559). The goal of the project was elaborating an institutional approach to the historiography of postcolonial theatre, with a particular focus on the involvement of internationally coordinated development and modernisation programmes in the postwar period. The research programme introduced the concepts of epistemic community, expert networks and technopolitics to theatre historical research as a means to historicise theatre within transnational and transcultural paradigms, and examine its imbrication with globalisation processes.

When you start to delve into this historical period, the significance of the role played by cultural education, and theatre in particular, becomes clear. Applying for an ERC advanced grant is a complex undertaking involving a principal investigator and postdoctoral and doctoral researchers, as well as administrative support. The more we became immersed in the topic, the clearer it became that we could only conduct an inquiry into the development of theatre by inviting young scholars from other regions to examine theatre history transnationally. Hence, in addition to the 'normal' set up, we acknowledge the contributions of our associated research fellows from Syria, Brazil, Turkey, Romania and elsewhere, some of whom are represented in this volume. Their regional expertise led to crucial insights into developments the core team could not cover. The contributions in this volume come from fellows and colleagues from other countries who were not directly involved in the project, but who contributed their expertise via workshops and presentations in the orbit of the project, and thus contributed to a further broadening of horizons.

The developing theatre project has produced several single-author monographs, some of them still in the process of publication. This volume, however, is a collaborative effort, presenting results and insights arising from five to six years of collective deliberation.

# Acknowledgements

We would like to take this opportunity to thank some of those who accompanied us, with impressive knowledge and composure, through the not-always easy administrative process of running an ERC project. Special thanks go to Jonas Tillinger, the University of Munich research officer responsible for ERC projects – his steady hand averted many a crisis. A special mention to Christina Lagao, who handled the administration of the project.

No thanks go to COVID-19, which caused significant disruption in the final two years of the project, when field trips, conferences and meetings were cancelled, archives closed and fellowships terminated, and all academic life went online. It is a testimony to the flexibility of the PhD students working on the project that they were able to adapt and to complete their dissertations.

We would like to thank the ERC, which demonstrated great flexibility in its responses to changing circumstances. At UCL Press we received excellent guidance throughout the production process from Chris Penfold and Jonathan Dore.

As is often the case, when research projects come to an end it feels as if they are epistemically unfinished. The questioning, creation of knowledge and critical reflections are not final. Thus, with this volume, we extend an invitation for further research on the topic of developing theatre. Knowledge is dynamic, epistemes are always in flux. Development never stops.

# Introduction
## Christopher B. Balme and Nic Leonhardt

Today, the stubborn divide between an affluent Global North and a relatively undeveloped Global South applies not only to indicators of health, education and income, but also to access to cultural and artistic institutions, most noticeably to professional theatre of the kind available in almost all developed nations. Access to theatre is very low on current government agendas, if it appears at all. This was not always the case, however. For approximately four decades, roughly between 1950 and 1990, theatre was seen as a key element not only of cultural development but also of world peace. During this period there was a significant investment of financial and human resources on both sides of the Iron Curtain. Promoting theatre and building professional theatre institutions became a goal of American philanthropic organisations, Eastern bloc assistance to aligned and non-aligned states, and government cultural policy in some newly decolonised nations. Against a background of newly emerging postcolonial states, international theatre organisations were formed, university theatre departments established, hundreds of grants dispensed, national theatres built and international arts festivals organised to showcase a new generation of artists from emerging countries. By the mid-1980s much of this efflorescence in the Global South had passed: attempts to create permanent ensembles had failed, theatres had turned to hosting mainly folkloric performances, leading artists had emigrated and international funding was being channelled into theatre for development projects with highly instrumental ends. While this narrative is perforce a simplification of varied processes and myriad differences, its broad thrust is accurate.

This book examines the complex transnational processes that led to an institutionalisation of theatre in emerging nations on an unprecedented scale. It is linked to a European Research Council project, 'Developing theatre: building expert networks for theatre in emerging countries after 1945', which undertook a fundamental re-examination of the historiography of theatre against the background of internationally coordinated development and modernisation programmes that linked funding organisations, artists, universities and governments in networks of theatrical expertise.[1] The authors of the contributions in this volume were closely associated with the ERC project from 2016 as senior researchers, doctoral students, affiliates and fellows; it was the shared, transcultural exchange between the authors on the complex thematic field of developing theatre that facilitated its epistemological reconsideration.

## Contested concepts

This book and the research project from which it draws are located in a highly contested semantic field. Terms such as 'development' and 'modernisation' – once watchwords of postwar optimism – are today often seen as the problem rather than the solution in terms of the gaping and persistent inequalities between Global North and South. In the early 1990s, four decades after Harry S. Truman heralded the 'development century' in the fourth objective of his 1949 inaugural address, Wolfgang Sachs announced in his influential *The Development Dictionary: A guide to knowledge as power* that 'the idea of development stands like a ruin in the intellectual landscape', and it was time 'to write its obituary'.[2] Three years later Arturo Escobar published his controversial critique of the term 'development', *Encountering Development: The making and unmaking of the Third World* (1995), in which he brought to bear Foucauldian discourse analysis in uncovering the epistemological structures behind 'development thinking', which functioned, he argued, as a screen for capitalist economics and Western domination. Such critiques led in turn to 'post-development' thinking, which sought to define discursive and praxeological strategies for transcending the development dilemma.[3]

Developmentalism, defined here as the development ideology, is a direct outgrowth of modernisation thinking, which began in the nineteenth century and dominated policy on newly independent nations on both sides of the Iron Curtain. The level of industrialisation and institutional diversity characteristic of Global North countries was regarded in teleological terms as the natural goal of all nations. In the 1950s, 1960s and 1970s, a series of metatheories were proposed that sought to accelerate the progress of newly decolonised nations towards this goal. Interventions such as Walt Rostow's *The Stages of Economic Growth: A non-communist manifesto* (1960), with its famous five phases, progressing from traditional societies to 'mass consumption', or Paul Rosenstein-Rodan's 1957 notion of the 'big push for development', gained dominance through a unique combination of academic research, policy-generating think-tanks and proximity to political power.[4] These monolithic concepts of modernisation eventually gave way to more nuanced understandings. At the end of the twentieth century sociologist S. N. Eisenstadt argued that the project of modernity should be seen in terms of culturally varied responses that he termed 'multiple modernities'.[5] He disputed the claim that Western patterns of modernity were the 'authentic' ones, while conceding that 'they enjoy historical precedence and continue to be a basic reference point for others'.[6] However, in the period in focus here – roughly 1950 to 1990 – the terms modernisation and development still enjoyed considerable discursive power, and even carried an air of inevitability. The central issue to be resolved among emerging nations was the relationship between existing cultural traditions and the exigencies of modernisation, which led to countless essays and books on the putative, antonymic concepts of tradition and modernity.

The aim of this volume is to explore how theatre became caught up in these debates. It examines postcolonial theatre from an institutional perspective. This institutional approach structures the volume, whose three sections define different aspects of institutionalism.

## Part I. (Un)sustainable institutions: building a theatrical epistemic community

'(Un)sustainable institutions' refers to the idea that in the postwar period institutional frameworks were promoted and sometimes realised with the aim of enabling a professional theatre culture. In this context, theatre needs to be investigated as an institution, in this case meaning a complex of norms regulating social action. Institutions invariably operate on the basis of laws, and affect collectives as much as individuals. The special dynamics of institutional normativity in the arts may be investigated, for example through the introduction of pedagogical institutions for artistic training. Whether privately organised or state run, such institutions exhibit by definition a degree of normativity and discursivity that permits us to examine precisely how local interpretations of mainly Western cultural practices were implemented. By the same token, we must ask how Western conceptions of training theatre artists – mainly actors, singers and dancers, but also directors, designers and others – were seen as being a part of cultural modernisation.

If we are to examine theatrical institutions we must define what we mean by 'institution', a notoriously difficult concept to pin down. Neo-institutionalist theory distinguishes between an institutional and an organisational level. The economist Douglass North famously described institutions as 'the rules of the game' in societies, and the 'constraints that shape human interaction'.[7] These rules or frameworks are embodied in organisations, so there exists continual interdependency between the abstract level of institutional frames and rules and the day-to-day maintenance of them in and through organisations. While in everyday speech we tend to use the terms institution and organisation inter-changeably, on the level of theory and analysis it is important to distinguish them.

Although we experience theatre through specific organisations, these organisations are largely influenced by institutional rules and frameworks, which change over time. For example, the common agreement that theatre is as an art form like painting, sculpture, literature and some forms of cinema is by no means a given but rather the result of processes of institutionalisation, the most significant of which is public investment in the arts. The touchstone is usually the call for a national theatre or its equivalent. This emerged from a global debate, which began in the nineteenth century, focused on classical music and the visual arts that sociologist and neo-institutional theorist Paul DiMaggio, looking at the US, termed the 'sacralization of the high culture model'. But, as he has noted, theatre, in the US at least, did not lend itself to the transcendent, quasi-religious discourse employed to sacralise classical music or the visual arts: 'Of all the art forms to which the high culture models extended, the stage was the most improbable; the most commer-cially successful; the one least in need, as it was organised during the nineteenth century, of elite patronage.'[8]

The focus of this book is the period after the Second World War, when theatre of the sacralised, high-culture variety was promulgated throughout the world, particularly in the newly decolonising and decolonised world. It was a process heavily imbricated with Cold War developments, and one primarily interested in creating institutions, or more precisely organisations, that would outlive individual artists and groups, although the latter were seen as conduits through which the process of institution building could be initiated. If we want to chart how theatrical institutions were instituted in postcolonial contexts, we must study the intersection of different institutional and organisational networks, which includes the establishment of professional organisations.

Professionalism is closely linked to the idea of belonging to and participating in the theatrical epistemic community. Coined by political scientist Peter M. Haas, the term 'epistemic communities' refers to networks of knowledge-based experts who advise policymakers and governments, usually on questions of scientific and technical complexity.[9] Epistemic communities manifest a high degree of international organisation in the form of professional associations, conferences, expositions and learned publications that are seldom restricted to a single country. For this reason, epistemic communities have become a favoured object in transnational historiography of the postwar period.[10] Although the concept was developed in the context of international relations, and most research into epistemic communities has focused on cases involving a high degree of technical scientific expertise, such as nuclear disarmament or environmental issues, the concept can be extended to cultural phenomena.[11] We argue that theatre artists, scholars, critics and pedagogues in the first half of the twentieth century saw themselves as members of such a community, and that they subsequently aspired to professionalisation, developed organisational structures and formed transnational networks of the kind that distinguish scientific and technical epistemic communities. The theatrical epistemic community constituted itself to promote a practice of theatre that cut across Cold War rivalries and coincided with decolonisation. It could also be argued that the same epistemic community ultimately disintegrated, splintering into many different subgroups with little or no international cohesion. The origins of the postwar theatrical epistemic community lie in the international movement known as theatrical modernism, whose foundational belief was the idea that theatre is an art form and not just a commercial enterprise, and hence of high cultural and, by extension, public value.

The introduction of sustainable, professional theatrical institutions in the Global South after 1945 was supported by a combination of national imperatives, philanthropy and international organisations such as the International Theatre Institute (ITI). The ITI was founded in 1948 by UNESCO on the initiative of UNESCO's first director general Julian Huxley and the playwright J. B. Priestley. The essays in this volume examine under what institutional conditions theatre – generally seen as a force for good – can be implemented and sustained. What role can the academy (understood in the broadest sense as encompassing university theatre departments and conservatories) play in the process of sustainable institution building? Individual chapters will highlight specific aspects and examples of institution building.

In the aftermath of the Second World War, amid growing superpower tension, the US embarked on a massive soft-power initiative to counter Soviet influence. During what is known today as the cultural Cold War, for the first time in the US's history substantial state funding for the arts was channelled abroad, not only through the State Department but also via covert channels. The latter were mainly funded and coordinated by the CIA, which established a network of front organisations to dispense American largesse. The most well-known of these was the Congress for Cultural Freedom (CCF), which played a central role in apportioning US funds in the 1950s and 1960s. Although mainly active in Western Europe, it also promoted the arts and literature in some developing countries.[12] American philanthropic organisations, especially the Rockefeller, Ford and Carnegie foundations, assisted in this hearts-and-minds war. While these foundations were not directly subordinate to the State Department or the CIA, their aims – establishing liberal democracy across the world – were often congruent, and the personnel interchangeable. From 1950 onwards, American philanthropic organisations channelled funds into developing countries to support the arts, especially theatre, specifically by building infra-structure, implementing drama programmes and supporting promising artists and scholars. The connections between philanthropic organisa-tions, American foreign and cultural policy, academic institutions, and individual artists and scholars were multitudinous and often difficult to grasp. Several chapters in this volume engage with philanthropy. Rashna Nicholson's essay (Chapter 4) analyses the involvement of international philanthropy in the Occupied Palestinian Territories after the 1993 Oslo Accords (although the first philanthropic contributions date from the mid-1980s). She argues that the 'NGOisation' of cultural development led ultimately to a phantom sovereignty dependent on foreign experts and funding agendas.

The International Theatre Institute (ITI) and the International Union for Puppetry Arts (UNIMA) played a central role in shaping the global theatre community during the Cold War. They contributed to the internationalisation of various theatre cultures during the postwar period, and as such are ideal subjects for a global theatre history of the Cold War. These two international organisations (IOs) built world networks by enabling theatre communities in the Global North, East and South to establish connections, despite the ideological divisions of the Cold War. In Chapter 1, Viviana Iacob and Rebecca Sturm show how the history of these IOs provides a means to understand how the Global North, East and South contributed to the theatrical epistemic community in the second half of the twentieth century. The chapter also proposes alternative trajectories for rewriting local theatre histories, and focuses on the response of UNIMA and the ITI to Cold War divisions and decolonisation by looking at the strategies put in place to establish a common ground for debate between the East and the West. Iacob and Sturm analyse the projects that came out of this modus vivendi, and their sustainability at both local and global levels.

Festivals have been cited as an important aspect of institutionalised religion in traditional African and indigenous societies. However, following colonisation, and particularly colonisation's extended influence from the late nineteenth century, festivals as a religious and cultural phenomenon underwent radical transformation in Africa. Not only were they reconstituted as a platform for the celebration of African identity and heritage, but also as spaces for protest, the acquisition of agency, and personal, community and cultural interaction. In Chapter 2, Gideon I. Morison and Judith Rottenburg examine selected cultural festivals staged on the African continent in the 1960s and 1970s as manifestations of a theatrical organisational field whose epistemic community, networks and modes of funding shaped both the nature of artistic practices within the field, and long-term institutional developments in the performing arts across the hosting African territories.

Theatre for development (TfD) as a theatre form sui generis emerged in the 1970s out of various activities and under differing labels. Theatre in education, popular theatre and community theatre predated TfD, and either reformed around the new term or contributed particular techniques or institutional contexts. In Chapter 3 Abdul Karim Hakib explores how these diverse practices were formed into an 'organisational field', a key term of neo-institutional theory that refers to sets of organisations distinguished by professionalisation, common goals and a high degree of isomorphism. The chapter traces how TfD consolidated itself institutionally through a series of seminal workshops in Zimbabwe (1983), Cameroon (1984) and Nigeria (1986), all of which involved practitioners and scholars from many African countries, as well as substantial support from foreign countries and international organisations, such as the ITI and UNESCO.

# Part II. Technopolitics

Technopolitics is a term used to connect the vectors of development thinking, the Cold War and decolonisation. Existing research into techno-politics has emphasised complex technical and scientific initiatives, such as hydroelectric dams and nuclear power, as they played out in the developing world.[13] We adapt the term to define theatre, especially of the modernist variety, as a technology introduced to or imposed on cultures where it was often an unfamiliar cultural practice. The term enables an examination of the 'unpredictable power effects of technical assemblages',[14] which could be applied to the construction of national theatres as well as to the intro-duction of theatre for development practices. The essays in the second part of the book expand the notion of technopolitics to include cultural infrastructure as being subject to the same imperatives as technical and scientific progress, whereby technology, broadly understood, is not just a tool but also a mode of politics. Through the construction of national theatres, the establishment of theatre academies and even the introduc-tion of new pedagogical tools such as the workshop, the Global North intervened in and promoted forms of cultural infrastructure that were deemed adaptable to any environment.

From the 1950s onwards several national theatres were established in sub-Saharan Africa. Their construction involved British colonial admin-istrations, American philanthropy and Chinese developmental aid. These buildings, still standing, bear the often literal scars of African history in the age of post-colony. While each theatre has its own particular history, they share certain common experiences that together can be read as an allegory of postcolonial history. The essay by Christopher Balme in Chapter 5 proposes a narrative bracketed by the seemingly contradic-tory terms 'modular modernity' and 'cultural heritage' – modernity with its promise of the new, cultural heritage with its ideology of preserva-tion. While apparently oppositional, these terms can be seen as two points on a continuum of Western and Asian influence on the African continent. There is a direct through-line connecting modular modernity with cultural heritage discourse of the post-Cold War period. The main example is the National Theatre in Uganda, which can read as a test case of shifting discourses and agendas in the context of the cultural Cold War and its long-term implications.

In Chapter 6, Ziad Adwan explores how his alma mater and former employer, the Higher Institute of Dramatic Arts (HIDA) in Damascus, achieved an exceptional degree of prestige in Syrian cultural life, and has been instrumental in building a theatrical infrastructure in Syria, where the medium was long regarded as foreign and incompatible with indigenous culture. Although operating under a dictatorship in a conservative country, HIDA enjoyed an unusual degree of curricular autonomy and free expression in a country that repressed other cultural and educational sectors. Based on the influential Russian Institute of Theatre Arts in Moscow, which in turn served as an institutional role model in many socialist countries, HIDA sought to integrate practical theatre training with the academic study of theatre. However, this created a difficult situation for theatre intellectuals and scholars. Syrian intellectuals were challenged by several factors – as in many socialist countries during the Cold War – chief of which was the ability to confront the status quo without being accused of disloyalty. Yet while HIDA became 'the place of the intellectuals' at a national level, the practice of critical intellectual inquiry by scholars and artists engendered controversies inside the institute between the acting and theatre studies departments. Adwan argues that the rise of commercial television and the success of accomplished alumni gave the institute its prominent position in Syria and in many other Arabic-speaking countries. These two seemingly antithetical developments – the rise of serialised television drama and the changing status of the intellectual – played a significant role in shaping the institute's image and curricula, and in determining perceptions of the critical intellectual in Syria.

Chapter 7, by Christopher Balme and Nic Leonhardt, explores how the workshop, one of the most ubiquitous terms and practices in the contemporary cultural sector, has its origins in early twentieth-century experimental theatre. The essay traces the workshop's shift from the nineteenth-century shop floor, where it was replaced by industrial factories, to pre-First World War university seminars in the US. George Pierce Baker's playwriting class at Harvard – the famous 47 Workshop – created a model for a theatre laboratory that slowly gained a following outside the academy. From there the workshop became a catchword for experimentation in the theatre and in the new media – radio and television. The chapter focuses on how American philanthropic organisations promoted the workshop in the 1950s and 1960s, both at home and abroad. The history and dissemination of the term and practice can be traced to a particular conjunction of factors within the US academy and philanthropy, both of which supported the rise of modernist theatre. This led in turn to a global distribution of workshop thinking. In this way a particular epistemic format, developed by and associated with non-conventional theatre forms, permeated contemporary thinking and pedagogical practice.

Since the middle of the twentieth century, several Broadway shows have been transported to Brazil. Between the 1960s and 1970s, musicals such as *Hello Dolly* (1966), *Hair* (1969) and *Man of La Mancha* (1972) built, in a contested way, an international theatre in Brazil. These pioneering productions introduced, albeit precariously, new forms of staging, new pedagogical techniques and an American repertoire to cities like São Paulo and Rio de Janeiro. In the 1980s, at the end of the Cold War, contextual changes enabled the expansion and stabilisation of this transnational flow of shows, to the point of constituting a prominent theatre market in Brazil. Following urban reform in New York, and the entrance of large entertainment companies such as Disney into Broadway, the strategy for exporting Broadway musicals to cities around the globe was consolidated into a business model. In Brazil the production of these shows was facilitated by new cultural legislation inspired by the US tax-exemption model, and through the expertise of a Mexican entertainment company with multinational operations in musicals. In Chapter 8, Gustavo Guenzburger and Bernardo Fonseca Machado explore the transnational networks that enabled the creation of a market for Broadway shows in Brazil in the second half of the twentieth century. They focus particularly on the effects of a law passed in 1991, known as *Lei Rouanet* after its initiator, that allowed companies to claim tax deductions on cultural funding, thereby shifting the coordinates of cultural policy to corporations. The essay's examination of the flows of techniques, people, formats and legislation reveals the contradictions and asymmetries of this cultural transit process and its problematic consequences.

## Part III. Expert networks

Technopolitics is typically enacted by networks of experts. The third section of the book maps the complexities and agency of such expert networks as they entered the arena of theatre. Within the expert network paradigm, experts are employed to act within networks centred on projects and policies, such as the construction of theatre buildings, and the establishment of national theatres and theatre academies. Following expert networks is both a subject and a method, the latter involving the reconstruction of expert networks in order to better understand the interrelated (path) dependencies that contributed to the emergence and sedimentation of particular theatrical practices and institutions. Such networks provide access to the nuts and bolts of institution building beyond the government policy papers, allegiances, dependencies and money flows that ultimately allow institutions to be instated.

The biographical essays in the third section of the book portray key experts who were active in the field of theatre mainly in the 1960s and 1970s. Methodologically, some of the essays employ network theory to demonstrate the high degree of interconnectedness between individuals and the organisations that facilitated their work. While the emphasis is on individuals who contributed to institution building as much as on personal artistic achievements, the essays attempt to contextualise individual achievements in the wider field of collective agency fostered by institutional infrastructures.

A driving force behind these expert networks was the Rockefeller Foundation, which for more than two decades after the Second World War supported theatre both inside and outside the US. In 1965 the foundation published a report on the performing arts, their impact on American society and strategies of supporting their economic blossoming. Entitled 'The performing arts: problems and prospects', the alleged motivation for the report, which was preceded in 1963 by a survey of American citizens, was recognition of theatre's potential for social and cultural good:

> Only in our time have we begun to recognize the arts as a community concern to be placed alongside our long-accepted responsibilities for libraries, museums, hospitals, and schools. In the two decades since World War I, our society has achieved material advances almost beyond belief. Yet man increasingly realizes that meeting basic physical needs falls far short of attaining the end objectives of life – the emotional, intellectual, and aesthetic satisfactions that constitute his higher needs. The arts today are more fully appreciated as one means by which man can achieve the satisfactions he seeks, and therefore are important, even essential, to the human mind and spirit.[15]

It is noteworthy that the Rockefeller Foundation devoted itself to supporting theatre, particularly in the two decades following the Second World War. Neither before nor after this period did the foundation invest in the performing arts to a comparable degree. In the US it was individuals and community theatres, and outside it was predominantly directors and theatre pedagogues, who benefited from Rockefeller Foundation funding.

In Chapter 9 Nic Leonhardt focuses on the Filipino playwright, director and pedagogue Severino Montano. With the help of a Rockefeller

Foundation grant for 'the development of drama in the Philippine Islands', Montano travelled the US and Europe in the 1950s, targeting theatres and people from which he hoped to gain knowledge for his theatre work in his home city of Manila. Although the Rockefeller Foundation's funding for Montano was relatively modest, it continued at a steady rate for a decade, supporting his theatre academy in Manila as well as his Arena Theatre, for which he had the ambitious plan to set up branches in Manila's more rural surrounding areas. The chapter illuminates Montano's professional development on the basis of the Rockefeller grant, as well as the foundation's funding policy in the field of theatre in the US and abroad.

Against the background of Turkey's accession to NATO in 1952, the US provided Turkey not just with military hardware but with cultural assistance via organisations such as the Fulbright Program and the Rockefeller and Ford foundations. The Rockefeller Foundation supported the training of young artists, and donated a total of US$792,000 to purchase new equipment and develop human resources. An important beneficiary of this funding was the scholar and critic Metin And, the subject of Hasibe Kalkan's contribution (Chapter 10). And began his arts career as a theatre critic, and taught theatre and cultural history at the Theatre Institute in Ankara. With his more than 50 books, and as a founding member of the department of theatre studies at Ankara University, he created a foundation for the emerging discipline of theatre studies in Turkey. He campaigned for a theatre that focused on Turkey's theatrical traditions as well as on Western models. And made important contributions to Ottoman and Turkish theatre history with his detailed research and publications, which are still standard works. He was also active internationally, teaching Turkish theatre at Justus Liebig University Giessen, and at the universities of Tokyo and New York. His work centred on reappraising the influence of Western theatre on Turkish theatre, while at the same time making traditional Turkish theatre – such as shadow theatre, meddah and Karagöz – better known abroad.

In Chapter 11, Clara de Andrade and Christopher Balme consider how the transnational networks of the Theatre of the Oppressed (TO) contributed to its institutionalisation and prevalence as one of the most practised theatrical methodologies worldwide. In order to understand the expansion of the method, developed by Augusto Boal, into a transnational network, the chapter offers definitions of the terms 'institutionalisation' and 'network' before providing a brief review of the history of the TO, its adaptation to French and Brazilian cultural policies, and the importance of TO centres to this process. The method's ability to adapt to diverse contexts and cultures, and especially to the social development field, demonstrate that the global network of the TO, more than just promulgating a theatrical method, became a vehicle for the circulation of policies connected to the idea of cultural democracy.

Chapter 12 examines the career of Cecile Guidote, who founded the Philippine Educational Theatre Association (PETA) in 1967 to support not only the development of Philippine theatre but also Philippine society. With these goals, PETA was part of a larger movement to use theatre as a tool of nation building in the decolonising world. Rebecca Sturm highlights how Guidote quickly established PETA within an international network of like-minded theatre artists. The support she secured from various sources – including UNESCO, the ITI, the Rockefeller Foundation and LaMaMa Experimental Theatre Club – resulted in the first Third World Theater Festival, hosted by PETA in Manila in 1971. When martial law forced Guidote into political exile in 1972, she worked with other exiles and theatre artists from minority ethnic groups in New York while PETA continued creating and performing plays in Filipino, both endeavours supported by the international contacts Guidote had established.

Throughout this book, US philanthropy looms large as a significant factor in the development and modernisation efforts of the 1950s and 1960s. Chapter 13, by Christopher Balme, focuses on Robert W. July, a field officer for the Rockefeller Foundation, who between 1958 and 1968 visited numerous countries in sub-Saharan Africa on an annual basis. His remit was to support the expansion of the humanities and social sciences in higher education and in cultural institutions such as museums and theatres. He kept extensive diaries of his travels and encounters with writers, theatre artists, academics and administrators, which provide an insight into how the Rockefeller Foundation imagined the future of art, culture and intellectual endeavour in the newly decolonised African nations. Over the course of his visits, July became convinced that dance and theatre were the most central, integrative art forms in Africa.

July had only praise for Efua Sutherland, the founder of Ghana's experimental Drama Studio, and encouraged the Rockefeller Foundation to support her. As a dramatist, director, teacher and cultural activist, Sutherland was a seminal figure in Ghana's theatrical and cultural landscape from the late 1950s until her death in 1996. In Chapter 14, Abdul Karim Hakib examines the pan-African networks that connected the Rockefeller Foundation, the Afro-Asian Writers Conference, W. E. B. Du Bois, Kwame Nkrumah, Wole Soyinka, Chinua Achebe, Langston Hughes and Martin Luther King, among others. The essay focuses on two foundational moments: the establishment of the Ghana

Drama Studio in the late 1950s, and the Pan-African Historical Theatre Project, which Sutherland advocated for throughout the 1980s.

## Notes

1  See https://developing-theatre.de/.
2  Sachs, 1992, 1.
3  Pietersee, 2000.
4  Rostow, *The Stages of Economic Growth*; Rosenstein-Rodan, 'Notes on the theory of the "big push"'.
5  While there are significant differences between 'modernity' and 'modernisation' (the former being a state and the latter a process), they are connected by the same teleological thinking that tends to arrange cultures and nations on a continuum leading to the 'convergence of industrial societies'. Eisenstadt, 2000, 1.
6  Eisenstadt, 2000, 3.
7  North, 1990, 3.
8  DiMaggio, 1992, 23.
9  Haas, 1992, 1.
10  See, for example, Clavin, 2005.
11  Davis Cross, 2013, 142.
12  For the activities of the CCF more generally, see Stonor Saunders, 1999; Benson, 1986.
13  See Mitchell, 2002; Hecht, 2011.
14  Hecht, 2011, 3.
15  Rockefeller Panel, 1965, v.

## References

Benson, Peter. *Black Orpheus, Transition, and Modern Cultural Awakening in Africa*. Berkeley: University of California Press, 1986.

Clavin, Patricia. 'Defining transnationalism', *Contemporary European History* 14 (4) (2005): 421–39.

Davis Cross, Mai'a K. 'Rethinking epistemic communities twenty years later', *Review of International Studies* 39 (1) (2013): 137–60.

DiMaggio, Paul. 'Cultural boundaries and structural change: the extension of the high culture model to theater, opera, and the dance, 1900–1940'. In *Cultivating Differences: Symbolic boundaries and the making of inequality*, edited by Michèle Lamont and Marcel Fournier, 21–57. Chicago: University of Chicago Press, 1992.

Eisenstadt, S. N. 'Multiple modernities', *Daedalus* 129 (1) (2000): 1–29.

Haas, Peter M. 'Epistemic communities and international policy coordination', *International Organization* 46 (1) (1992): 1–35.

Hecht, Gabrielle. 'Introduction'. In *Entangled Geographies: Empire and technopolitics in the global Cold War*, edited by Gabrielle Hecht, 1–12. Cambridge, MA: MIT Press, 2011.

Mitchell, Timothy. *Rule of Experts: Egypt, techno-politics, modernity*. Berkeley: University of California Press, 2002.

North, Douglass. *Institutions, Institutional Change and Economic Performance*. Cambridge: Cambridge University Press, 1990.

Pietersee, Jan Nederveen. 'After post-development', *Third World Quarterly* 21 (2) (2000): 175–91.

Rockefeller Panel. *The Performing Arts: Problems and prospects*. New York: McGraw-Hill, 1965.

Rosenstein-Rodan, P. N. 'Notes on the theory of the "big push"'. In *Economic Development for Latin America*, edited by H. S. Ellis, 57–81. London: Palgrave Macmillan, 1961. https://doi.org/10.1007/978-1-349-08449-4_3.

Rostow, W. W. *The Stages of Economic Growth*. Cambridge: Cambridge University Press, 1960.

Sachs, Wolfgang, ed. *The Development Dictionary: A guide to knowledge as power*. Second edition. London: Zed Books, 1992.

Stonor Saunders, F. *Who Paid the Piper? The CIA and the cultural cold war*. New York: New Press, 1999.

Part I

# (Un)sustainable institutions: building a theatrical epistemic community

# 1
# Global theatre players during the Cold War: the ITI and UNIMA

Viviana Iacob[1] and Rebecca Sturm

The International Theatre Institute (ITI) and the International Union for Puppetry Arts (UNIMA) played a central role in shaping the global theatre community during the Cold War. They contributed to the internationalisation of various theatre cultures during the post-1945 period, and as such are ideal subjects for a global theatre history of these years. These two international organisations (IOs) built trans-regional networks by facilitating connections between theatre communities in the Global North, East and South despite the ideological divisions of the Cold War. This chapter explores specific moments in the history of these IOs in order to illustrate how the Global North, East and South contributed to the theatrical epistemic community in the second half of the twentieth century. We analyse these organisations' responses to Cold War divisions and decolonisation by looking at strategies and projects designed to establish a common ground for debate and initiate the professionalisation of theatre practice at a global level.

The role of theatre IOs as creators of epistemic communities and arenas for East–West interaction during the Cold War has received greater attention in the last decade, such as in Daniela Peslin's study of the Theatre of Nations festival[2] during its Parisian tenure; Charlotte Canning's ground-breaking study of American theatre internationalists and the USA's involvement in the creation and activities of the ITI into the 1960s;[3] Hanna Korsberg's article on the eighth world congress of the ITI held in Helsinki in 1959, and the opportunity the event provided to non-aligned Finland;[4] and Viviana Iacob's examination of Romanian engagement with the ITI and the comparable influence theatre experts from socialist countries had on the organisation.[5] Volumes such as *Theatre, Globalization and the Cold War* edited by Christopher Balme and Berenika Szymanski-Düll addressed the Cold War as a global phenomenon that impacted theatre cultures not only in the Global East and West but also in the Global South. While this book does not specifically discuss the role of international organisations in the globalisation of theatre during the Cold War, in their introduction the editors state that IOs appear to form different facets of a theatrical epistemic community that only took concrete institutional form after 1945.[6]

Elsewhere, Christopher Balme advocated for the need to re-examine theatre history during the postcolonial era 'against the background of internationally coordinated "development" and "modernisation" programmes that linked funding organisations, artists, universities, and governments in networks of theatrical expertise'.[7] Balme also argues that while the establishment of an epistemic community is a symptom of modernisation – an ideology that was equally dominant on both sides of the Cold War – the backlash against such theatrical ideologies is equally global. Thus, cultures from the Global South engaged in the rediscovery and reinvigoration of autochthonous performance forms.[8] IOs became important arenas in which traditions and practices from the decolonising states were introduced and debated.

Moreover, during the Cold War, international theatre organisations were exemplary sites for the circulation and adaptation of expertise, the cornerstone of theatre professionalisation. While both the West and East were equally invested in exporting their version of expert knowledge, IOs provided a forum where Global South representatives could access both approaches. As a result, practitioners from the so-called Third World were able to craft a wide range of syncretic practices to showcase the local specificities of their cultures within the global epistemic community.

By looking at the training and exchange programmes developed by the ITI and UNIMA in the last three decades of the Cold War period, this chapter shows that IOs offered viable meeting points for the Global North, East and South. As suggested by the scholarship outlined above, contributions from various parts of the postwar world necessitates research into primary resources spanning the archives of international organisations and local institutions. It also requires corroborating these findings with the publications produced by IOs, including journals, bulletins, catalogues and collective works published by their headquarters, issued by local centres or authored by organisational members or individual representatives. This multiplicity of viewpoints accounts for discrepancies, and balances out narratives produced during and after the Cold War. For example, throughout the Cold War period, UNIMA publications did their best to equally represent Eastern and Western approaches to puppetry and their contributions to the development of the organisation. However, the publications produced after the collapse of the Eastern bloc show the tensions between the two sides much more vividly.[9]

UNIMA and the ITI play a special role among theatre IOs created after 1945. They emerged from the ashes of the Second World War, and by the end of the 1960s had created networks of practitioners around the world. This growth was plagued by miscommunications, misunderstandings and projects that did not come to fruition. However, the development of these IOs also reflects a huge number of interactions and entanglements that form a history of theatre and globalisation during the Cold War comprising forgotten circulations and contributions.

In the late 1950s and early 1960s both UNIMA and the ITI underwent a process of reciprocal acculturation[10] between the two ideological camps of the Cold War. The 1970s and 1980s followed suit with self reflection and a re-evaluation of strengths and weaknesses. These processes not only entailed coming to terms with the fact that the Cold War was a global phenomenon, but also required the reconceptualisation of what theatre meant or stood for as a result of engaging with an extensive array of Global South performing traditions. In 1974 Henryk Jurkowski, the general secretary of UNIMA, wrote:

> it is obvious the concept of puppet theatre as an artistic enterprise is not sufficient if we want to understand and encompass all currents in the world of puppetry ... we must expand our understanding of the theatre's functions so as to encompass all theatrical phenomena of importance to world culture.[11]

The ITI was created in 1948, heavily inspired by the Société Universelle du Théâtre (SUDT) established in 1927. UNIMA was founded in 1957, although it rekindled an interwar association established in Prague in 1929. At their inception, these IOs were Eurocentric. In the interwar period, for UNIMA the world meant Europe, the United States and Japan. In 1927 the SUDT comprised European and American founding members, along with representatives from Brazil, Chile and China.[12] It took more than half a century for these IOs to abandon their Euro-Atlantic outlook.

In the case of both organisations, their desire to engage with the Global South was intrinsically connected to the political vicissitudes of the Cold War period. Although they were separate entities, their trajectories often merged, reflecting the overall state of the organisational field[13] during the period.

## Entangled histories: building global expert networks

Undoubtedly, the success of these IOs in connecting the world during the Cold War had much to do with their interwar histories, as they were able to build upon existing networks and knowledge. However, it was the start of the detente in the mid 1950s that made possible both the rebirth of UNIMA and the ideological rapprochement between members from the East and West within the ITI.

The ITI was created under the auspices of UNESCO, with national branches in each UNESCO member state, a structure of working committees, an annual congress and, from 1957, an international festival, the Theatre of Nations. The ITI's chief architect Maurice Kurtz was heavily inspired by the SUDT, which had been founded by French director and actor Firmin Gémier under the aegis of the International Institute for Intellectual Cooperation (IIIC), the League of Nation's advisory cultural organisation and UNESCO's precursor. From 1927 to 1938, SUDT held 11 congresses, many of them accompanied by a festival. Gémier's arguments on why the specific qualities and practices of theatre made it especially suited for internationalist aspirations[14] were mirrored in English playwright and critic J. B. Priestley's opening address at the first ITI congress:

> The particular nature of the theatre compelled those concerned with it to deal with real human beings concretely and intimately … From the theatre, people could learn how others were living, thinking and feeling. For success in the theatre, it was necessary to have knowledge of common human nature, to have sympathy with it and faith in it.[15]

But if the internationalist spirit of the interwar period inspired the ITI's founders, the Cold War presented a significant obstacle to their endeavours. In 1948 Prague was chosen as the host of the first ITI congress. The same year, the communist party took power in Czechoslovakia, which drew the ITI into the maelstrom of early Cold War tensions.[16] By the end of the 1950s, however, the Soviet Union and the majority of Eastern European countries had become ITI members.[17] During these years, the inclusion of Global South performing traditions was clearly not a priority for the ITI. Nevertheless, events such as the conference on popular theatre in Bombay[18] and the formation of the Latin American Theatre Institute to some extent opened up the organisation to contact with other continents. Around the same time, the Theatre of Nations festival had made the international community aware of performing traditions outside the Euro-Atlantic context.[19]

These trans-regional encounters brought the shock of exposure and the elation of discovery to audiences and participants alike. They also steered the ITI towards a process of expanding the modernist text-based theatre model. The ITI had after all been founded on an understanding of theatre centred on European professional forms. At the first meeting of theatre experts in Paris in 1947, J. B. Priestley, one of the organisation's founders, dismissively said 'there were whole continents which had no national theatre', and that having 12 founding countries therefore made the ITI an entirely viable enterprise.[20]

For the ITI, overcoming its original Eurocentric bias was a decade-long process, much of which was carried out under the guidance of UNESCO. A considerable shift occurred from the 1960s onwards, when decolonisation prompted the UN and UNESCO to focus on development.[21] The ITI started to take a more active approach in supporting African states,[22] and the number of events organised by Global South countries under the umbrella of the ITI increased. In 1961 the University of the Theatre of Nations was established. Despite changes in direction and affiliation, interruptions, detours and trial runs, the university was probably the ITI's most successful fellowship programme focused on exchange and training between different regions of the world. Between 1961 and 1965, fellows from 37 Global South countries attended the programme,[23] and the teachers involved came from equally diverse cultural backgrounds.

Nevertheless, it was not until the early 1970s that the organisation created a committee dedicated to Global South theatre. With the second UN development decade,[24] UNESCO-affiliated organisations were further encouraged to support cultural development in the Global South.[25] The Committee for Third World Theatre (CTWT) was first discussed in 1971 during the ITI congress in London and officially established at the subsequent congress in Moscow. The creation of the CTWT was predicated on the need to increase the profile of Global South performance traditions and interests within the ITI. It was less a project and more a framework within which experts, local ITI centres and governments from the Global South could make their voices heard, albeit not without difficulty. The CTWT's most successful endeavour

in this respect was a series of 'Third World' festivals and accompanying conferences. The first was organised in the Philippines in 1971
and the second in Iran in 1973. Even though these events were not
free of conflict, the CTWT nevertheless allowed practitioners from the
Global South to internationalise their theatre agendas. It also provided
outside parties – the so-called CTWT consultants from the Global North
and Global East, such as Ellen Stewart of the United States and Fritz
Bennewitz of the German Democratic Republic – with an important
platform that legitimised their own Global South projects.[26]

The ITI's international agency depended on the initiatives
and financial contributions of its national centres. As a class-A non-
governmental organisation (NGO), the ITI benefited from UNESCO's
financial support when, for example, maintaining the secretariat or
producing its journals. However, the international events planned under
the umbrella of the ITI were only possible because local cultural institutions took on the majority of the expenses. The best example of this
is the Theatre of Nations festival, which was financed by the French
government for 18 years. When that support came to an end, the gauntlet
was picked up by the Polish ITI centre and the Polish government.[27]

The same approach applied to Global South members. Here,
however, UNESCO did much to bridge the socioeconomic gap, and
overcome, to some extent, the competition and clashes between representatives of the two ideological camps of the Cold War. Examples
include the international competition for dramatic works from Arab
countries (1968), the workshop on the social role of theatre in Africa
(Lagos 1978) and the workshop on theatre for development (Lusaka
1979). UNIMA had similar fiscal limitations. Its training programme was
financially dependent on contributions from socialist countries, and its
foremost training institute was only established when the French UNIMA
centre secured state funds. Still, the connections, contacts and conversations that inspired these projects were developed within and because of
the framework provided by both the ITI and UNIMA.

The ITI's turn to the Global South, coupled with exchange fellowship
programmes focused on professional training, inspired similar approaches
among other theatre IOs. This organisational mimicry[28] applied to UNIMA
too, even though it occupied a special place among theatre IOs. The
founding of both UNIMA and the ITI during the Cold War was inspired by
and built upon interwar avatars. Nevertheless, the ITI retained the role
of leader among theatre IOs, a status predicated on its relationship with
UNESCO. From the time of its foundation, the ITI enjoyed a relationship
with UNESCO that no other theatre NGO had during the Cold War period.

Unlike them, it was assigned category-A consultative status (close collaboration and consultation), a privilege shared by about 40 other international NGOs until 1980.[29] UNIMA representatives Jan Malík and Max Jacob attempted and failed to establish contacts with UNESCO prior to the fifth UNIMA congress in Prague in 1957.[30] When their inquiries went unanswered, UNIMA contacted the ITI. In 1960 UNIMA became a member of the ITI, and its leadership declared that the organisation was 'thus affiliated with UNESCO'.[31] Over the years, the ITI journal *World Theatre* published articles on puppetry and UNIMA's achievements on numerous occasions.[32] Until the late 1980s, UNIMA consistently lobbied UNESCO about becoming an affiliated NGO. The ITI's leading position among performing arts IOs was further consolidated when its leadership founded the liaison committee for theatre IOs. The committee became a platform for such organisations, enabling them to stay informed about each other's projects and engage in collaborative initiatives.[33]

Echoing the ITI's opening toward the Global South, UNIMA created its own committee for puppet theatre in the Global South in 1976 during its Moscow congress. Of course, as was the case with the ITI, UNIMA's involvement with postcolonial spaces did not begin that year. Like the ITI, UNIMA had first established contacts in the Global South in the late 1950s, but unlike the ITI, in the postwar years UNIMA engaged in an internationalism that stemmed from its interwar roots. Fashioned in the image of the UN and UNESCO, the ITI would only accept fully formed national centres into its ranks. By contrast, UNIMA was open to individuals and companies, resulting in a more diverse and malleable institutional makeup and allowing practitioners from countries including India,[34] Japan[35] and China[36] to join UNIMA long before these states founded their own national centres. This interest in world puppetry was part of UNIMA's creed from the time of its first iteration in 1929. Despite the fact that the majority of its members were European, from the beginning UNIMA's leadership had a strong academic interest, and was successful in gathering information on a variety of puppetry traditions from around the world. Its founders focused not only on the historicisation of puppetry but also on collecting and researching puppetry-related artifacts. Thus, UNIMA amassed a huge amount of knowledge on puppet theatre traditions following the interwar years. During this period, the Czech journal *Loutkár* provided a window onto puppetry arts from the Near, Middle and Far East. With the creation of UNIMA, *Loutkár* became the IO's official journal.

However, building a global organisation requires more than academic interest. While UNIMA's founders were aware of puppet traditions outside the European context through their research and collecting activities, engaging with such traditions was a goal UNIMA only established in the late 1950s. The postwar years offered former interwar members the opportunity to rekindle ties and resuscitate the organisation. At the same time, the IO sought to expand its membership and its connections to cultures beyond the Euro-Atlantic context.

In the second half of the 1950s, the push for non-alignment in the Cold War world also impacted UNIMA. In 1957, the year of the organisation's re-founding, Indian practitioner Meher R. Contractor became the first representative of a Global South country to be part of the UNIMA presidium.[37] After a puppet show she produced in Delhi, Contractor was invited to Prague by the Czechoslovak ambassador to India.[38] Her presence at the first UNIMA congress reflected the weight state socialist cultures carried in the organisation. This dynamic was strikingly evident at the first international puppetry festival in 1958, organised in Bucharest in tandem with UNIMA's fifth congress. It brought together participants from both the socialist camp and the West in addition to an impressive number of practitioners and theoreticians from the Global South. The latter came from Mongolia, India, the United Arab Republic, Argentina, the Democratic People's Republic of Korea, the Democratic Republic of Vietnam (festival participation), China and India (festival film section).[39] The 1958 gathering is mentioned in all UNIMA publications that refer to the history of its festivals, and was a watershed event in international puppetry.

The first international puppetry festival also served to highlight the systemic imbalances within UNIMA. The orchestrators of the organisation's revival were well aware of this situation. When Jan Malík, former secretary of the interwar UNIMA, proposed to his Western colleagues the re-establishment of the IO at the 1957 Brunswick festival, those involved understood that a balance between East and West had to be carefully maintained if the IO was to survive the bitter Cold War competition. This equilibrium was supposed to be achieved through a series of gentleman's agreements regarding UNIMA offices and events.[40] Over the years, and on numerous occasions, UNIMA representatives asserted that their association was apolitical, but the Cold War context invalidates this statement. Many of UNIMA's festivals and congresses were supported by socialist governments as they sought international visibility and prestige. Furthermore, in the case of East European countries, the performing arts establishment played a central role in the post-1956 drive to export socialist cultures to the rest of the world.[41]

The festivals organised by UNIMA, like the Theatre of Nations festival, constituted catalysts for engagement with the Global South.

The Bucharest festival set a standard for future events in terms of both approach and the number and diversity of participants. At the 1969 congress in Prague, Jacques Félix, at the time vice president of the UNIMA French centre, requested that he and his Charleville-Mézièrs company organise the next congress and festival.[42] His intention was to create an event of even greater magnitude than Margareta Niculescu's 1958 gathering.[43] The 1969 and 1972 UNIMA congresses and the 1972 festival were for Félix and Niculescu the starting point of a long collaboration. These encounters led to the foundation in Charleville, in 1981, of the International Institute for Puppetry, the first research and training centre in the field created in Western Europe.

The growing number of newly independent nations in the Global South, combined with growing global interdependencies, prompted UNIMA, like the ITI, to expand its network to encompass various regions and performance traditions. In the early 1970s UNIMA set out to catalogue theatre traditions around the world.[44] Meher R. Contractor, Taiji Kawajiri and Henryk Jurkowski played an instrumental role in the organisation's global approach to puppetry traditions, but it was Michael Meschke, a Swede, who changed the face of UNIMA in terms of its interconnectedness. In 1972 Meschke was elected to the executive committee and in 1976 he became vice president of UNIMA. Four years later, he chaired UNIMA's committee for the Third World. As soon as he became a member of the IO's executive committee, he proposed a rehabilitation programme for UNIMA[45] that aimed to expand the concept of puppet theatre. Throughout this period, he conducted extensive research trips to East and Southeast Asia, becoming more and more familiar with the regions, traditions and practitioners he sought to include in UNIMA's activities.

The 1972 congress and festival in Charleville-Mézièrs, and the 1976 congress in Moscow, were landmark moments for UNIMA. Not only were the organisation's new statues passed in 1972,[46] but four years later the organisation created its most important permanent commissions: the Commission for Publications, led by the Hungarian Dezsö Szilágyi; the Commission for Professional Training of Young Puppeteers, led by Romanian Margareta Niculescu; and the Third World Commission, led by Meher R. Contractor.[47]

The Moscow congress addressed, for the first time, the development of puppet theatre in the Global South. The means by which UNIMA could support artists from these regions was discussed, and the influence of Soviet and East European members in drafting these proposals was significant. UNIMA offered aid in the form of stipends, and the organisation of seminars and meetings of puppeteers from Africa, Asia and Latin America, the funds for which were to be provided by UNESCO in collaboration with socialist countries. The organisation also proposed distributing information to cultural bodies in the Global South, underlining the role puppet theatre played in the education and cultural development of children. The congress emphasised the importance of state funding for puppet theatres in connection with this issue.[48]

The reference to socialist countries in the Moscow congress report might seem partisan, but at the time the puppetry establishment in Eastern Europe had significant experience of sharing expertise with the Global South.[49] The fact that an initiative to create a commission specialising in training came from a Romanian should be no surprise. As early as 1972 Margareta Niculescu proposed a fellowship programme for specialisation in puppetry. She was supported in her endeavour by Czechoslovak and Swedish representatives. By 1976 the project offered puppeteers from Argentina the chance to study in Romania; those from Ghana the opportunity to study in Romania, Czechoslovakia and Hungary; and those from India the opportunity to study in Sweden. In 1979 the programme for postcolonial states expanded, with Bulgaria, Romania and Hungary offering two grants each, and Sweden continuing to provide one fellowship.[50]

The fellowship programme also points to the paradoxical issue of development aid within theatre IOs. While representatives from the Global South asked for the IO's help in matters of training – pleas to which UNIMA members were open – the programmes offered in the late 1970s did not necessarily meet needs or expectations. For instance, at the Moscow congress in 1972 it was noted that:

> … in Ghana, only the puppeteer troupes are financially independent. Today they are approaching the UNIMA centres around the world to address the problem of training puppeteers in the Third World and award scholarships to people from these countries who are interested in puppet theatre. The future of puppeteers depends on the training system.[51]

However, a report published in UNIMA's journal on the experience of Ghanaian youth in Czechoslovakia[52] recounted disgruntledly their interest in creating puppets but not in directing or stage design.[53] Dadi Pudumjee, the Indian puppeteer who received a fellowship at Michael Meschke's theatre, was rather critical of the experience. Puppet manipulation could be learned only during the production process, which was focused on the final visual effect of the performance rather than on the craft of handling puppets.[54]

Nevertheless, UNIMA members seemed to be very conscious of the issues raised by postcolonialism, arguably more so than any other theatre IO. In 1982, following a research tour across Indonesia, Thailand, Burma, Japan and India, Michael Meschke argued that to escape the image of UNIMA as a circle of European friends, the organisation had to be restructured to properly reflect global diversity and complexity.[55] Two years later, the secretary general's report at the organisation's 14th congress noted that the Third World commission should 'exercise great prudence to avoid being taxed with paternalism or cultural imperialism',[56] reflecting a constant engagement with contemporary globalities on the part of UNIMA's governing body. While the ITI attempted to do the same (see, for example, the CTWT), its structure seemed to constitute an impediment because of its exclusive focus on nation-states. It seems that UNIMA's much more malleable makeup, which included individual practitioners and companies in addition to national centres, allowed for a more flexible interaction with the world.[57]

UNIMA's training commission also changed the organisation. While the fellowships offered in the 1960s and 1970s were mainly assigned to socialist countries, the creation of the international puppetry institute in 1981 altered this state of affairs and jumpstarted a new era in puppetry training. The institute was supported by UNIMA's vice president Henryk Jurkowsky and chaired by its experts Jacques Félix and Margareta Niculescu with funding provided by the French state, the Ardenne-Champagne region and the Charleville-Mézières city council. The institute was imagined as a hub for performances, exhibitions and internships for puppeteers from France and the rest of the world. In one of the many brochures describing the institute and its projects, its director, Margareta Niculescu, stated emphatically that the organisation was unique in Western Europe, and that before its creation puppeteers in that part of the world could only train on the job, an approach discussed earlier in connection with the Swedish training fellowship offered to Dadi Pudumjee.[58]

The institute's leadership set out to imagine a new pedagogy, one that would bring together and distil the experiences of a significant number of practitioners and theoreticians from across the globe. The institute was a launching pad for the creation of the French National Graduate School for Puppetry Arts six years later, the first higher education institution in the field with a global profile created during the Cold War.[59] The institute and the graduate school used the wide array of contacts gathered by UNIMA members since its re-founding in 1957, and by the late 1980s Czechoslovak, Chinese, Polish, Romanian, Bulgarian, Swedish, Indonesian and Japanese experts taught courses attended by young practitioners from Iceland, South Korea, the USA, Sri Lanka, Brazil, Iran and Morocco.

## Conclusion

By the end of the Cold War, the ITI with its Theatre of Nations festival and university, as well as UNIMA and its international puppetry institute, had created a network of experts that contributed to the professionalisation of theatre at a global level. These IOs brought about the institutionalisation of an epistemic community that continued to be relevant after the fall of the Iron Curtain. The two IOs professed different types of internationalism, with the ITI basing its activity on the national centres, and UNIMA militating for interconnectedness by way of a conglomerate of individuals, companies, associations and local centres. However, both organisations were simultaneously agents of decolonisation and neo-colonialism. They opened up to the Global South and supported theatre development in newly independent countries, but they did so by promoting an essentially European professional model. During the 1970s and 1980s the two IOs did much to embrace a more inclusive idea of theatre, and reflected on their own limitations with respect to their engagement in the Global South. Arguably, UNIMA did a better job than the ITI, mainly because of its more flexible internal organisation. Still, it is hard not to read the histories of the ITI and UNIMA as a series of conflicts between various traditions from the Global South, East and North. Confrontation does not mean failure, however. The exchanges facilitated by the ITI and UNIMA generated relationships, conversations and mutual learning, making them the foremost international forums of global theatre circulation during the Cold War.

## Notes

1   Viviana Iacob acknowledges the support of the Alexander von Humboldt Foundation within the scope of a Fellowship for Postdoctoral Researchers between May 2020 and July 2022.
2   Peslin-Ursu, *Le Théâtre des Nations*.
3   Canning, 2015.
4   Korsberg, 217, 151–64.
5   Iacob, 2018, 184–214.
6   Balme and Szymanski-Düll, 2017, 10–11.

7 Balme, 2017, 126.

8 Balme, 2020, 286.

9 The change to the organisation's statutes was described during the Cold War years across an array of UNIMA publications as designed to cultivate a more democratic organisation. Decades later, however, Michael Meschke recalled Soviet representative Sergueï Obraztsov reacting to the proposed amendment in a similar manner to Nikita Khrushchev's notorious outburst during the 1960 UN assembly. The proposal to change UNIMA's statutes came from the Czechoslovak delegation in the wake of the Prague Spring 1968 (Meschke, 2019, 183).

10 Iacob, 2018, 194.

11 Jurkowski, 1974, 5–6.

12 UNESCO, 1948, 29–31.

13 DiMaggio and Powell, 1983, 147–60.

14 Canning, 2015, 162.

15 UNESCO, 1948, 5.

16 Canning, 2015, 172–6.

17 Iacob, 2018, 188.

18 The ITI Indian Centre was created in 1950. In 1956 the ITI journal *World Theatre* dedicated an entire issue to theatre in India (5/2). In 1957, India was represented for the first time at the Theatre of Nations festival.

19 The first three seasons of the Theatre of Nations festival featured companies from India, Japan, Ceylon, China, Morocco, Argentina, the Philippines and Haiti.

20 UNESCO, 1947,10.

21 Pavone, 2008,10.

22 Iacob, 2022, 71.

23 ITI Archive, Paris, *ITI/UTN/UIT*.

24 United Nations, 1970, 39–49.

25 Adiseshiah, 1970, 7.

26 See Rebeca Sturm's chapter on Cecile Guidote in this volume.

27 See ITI Archive, *Specification of Costs for the Theatre of Nations Warsaw, 1975*.

28 Iacob, 2024.

29 Among the other theatre NGOs, only the International Association of Theatre Critics (IATC) achieved B status (relations on information and consultation) with UNESCO during the Cold War period (BArch DR107/6, *Analyse des Standes der bisherigen Tätigkeiten in den NGO's der [sic] Kulturbereiches, Stand vom 1. September 1978*).

30 Sammlung Puppentheater/Schaustellerei des Münchner Stadtmuseums, Hohnsteiner/Max Jacob/Unima-Angelegenheiten, Nr. 1439, Malík, Jan, *Letter to Max Jacob*, 4.5.1958 and *Programm. III. ordentliche Sitzung des Vorsitzes der UNIMA in Paris, den 7. und 10. VI. 1959*, 7.

31 Sammlung Puppentheater/Schaustellerei des Münchner Stadtmuseums, Hohnsteiner/Max Jacob/Unima-Angelegenheiten, Nr. 1439, *History of UNIMA*, 9.

32 The 1958 festival was discussed, for example, in ITI's journal *World Theatre* 8, 1959.

33 Henryk Jurkowski, the general secretary of UNIMA, was present at the 1973 ITI congress in Moscow where he took the opportunity to discuss Global South puppetry issues with representatives from the recently decolonised countries who participated in the congress (Sammlung Puppentheater/Schaustellerei des Münchner Stadtmuseums, UNIMA Nr. 661, *XVII Moskau Kongress 1976, Vorträge*, 9).

34 Meher R. Contractor was a UNIMA member from 1957, but the Indian UNIMA centre was only created in 1982.

35 Japan's first participation in UNIMA dates to 1930. However, the Japanese UNIMA centre was created in 1967.

36 China participated in UNIMA events from the beginning of the 1980s, but the national centre for UNIMA was created in 2002.

37 Sammlung Puppentheater/Schaustellerei des Münchner Stadtmuseums, UNIMA Nr. 661, *Record of the proceedings of the Conference of UNIMA, Wednesday, December 4th 1957, Bulletin UNIMA*.

38 'Femmes en vedette', *UNIMA France* 69, 1980, 29. The same article mentions that soon after the gathering in 1957, Meher R. Contractor received a fellowship from the British Council. Contractor is a good example of the balancing act between East and West that Global South representatives engaged in.

39  Romanian State Archives/Institute for Cultural Relations with Foreign Countries collection, *UK file no. 342/1951–1958*, 11–26 and Sammlung Puppentheater/Schaustellerei des Münchner Stadtmuseums, UNIMA Nr. 661, *Participants list at the 1958 Festival, Bucharest*.
40  Erbelding, 2019.
41  Iacob, 2024.
42  Chopplet, 1985, 19.
43  Global South participants in the 1972 world festival came from Algeria, Argentina, India, Morocco, Kenya and South Africa.
44  In 1977 Michael Meschke addressed a letter to the ITI congress in which he requested the cooperation of ITI national centres to help UNIMA identify struggling artists in Global South countries. He hoped that this international support would 'draw the attention of national cultural authorities to the art of puppetry, threatened to disappear' (ITI Archive, Paris, UNIMA Correspondence, Meschke, Michael, *To the ITI Congress of Stockholm 1977*).
45  Meschke, 2019, 184.
46  PAM Archive, *11e. Congrès International de Marionnettes – Charleville, Conférence de Presse du 23 et Assemblée Générale du 25 Septembre 1972*.
47  Mäser, 1980, 38. See also the general secretary report on the 13th Congress, *UNIMA Informations*, 1981, and the general secretary report on the 14th congress, *UNIMA Informations* special issue on the Dresden Congress, 1984.
48  ITI Archive, Paris, UNIMA Correspondence, I. Zharovtseva, *The 12th congress of the UNIMA*, 4.
49  Iacob, 2024.
50  These fellowships were created for the Global South – India, Argentina, Ghana and Togo (General Secretary of UNIMA Report, 13th Congress, 17–25).
51  'In Ghana sind allein die Puppenspielertruppen finanziell unabhängig. Heute wenden sie sich an die UNIMA Zentren der ganzen Welt mit der Bitte, das Problem der Ausbildung von Puppenspielern in der dritten Welt und die Stiftung von Stipendien für Menschen aus diesen Ländern, die sich für das Puppentheater interessieren, zu erörtern. Die Zukunft der Puppenspieler hängt vom Ausbildungssystem ab.' Translation by the authors (Sammlung Puppentheater/Schaustellerei des Münchner Stadtmuseums, UNIMA Nr. 661, *17th Moskau Kongress 1976, Vorträge*).
52  These fellowships led to the opening of a training school in Accra, the International Puppetry School. Peretu and Ebikebina, *'Ghana'*.
53  Vavruška, 1977, 47–8.
54  Pudumjee, 1977, 46–7.
55  Meschke, 1982, 28.
56  The Secretary General's Report on the 14th Congress Held in Dresden East Germany, 12.
57  For example, local centres were seen as cumbersome (General Secretary of UNIMA Report 13th Congress, Washington, 23).
58  PAM Archive, *Brochure de présentation des activités, Institut International de la Marionnette, Expositions-Spectacles-Rencontre-Stages*, 8.
59  PAM Archive, *Première brochure de présentation et d'inscription de l'Ecole Nationale Supérieure des Arts de la Marionnette*.

# References

## Archival sources

BArch DR107/6, 1978, *Analyse des Standes der bisherigen Tätigkeiten in den NGO's der [sic] Kulturbereiches, Stand vom 1. September 1978*.
ITI Archive, Paris, *ITI/UTN/UIT*.
ITI Archive, Paris, 1975, *Specification of Costs for the Theatre of Nations Warsaw*.
ITI Archive, Paris, UNIMA Correspondence, Meschke, Michael, 'To the ITI Congress of Stockholm 1977'.
ITI Archive, Paris, UNIMA Correspondence, I. Zharovtseva, (Executive Secretary of the Soviet UNIMA Centre, Member of the UNIMA Executive Committee) *The XIIth congress of the UNIMA*.

PAM Archive, 1972. *11e. Congrès International de Marionnettes – Charleville, Conférence de Presse du 23 et Assemblée Générale du 25 Septembre 1972*. Accessed 6 September 2022. https://lelab.arts delamarionnette.eu/visionneuse.php?lvl=afficheur&explnum=23834#page/1/mode/2up.

PAM Archive. *Brochure de présentation des activités, Institut International de la Marionnette, Expositions-Spectacles-Rencontre-Stages*. Accessed 6 September 2022. https://lelab.artsde lamarionnette.eu/visionneuse.php?lvl=afficheur&explnum=25112#page/1/mode/2up.

PAM Archive. *Première brochure de présentation et d'inscription de l'École Nationale Supérieure des Arts de la Marionnette*. Accessed 6 September 2022. https://lelab.artsdelamarionnette.eu/visionneuse.php?lvl=afficheur&explnum=25171#page/1/mode/2up.

Romanian State Archives/Institute for Cultural Relations with Foreign Countries collection, *UK file no. 342/1951–1958*.

Sammlung Puppentheater/Schaustellerei des Münchner Stadtmuseums, 1976, UNIMA Nr. 661, *XVII Moskau Kongress 1976, Vorträge*.

Sammlung Puppentheater/Schaustellerei des Münchner Stadtmuseums, 1957, UNIMA Nr. 661, *Record of the proceedings of the Conference of UNIMA, Wednesday, December 4th 1957, Bulletin UNIMA*.

Sammlung Puppentheater/Schaustellerei des Münchner Stadtmuseums, 1958, UNIMA Nr. 661, *Participants list at the 1958 Festival, Bucharest*.

Sammlung Puppentheater/Schaustellerei des Münchner Stadtmuseums, Hohnsteiner/Max Jacob/ Unima-Angelegenheiten, Nr. 1439, *History of UNIMA*.

Sammlung Puppentheater/Schaustellerei des Münchner Stadtmuseums, 1958, Hohnsteiner/Max Jacob/Unima-Angelegenheiten, Nr. 1439, Malík, Jan, *Letter to Max Jacob. 4 May 1958*.

Sammlung Puppentheater/Schaustellerei des Münchner Stadtmuseums, 1959, Hohnsteiner/Max Jacob/Unima-Angelegenheite, Nr. 1439, *Programm. III. ordentliche Sitzung des Vorsitzes der UNIMA in Paris, den 7. und 10. VI. 1959*.

UNESCO. *Summary Report of the Third Meeting Held at UNESCO House, 19 Avenue Kléber, Paris 16e, on Tuesday, 29th July 1947, at 3.15 p.m.* 1947. Accessed 6 September 2022. https://unesdoc. unesco.org/ark:/48223/pf0000141480.

UNESCO. *Report on the First Congress of the International Theatre Institute*. 1948. Accessed 6 September 2022. https://unesdoc.unesco.org/ark:/48223/pf0000147375.

United Nations. *Resolution 2626. Resolutions Adopted on the Reports of the Second Committee. United Nations General Assembly – Twenty-fifth Session. 39–49*. 1970. Accessed 6 September 2022. https://undocs.org/A/RES/2626%20(XXV).

## Published sources

Adiseshiah, Malcolm S. 'The crisis in development', *UNESCO Courier* 23/10 (1970): 4–14.

Balme, Christopher. 'Theatrical institutions in motion: developing theatre in the postcolonial era', *Journal of Dramatic Theory and Criticism* 31 (2) (2017): 125–40.

Balme, Christopher. 'Theatre-historiographical patterns in the Global South 1950–1990: transnational and institutional perspectives'. In *The Routledge Companion to Theatre and Performance Historiography*, edited by Tracy C. Davis and Peter W. Marx, 269–89. London: Routledge, 2020.

Balme, Christopher and Szymanski-Düll, Berenika. 'Introduction'. In *Theatre, Globalization and the Cold War*, edited by Christopher Balme and Berenika Szymanski-Düll, 1–22. Cham: Palgrave Macmillan, 2017.

Canning, Charlotte. *On the Performance Front: US theatre and internationalism*. Basingstoke: Palgrave Macmillan, 2015.

Chopplet, Bernard. 'Charleville…au fils des festivals'. In *Charleville…au fil de la marionnette*, edited by Bernard Chopplet and Pierre Huard, 15–72. Lyon: La Manufacture, 1985.

DiMaggio, Paul J. and Powell, Walter W. 'The iron cage revisited: institutional isomorphism and collective rationality in organizational fields', *American Sociological Review* 48 (2) (1983): 147–60.

Erbelding, Mascha. 'Built on glass: the restoration of UNIMA after 1957 from a (West) German perspective', Conference paper delivered at *The Role of UNIMA in the Recognition, Development and Importance of Puppetry in the 20th Century and its Visions for the 21st Century* (7 June 2019). Prague, Czech Republic. https://unima.idu.cz/en/conference/.

Iacob, Viviana. 'Scenes of Cold War diplomacy: Romania and the international theatre institute, 1956–1969', *East Central Europe* 45 (2018): 184–214.

Iacob, Viviana. 'The University of the Theatre of Nations: explorations into Cold War exchanges', *Journal of Global Theatre History* 4 (2) (2022): 68–80. https://doi.org/10.5282/gthj/5155.

Iacob, Viviana. 'Cold War mobilities: Eastern European theatre going global'. In *Performing the Cold War in the Postcolonial World: Theatre, film, literature and things*, edited by Christopher Balme, 43–67. New York: Routledge, 2023.

Jurkowski, Henryk. 'Responsibility', *UNIMA Informations* (1974): 4–8.

Jurkowski, Henryk. 'General Secretary of UNIMA report XIIIth Congress, Washington', *UNIMA Informations* (1981): 17–25.

Korsberg, Hanna. 'Creating an international community during the Cold War'. In *Theatre, Globalization and the Cold War*, edited by Christopher Balme and Berenika Szymanski-Düll, 151–64. Cham: Palgrave Macmillan, 2017.

Larose, François (translation). 'Femmes en vedette', *UNIMA France: bulletin de la section française de L'Union Internationale de la Marionnette* 69 (September 1980): 28–9.

Mäser, Rolf, ed. *Puppentheater International: 50 Jahre UNIMA/International Puppet Theatre: 50 Years of UNIMA*. Berlin: Henschelverlag Kunst und Gesellschaft, 1980.

Meschke, Michael. 'Asia 1982: a report from a journey', *UNIMA Informations* (1982): 22–9.

Meschke, Michael. 'A few memories and experiences from UNIMA'. In *UNI..What? UNIMA! Czech Contributions to the History of the International Puppetry Organization*, edited by Nina Malíková, 174–89. Prague: Chudin Puppetry Museum, 2019.

Pavone, Vincenzo. *From the Labyrinth of the World to the Paradise of the Heart: Science and humanism in UNESCO's approach to globalization*. Lanham, MD: Lexington, 2008.

Peretu, Ebikebina. 'Ghana', *World Encyclopaedia of Puppetry Art*. UNIMA. Accessed 6 September 2022. https://wepa.unima.org/en/ghana/.

Peslin-Ursu, Daniela. *Le Théâtre des Nations: Une aventure théâtrale à redécouvrir*. Paris: Harmattan, 2009.

Pudumjee, Dadi. 'On my UNIMA scholarship in Sweden', *UNIMA Informations* (1977): 46–7.

UNIMA. 'The Secretary General's report on the XIVth Congress held in Dresden Germany', *UNIMA Informations* Spécial XIV Congrès (1984): 8–16.

Vavruška, Eduard. 'On UNIMA scholarship for Ghanaian puppeteers in Czechoslovakia', *UNIMA Informations* (1977): 47–8.

2

# Infrastructures for a Black/African renaissance: cultural institution building and organisational frameworks in selected postcolonial Pan-African festivals

Gideon I. Morison and Judith Rottenburg

In April 1966 the first Pan-African cultural festival attracted an estimated 20,000 visitors to Dakar.[1] Only six years after most African countries had gained independence from the former colonial powers, this event transformed the Senegalese capital into a vibrant meeting point for artists, intellectuals and politicians. They came from a variety of African countries as well as the global African diaspora, from Europe, the US and the Soviet Union. For almost a month, this cultural gathering of unprecedented scale hosted events of various artistic disciplines – theatre, dance, music, visual art, literature, cinema – as well as a well-attended conference at the National Assembly over the course of a week. In a celebratory speech, the Senegalese poet and first president Léopold Sédar Senghor proclaimed that 'if we have assumed the terrible responsibility of organising this festival, it is for the defense and illustration of negritude'.[2] At the same time, he made sure to emphasise that the return to Black culture should ultimately allow Black people to take a new place in the modern world: '… in order to dialogue with others … we, Black people, must finally be ourselves in our dignity: in our recovered identity'.[3] In this sense, he called the festival 'a far more revolutionary enterprise than the exploration of the cosmos: the elaboration of a new *humanism* which this time will include the totality of men on the totality of our planet earth'.[4]

Against the background of centuries of slave trade and colonisation, the First World Festival of Negro Arts in Dakar (Premier Festival

Mondial des Arts Nègres, also referred to as FESMAN) was conceived as a framework to vindicate African cultures and celebrate their return to the stage of history with the advent of newly independent African nations. It would become the first in a series of large-scale cultural festivals on the continent, and served to some extent as an organisational model for such festivals. In 1969 Algeria hosted the Pan-African Cultural Festival in the city of Algiers (Le premier festival culturel panafricain d'Alger, also referred to as PANAF), which was followed by the Zaire '74 festival in Kinshasa in 1974. Finally, in 1977, Nigeria staged the particularly ostentatious Second World Black and African Festival of Arts and Culture (FESTAC) in Lagos. All of these festivals generated huge financial and ideational investment, and contributed, not without conflict or controversy, to a renaissance of Black/African culture. They also fostered a pan-African unity and a transatlantic Black consciousness at the dawn of independence. Despite their inherently ephemeral nature, they had a lasting impact on the host cities and countries, and beyond.

Drawing on postcolonial and decolonial perspectives, this chapter maps transformations in the cultural landscape of the continent, especially in West Africa, related to pan-African cultural festivals. Specifically, this chapter examines these festivals as platforms of an expanding organisational field whose epistemic community, networks and modes of organisation shaped both artistic practices within the field, and long-term institutional developments of the arts across their host territories. By examining the programme contents, venues and institutions that enabled the hosting of these hallmark African postcolonial festivals, their contributions to cultural practices and institutional legacies shall be highlighted. The Pan-African Historical Theatre Project (PANAFEST), a festival held in Ghana every two years since 1992, will be discussed as a successor to the festivals of the 1960s and 1970s.

## The Pan-African cultural festival: some genealogies of a postcolonial format

Festivals are an essential aspect of institutionalised religion in indigenous African societies. As John Mbiti described in his *Introduction to African Religion* in 1975, rituals, festivals and ceremonies not only embody or 'act out' societal values and beliefs, but also communicate them to the younger generations.[5] They typically involve dancing, mask wearing, feasting, making offerings and sacrifices, praying, blessing people, and general jubilation,[6] and function as a platform for community renewal, spiritual awakening, entertainment, and creative and artistic expression.

Like traditional festivals, contemporary festivals are special-status events that are celebrated as holidays, during which formal duties, tasks and everyday routines are abandoned. The unique status of festivals tends to remind participants of the important things and moments in life. Beyond serving as platforms for communal interaction, cohesion, learning and socialisation via a range of activities, contemporary festivals take place in specific locales, focusing on a particular theme. They derive their festive contents from the wealth of cultural milieus in the societies in which they are staged, including but not limited to artistic forms such as drama, dance, music, film, art and crafts. As such, cultural festivals contain potentialities for the reinvention of national and regional identities, and for the promotion of the culture-led regeneration of urban spaces. They could also be developed as representative of ideas of a nation, and become sites of its performative construction.

Contemporary festivals have been conceptualised and organised to promote identity, cement cultural heritage, and facilitate social integration and belonging, as well as foster strategies for tourism development and economic investment.[7] History in particular has become a central ingredient in the institutionalisation and organisational framework of contemporary festivals, which are, according to Torunn Selberg, 'staged and reused for purposes other than the acquisition of knowledge'. Legacies of historical occurrences – including local events, individuals, myths and other forms of narrative – are frequently appropriated, ritualised and actualised in the performative agendas of contemporary festivals.[8] Consequently, while historical festivals generally tend to emphasise the uniqueness of their host community, they also attempt to negotiate, frame or structure historical legacies as a sort of melting pot of local and global narratives. Under such circumstances, the uniqueness of local narratives is dramatised or presented as standing in dialogue or protest (or sometimes both) with narratives relevant to current global circumstances, to ensure success.

African postcolonial festivals were an offshoot of the African cultural renaissance, and the festivals' overarching goals reveal the institutional and organisational frame to be in alignment with this movement, namely: decolonising intellectual discourses of Black/African identity and heritage; building institutions for promoting postcolonial visions for the cultural, political and socioeconomic development of the Black world; and reuniting the continent with the global diaspora, as well as showcasing African cultural capital and talent via theatrical performances including dance, music, drama, film, literature and the visual arts. Besides the celebration of Black/African identity and heritage, these festivals were also spaces of protest and agency, and sites for personal community and cultural interaction.

While the format of the large-scale Pan-African cultural festival has been interpreted as a 'resumption and revenge' of the European model of the world's fair at a time of industrialisation and colonialism,[9] the genesis of the postcolonial Pan-African festival is traceable to deliberations and negotiations at two major conferences – the Congress of Black Writers and Artists, held in Paris in 1956 and Rome in 1959. Organised under the auspices of the publishing house and journal Présence Africaine, and in the case of the second congress the newly founded Société africaine de culture (SAC), these conferences brought together prominent African intellectuals, writers, artists and politicians to critically examine the state, impact and future of African culture as part of the continent's sociopolitical and economic liberation and development. They are not the only precursors, but they are particularly important ones; Elizabeth Harney has pointed to a number of other festivals, exhibitions and conferences that preceded and anticipated the large-scale Pan-African festivals.[10]

The first of these congresses, held at Sorbonne University from 19–22 September 1956, revolved around the theme 'the Crisis of Negro Culture', with attempts made to define and position Black/African cultural discourse within the rubrics of race, politics and historical commonality vis-à-vis the ideological and theoretical positions that undergirded the negritude movement. The significance of the 1956 congress lies in the fact that it provided a conceptual path for the institutionalisation of African postcolonial festivals, as well as establishing a path-dependent example of what would later become a central nucleus of these festivals – the colloquium – whose methods of organisation were perfected at the congress in Rome. The founding of the SAC, an association that aimed to promote African culture and was closely linked to the publishing house Présence Africaine and its founder Alioune Diop, was a direct outcome of the first congress in Paris.[11]

Building on the foundations laid by the 1956 congress, the second Congress of Black Writers and Artists discussed 'the Unity and Responsibilities of Negro-African Culture'. The agenda for this consensus-building congress was broadly divided into two parts: the foundations of African culture and the likelihood of achieving unity and solidarity, and the tasks and responsibilities of each discipline and art form in the actualisation of African unity.[12] Although no further archival sources have been found so far, there are indications that here the colloquium was accompanied by a small music programme and visual arts exhibition, organised by the Senegalese artist Papa Ibra Tall.[13]

In his analysis of the Rome congress, Yohann Ripert avers that the focus of the event differed from the Paris congress in that it moved from 'scholarly discussions to political preparations for a postcolonialism at its fingertips'. Thus, the Rome congress is usually referenced as the point at which African postcolonial festivals were inaugurated via the participants' recommendation that 'the congress must establish an essential part of its activities, a festival to be held during the next congress meeting … The festival must include singing, drumming and dancing, and perhaps also drama and poetry readings. These would have to take place when the congress is in session.'[14]

This recommendation led to the the First World Festival of Negro Arts, which after several delays finally took place in Dakar in 1966. By then most African countries had gained independence, and the series of Pan-African festivals that would unfold on the African continent over the next decade reflected these new conditions.

## Performances of renaissance: instituting and framing African postcolonial festivals

Although the bulk of African postcolonial festivals were planned and hosted as independent events, Dominique Malaquais and Cedric Vincent have demonstrated a 'mutual entanglement' between these festivities. They argue that African postcolonial festivals constituted 'one vast and shape-shifting festival that travelled across time and space', providing spaces for political-cum-developmental continuities across the Black/African world from the 1950s to the present.[15] Following this broad perspective, the African postcolonial festival resembles a mobius strip, folding over itself to produce multiple forms and meanings, thus enabling the recurrence and repeat utilisation of ideas, symbols and processes that unfold in mimetic forms, acquiring new appearances and significations. However, it is critical to contextualise the nuances that underlined the objectives, goals and organisational structures or framings of each festival.

FESMAN in Dakar was supported by investment from the SAC, UNESCO and the Senegalese government led by Léopold Sédar Senghor, as well as by contributions from France.[16] It started with the large-scale colloquium entitled 'Function and significance of African negro art in the life of the people and for the people', which had been prepared at a pre-conference in Paris in 1964 and was financed by UNESCO.

The conference was held at the National Assembly from 30 March to 8 April 1966, and brought together eminent scholars and artists mostly from Africa, Europe and the US.[17] Many newly built cultural institutions served as venues for the festival: the Théâtre National Daniel Sorano; the Senegalese Workshop of Decorative Arts in Thiès, which had opened in December 1965 as an addition to the National Arts Institute in Dakar; the artisanal market of Soumbedioune; and the UNESCO-financed Musée Dynamique (Dynamic Museum), a modernist museum building based on the shape of a Greek temple, with an interior influenced by the Ethnographic Museum in Neuchâtel, Switzerland. A monumental exhibition of classical African art, financed by France and organised by a 'mixed committee', inaugurated the museum during the festival before travelling to the Grand Palais in Paris.[18]

The festival took place against a background of economic weakness. The priority was to present Senegal as a young, progressive nation – at the expense of both the average and poor Senegalese population – and to provide a platform for international visitors to debate major cultural and historiographical issues in Dakar. In the months prior to the festival, dramatic measures were taken to modernise the cityscape: new avenues were created, shanty towns (bidonvilles) demolished and numerous new buildings and hotels built.[19] The festival documentary by African-American filmmaker William Greaves, which was sponsored by the US Information Agency, vividly conveys an impression of smooth progress.[20] However, to cultivate this impression, Senegalese troops drove beggars and other 'undesirables' off the streets, cordoned off impoverished urban areas and closed the university to prevent student unrest, as Elizabeth Harney describes.[21]

Despite its elitist and exclusive character, FESMAN played a pivotal role in supporting global Pan-African efforts to boost the African cultural renaissance, creating a valuable intellectual and political climate for Black/African people of different nationalities to 'explore their common experiences without perceiving themselves as special people who shared a fixed nationality and identity'.[22] However, the organisation and delivery of FESMAN generated various reactions and criticisms. The major misgivings about FESMAN revolved around Senghor's unilateral enthronement of negritude as the preeminent ideological vision for African emancipation, and the overt privileging of culture over political, economic and liberational activism. Critique also concerned the exclusionary limits of participation, which not only denied representation to a large proportion of Black/African liberation movements, but also limited access to some Black/African dissidents and critics.[23]

These misgivings resulted in PANAF in Algiers in 1969, one of the most revolutionary and representative Pan-African gatherings of the twentieth century. The structure of PANAF was similar to that of FESMAN, and included a theatre, music and performance programme, visual arts exhibitions, film, literature, and a major conference. The organisers of PANAF sought and attracted participation from all member countries of the Organisation of African Unity (OAU), Black diaspora movements across the globe, national liberation movements in Africa and delegations from the Middle East and Asia.[24] Unlike FESMAN, the organisational agency of PANAF was directed towards demonstrating the inextricable link between culture and the ideological battle to liberate Africa from colonialism, neocolonialism and imperialism.[25] Accordingly, the Algiers conference moved away from the detached discussions of Dakar to take into account the more political dimensions of cultural debates.[26] In contrast to Dakar, the PANAF festival venues were easily accessible, as Tsitsi Ella Jaji describes. Ten temporary stages were built in public squares across the city, allowing direct contact between the visiting performers and working-class Algerians, as captured in William Klein's documentary film.[27]

As if to demonstrate its revolutionary credentials and radical spirit, negritude was consistently criticised as 'racial essentialism and neo-colonial pacifism', and thus rejected as a pathway for African development and progress.[28] In its stead, the event produced a Pan-African Cultural Manifesto as a guide to Africa's radical cultural practice and revolu-tionary postcolonial future.[29]

Following FESMAN and PANAF, the next major postcolonial festival was scheduled to take place in Lagos in 1970, conceived as a continua-tion of FESMAN. However, due to a combination of the Nigeria-Biafra War (1967–70) and organisational lapses, the event was delayed until 1977. Meanwhile, Zaire '74 in Kinshasa emerged as a gap-filling or precursor event to Lagos '75, later hosted as FESTAC '77. The Zaire '74 festival arose from Hugh Masekela and Stewart Levine's proposal to hold a three-day Black/African music festival as a prelude to the boxing match between Muhammad Ali and George Foreman, which came to be known as 'The Rumble in the Jungle'.

In keeping with earlier festivals, the main aim of Zaire '74 was to facilitate interaction, solidarity and cultural exchange between Black and African musical icons from the US, South America and the Caribbean and their African counterparts, particularly Zairians. It also sought to link sounds from the Black diaspora – including blues, rumba, jazz and soul – with a diverse range of African rhythms, while also encouraging collaboration between the artists responsible for these cultural products. According to Ron Levi, the festival united 'Black power' with 'soul' power at a time when both were at their peak, and together with The Rumble in the Jungle showcased the glory of Black culture and Mobutu's regime.[30] Thus, Zaire '74 could be described as a festival where the co-mingling of statist and commercial agendas led to a different expression of the African cultural renaissance – authenticity, or Mobutuism.

Due perhaps to Mobutu's involvement and influence (vis-à-vis his projects of political and cultural nationalism), Zaire '74 has attracted little critical attention, even though it arguably falls within the bounds of the transnational cultural productions that emerged in Africa from the late 1960s onwards. Organised as a 'purely sound event' with little or no relationship with the broad landscape of cultural discourse, Zaire '74 deserves a place within the continuum of global African postcolonial festivals due to the characteristics it shares with the more prominent cultural festivities, including a transnational vision of Pan-Africanism, Pan-African solidarity, and elements of African cultural nationalism and renaissance, as well as the valorisation of decolonisation and imperialism. Despite its limited organisational frame, Zaire '74 embodied an emerging trend that brought statist political agendas and investment (especially investment in the building of institutions and events) into the cultural field in the postcolonial Africa of the 1960s and 1970s.

In contrast to the peripherality of Zaire '74, FESTAC, held in Lagos in 1977, has been acknowledged as the 'grandest' of all the era's African postcolonial festivals. Financed by Nigeria's recent oil boom[31] and taking place in the aftermath of the ideological rivalry that followed FESMAN and PANAF, FESTAC '77 was organised from a moderating frame – one meant to reconcile the extreme ideological positions on Black/ African renaissance while steering the focus of Black/African cultural empowerment towards technology-driven modernity.[32] As evidenced by the festival's opening addresses, Nigeria's president Olusegun Obasanjo, and indeed the festival organisers, tied the success of the Black/African renaissance journey to political awareness, and historical and cultural restoration to a concomitant restoration of the links between culture, creativity and mastery of modern technology and industrialism. In his opening address Obasanjo proclaimed that Africans needed to embrace technological progress:

> What is of paramount importance is to recognise and give modern technology which is the base of Western dominance, its due place. Modern technology is indispensable to our march forward, but the

acquisition of technology does not mean a break with the past …
We must dedicate this festival to ensuring that black and African
peoples all over the world become aware of what it takes to change
the lot of our peoples and industrialization and technological
advance are our essential imperative. Just as our ancestors have
made a timeless impact in the development of aesthetic cultural
artefacts, we too have the task to bring this inherent creative power
to bear on the mastery of industrial progress.

In his message at the opening of the FESTAC '77 colloquium, Obasanjo
framed the Black world's dependency status as an historical condition
that could be addressed not through 'excursion into the past' and 'self-
glorification and self-justification' but through achieving 'originality in
our thoughts' and mastery of 'technological creativity', functioning as 'a
tool for increasing the share or affluence which science and technology,
and the social sciences make possible in today's world'. For Obasanjo,
only this intellectual achievement and developmental pathway would
earn the Black/African world 'the dignity we crave for, the recognition
we seek and the liberation we are struggling to achieve'.[33]

Like PANAF, the colloquium of FESTAC '77 supported a rich blend
of critical discourse, intellectual engagement and intervention on the
theme of 'Black Civilization and Education'.[34] The Lagos Programme –
an outline of implementable goals covering all the sub-themes of
the colloquium – emerged from the colloquium as a development
policy document for the Black/African world.[35] The extent to which
these recommendations were implemented or incorporated into the
development agendas of various Black/African countries is debatable,
but as no African country can thus far be described as industrialised, it is
safe to assume the technology-driven pathway projected at FESTAC '77
did not find widespread adoption.

Overall, FESTAC '77 represented the last of the statist-led Black/
African postcolonial festivals in which culture inspired a modernising,
progressive developmental path leading towards a glorious destiny for
the Black/African world. More than anything, the cumulative exploration
of these special cultural events from the late 1960s and 1970s shows how
a spectrum of ideas brought individuals together in movements and
networks for the recuperation of Black/African history, heritage and
civilisation – movements and networks that sought to map a modernised
African world and elevate a hitherto denigrated Black/African culture to
an enviable position among global cultures. Although Ethiopia was the
designated host of the next African postcolonial festival, scheduled for

1981, it did not go ahead due to a chain of events including famine in the Horn of Africa that extended from the late 1970s to the mid-1980s and a serious political crisis, thus bringing to an end the era of grand African festivals – something development economists have described as 'deinstitutionalisation'.[36] The deinstitutionalisation of grand, state-sponsored African postcolonial festivals was the result of a complex interplay of economic, political and unsustainable institutional forces that emerged in the 1980s.

Described by the World Bank as a 'lost decade' in Africa,[37] the 1980s bore witness to a raft of changes driven by sociopolitical and economic crises, including social uprisings, protests, civil conflicts, coups d'état, military and civilian dictatorships, austerity measures, and famine. It was a period in which the inspiring visions of hope for the continent – revolving around rapid modernisation, political stability, economic and social progress, prosperity, development, and optimism in the early years of decolonisation – were gradually and extensively replaced by new waves of struggle against autocratic regimes, economic decline and rising public debt.[38] In addition to these regressive scenarios, major (Western) financial institutions such as the World Bank, the International Monetary Fund (IMF) and the United States Agency for International Development (USAID) imposed so-called 'necessary conditions' as requirements for the extension of international credit facilities to the Global South, thus forcing African countries to adopt these institutions' structural-adjustment and economic-stabilisation programmes.[39] The underlying purpose of these programmes, and the agenda of the institutions that sponsored them, was to engineer the liberalisation of African economies as a part of synchronised efforts to roll back Soviet influence in sub-Saharan Africa and impose a free-market economic framework. However, this economic imposition was not without consequences, as for the most part it led to a sharp decline in government investment in the cultural sector across Africa.[40] Thus, funding for cultural events, such as festival organisation and other art-related programmes, either became severely limited or was diverted into the servicing of what were often considered more 'critical sectors'. Nevertheless, it was in this challenging atmosphere that ideas for a new Pan-African festival in Ghana were expressed in Efua Sutherland's paper 'Proposal for a Historical Drama Festival in Cape Coast' (see also chapter 14).

PANAFEST was conceived by Sutherland as a cultural project that would extend the frontiers of theatrical production within the context of the national theatre movement. Put differently, the festival's conceptual goals were directed towards consolidating the achievements of the national theatre movement by linking developments in theatre to festival making, and progressively connecting this emergent theatrical development in creative collaboration with outputs across the continent, and with Black/African communities in the diaspora.[41] This conceptual vision is evidenced by the fact that the proposal for the festival was submitted through the drama unit of the Institute of African Studies in 1980, undergoing a gradual (ultimately eight-year) vetting process from the regional to the national government, attracting a network of supporters along the way.

However, it was not until the proposal was modified and rechristened, and the focus expanded to demonstrate its economic viability or potential to the state, that investment in its actualisation and institutionalisation was mobilised. Instead of its institutionalisation as a historical theatre festival as initially conceptualised by Sutherland (and actualised in the first two iterations of the festival), the event was reconceived as a Pan-African cultural event accommodating not only the exhibition of other artistic and cultural productions, but also providing space for intellectual discourse on African history (addressing dialogic engagements or contact between Africans on the continent and those in the diaspora) and tourism-product development.[42] While acknowledging this conceptual recasting, Sutherland avers that the event has expanded over time from the original, centralised vision of 'reconciliation and reunification' via the theatricalisation of (slave) history[43] to one that incorporates tourism-development projects such as Emancipation Day, the Joseph Project and the Year of Return initiative (among other statist homecoming projects), thus enabling the Ghanaian state to 'exploit the country's abundant points of interest, such as the former slave trading forts, as well as its well-known history of Pan-Africanism for economic progress'.[44]

As a biannual cultural event combining history, heritage and culture in an attractive tourist product, PANAFEST, along with the other statist homecoming projects mentioned above, functions as a veritable contact zone between the continent and its diaspora. Organised under broad, recurrent themes – the 'Re-Emergence of African Civilization' and 'Uniting the African Family' – PANAFEST seeks, among other things, to revise the historical narrative of the slave trade by confronting or 'exorcising the trauma' associated with it in an attempt to engineer 'reconciliation and reunification' between the continent and its diaspora, and to encourage the exchange of ideas, skills and expertise, along with direct economic investments or partnerships, to support the development of a shared or mutually beneficial future. While it shares ideological roots, overarching goals and proximate objectives with the ideals of Pan-Africanism, drawing organisational continuities from FESMAN, PANAF and FESTAC, PANAFEST operates essentially in a different sphere to its predecessors. Whereas the first generation of modern art festivals in Africa exhibited 'carefully balanced goals to tourism with concrete political objectives related to specific transnational communities' as representations of a decolonising impetus across the continent, PANAFEST and related second-generation African postcolonial festivals represent 'new forms' of cultural production and circulation in an increasingly fragmented yet globalised world space.[45] Not only are these new events exposed to the vagaries of free-market and liberal commercialisation, they are often incorporated into the complex, contested dynamics of the hosts' (trans)national political and developmental agendas. In view of such imbrications, Katharina Schramm argues for the 'potential promise of economic development' and the utility of the cultural sphere as an arena for legitimation, particularly for the 'government in charge', rather than a genuine interest in the performing arts, to be the dominant driver in actualising the festival.[46]

## Institutional legacies of Pan-African postcolonial festivals

Embedded in African postcolonial festivals is a whole gamut of events conceptualised and actualised under the canopy of the African (cultural) renaissance as an amalgamation of movements, of which Pan-Africanism emerged as an overriding ideology. Pan-Africanism accommodated theoretical conceptions that emphasised ideals of African liberation and development while also centre-staging the connected histories and heritage of the Black/African world and its contributions to humanity. Taken together, these events showcased various layers of African cultural riches across theatrical (dance, drama, music and film), visual (art, crafts and architectural design) and intellectual (literature and research) domains, and at the same time facilitated the building of institutions, via statist intervention, for the promotion of Black/African civilisation and cultural, sociopolitical and economic development across the Black world.

Preparations for these events resulted in what could be described as a golden era of funding and cultural investment in postcolonial Africa. Coinciding with the Cold War – during which culture, especially theatre, played a critical role in the battle for supremacy in the global conflict – the level of investment in the cultural sector by African governments in the 1960s seems to confirm the observation that 'the Cold War period saw an unprecedented expansion of public funding of the arts, especially the performing arts'.[47]

The institutions that hosted FESMAN in Dakar continue to shape the cultural landscape of Senegal, an exception being the Musée Dynamique, which operated as a museum only until 1988 (excepting a five-year spell as a dance school) before being declared the seat of the Supreme Court by president Abdou Diouf.[48] To this day, there are calls to move the court and use the building for its original purpose. In recent years a new theatre, the Grand Théâtre National de Dakar, and museum were built in Dakar via Chinese investment. The scale of these buildings makes the elder institutions look small. In particular the Museum of Black Civilisations, which opened in 2018, can be considered a legacy of FESMAN, and the cultural policies of its time more generally, insofar as it represents a belated realisation of a museum project envisaged by Senghor to embody his ideas on negritude and Black civilisation.[49] It was president Abdoulaye Wade who finally helped bring the long-planned museum into existence, and who also invested in a revitalisation of the 1966 festival, FESMAN 2010, held in Dakar under the theme of African renaissance.[50] However, the strongest sense of continuity with FESMAN 1966 can be felt at the visual arts biennale Dak'Art, which was founded during Abou Diouf's presidency in 1992 and has since established itself as Africa's most important visual art biennial. It regularly attracts thousands of visitors to Dakar, and provides a contemporary platform for transatlantic Pan-African art and debate.

The first Pan-African Cultural Festival (PANAF) in 1969 played an important role in the 'spatio-political' development of Algiers, as Anna Jayne Kimmel explains:

> The city committed to material upgrades in preparation for the festival, including illuminating the streets with new cables for lighting, expanding the sanitation infrastructure, as well as constructing several temporary hospitals, lodgings, and infirmaries. Live theatres and cinemas were equipped with the latest technology to accommodate the technical needs of the artists.[51]

Furthermore, the festival's colloquium produced the Pan-African Cultural Manifesto as a guideline for the decolonisation of Black/African cultural and political spaces – a precursor to the institutionalisation of so-called 'cultural policies' across the continent in the 1970s. The festival also influenced the establishment of the Pan-African Federation of Filmmakers (FEPACI), under whose aegis the Pan-African Film and Television Festival of Ouagadougou (FESPACO) became instituted. In 2009, a second Pan-African Cultural Festival was staged in Algiers.

FESTAC '77 was directly responsible for several structural and institutional projects, including the formation of the National Council for Arts and Culture (NCAC) and the festival that became associated with it, the National Festival of Arts and Culture (NAFEST); the National Theatre; the Centre for Black and African Arts and Civilization (CBAAC); and the federal housing estate Festac Town.[52]

It would probably be premature to try to ascertain the direct institutional legacies of PANAFEST, given that the festival is ongoing. However, there can be no denying that the emergence of PANAFEST – inspired by and building on the legacies of FESMAN, PANAF and FESTAC '77, all of which strengthened interactions between continental Africans and the Black/African diaspora – has brought tourism and economic collaboration into the purview of African postcolonial development. Ghana's success in blending its precolonial slave-trade history, ecological conservation and Kwame Nkrumah's Pan-African legacy – in addition to the modernisation of traditional festivals – into a tourist marketing strategy that has transformed the country into the destination of choice (the gateway to Africa) for the Black/African diaspora is both admirable and, in its blatant commercialisation, problematic. The emergence of PANAFEST as an embedded component of Ghana's tourism-development initiative, and the derived economic benefits in the cultural, creative and hospitality sectors, could be cited as direct legacies of the festival.

## Situating African postcolonial festivals in the globalisation of African cultural productions: a concluding prognosis

If one were to attempt to evaluate African postcolonial festivals, either in terms of a single event or from the perspective of the idealism that undergirded their organisational goals and objectives, one could paint a portrait of colourful spectacles that produced little tangible evidence of progress despite massive financial and ideational investment. However, analysing these events alongside the African renaissance as confluences of connected ideas, people and movements towards the actualisation of proximate objectives or goals, one begins to see the extent to which these events influenced the deconstruction of Eurocentric ideas of African identity, heritage and civilisation, and the transformation of culture from the threshold of proscription to acceptance, thus building networks for the global circulation of cultural productions. Even though negritude has been thoroughly critiqued for its racial essentialism, the movement's centrality in the projection of African culture cannot be denied. In his study *In Search of Africa*, Manthia Diawara captures this contribution thus:

> Negritude, as part of decolonisation, was important because it gave black people in France their first opportunity to assert themselves in the political, psychological and artistic spheres. This would later lead to the independence of several African countries, with Negritude writers among the heads of state. Negritude enabled African and the Caribbean, for the first time, to deploy blackness as a positive concept of modernisation: be proud of your ancestry, discover the beauty of blackness, and let Negritude unite you against colonialism.[53]

From the conception and actualisation of the first and second Congress of Black and African Writers and Artists to FESMAN, the idea for Black/African postcolonial festivals emerged as a cultural project in the 1950s, drawing coeval intellectual contributions from an aggregate of movements under the aegis of Pan-Africanism for the Black/African renaissance. The conceptual networks for these events brought together actors, cultural experts, politicians and artist-scholars including Aimé Césaire, Leon-Gontran Damas, Leopold Senghor, Richard Wright, Mercer Cooke, Frantz Fanon and Alioune Diop. Diop ultimately emerged as a central broker in the network by creating a circulatory apparatus – the periodical *Présence Africaine*, which linked the theoretical ideals of negritude with the Pan-African diaspora – and by playing a central role in the organisation of both FESMAN and FESTAC. FESMAN established the organisational framework or structure – the colloquium, a performance programme, and exhibitions (see Morgan Kulla's 'The politics of culture: the case of FESTAC') – that subsequent festivals followed (PANAF and FESTAC), attempted to follow (Zaire '74) or adapted in some form (PANAFEST). While PANAFEST may not be an exact fit in terms of agenda and the scale of organisation with FESMAN, PANAF and FESTAC, what connects its conceptual network with that of these first-generation festivals are its ties to Pan-African aspirations via the utilisation of 'modern' festivals as a 're-membering' enterprise, combining political and economic development, solidarity, cultural recuperation, and collaboration between the continent and the global diaspora.

Criticism of these events has focused on the enormous economic cost, corruption and waste (in the case of FESTAC), and various schisms within the events' organisational structures, but their institutional legacies suggest an era of immense investment and institution building in the cultural sector. Thus, the development of these events followed a general trajectory where ideas from artist-scholars drew statist and private patronage (via a process of institutional building) that enabled collaboration between artists, governments, public agencies and participants towards the actualisation of these events. As legacies of the African renaissance and African postcolonial festivals, these emergent cultural institutions – though largely overdependent on subsidies and government patronage, and vulnerable to operational challenges arising from the lack thereof – seem to have enabled the circulation and penetration of African culture as seen in the cultural and creative industries, especially in music (Afrobeats, Amapiano, etc.), film (Nollywood, Ghollywood, Sollywood, etc.) and literature. The explosion of African culture onto the global stage draws on the flow of capital, talent, skills, technology and collaboration between the continent and its global diaspora – a central commitment of the African renaissance and the festivities that became associated with it.

## Notes

1   Ficquet, 2008, 22.
2   Senghor 1977 [1966], our translation, 58.
3   Senghor 1977 [1966], our translation, 62.
4   Senghor 1977 [1966], our translation, 58.
5   Mbiti, 1975, 136.
6   Mbiti, 1975, 137.
7   See Selberg, 2006.
8   Selberg, 2006, 298.
9   Ficquet, 2008, 22. See also Apter, 2005.
10  Such as the Biennale de la Méditerranée in Alexandria in 1955, the Afro-Asian Writers' Conference in Tashkent in 1958, the First International Congress of Africanists in Accra, Ghana in 1962, and the First International Congress of African Culture at the Salisbury National Gallery in Zimbabwe (then colonial Rhodesia). See Harney 2004, 263 and Harney, 2016, 180–1.
11  Aka-Evy, 2007.
12  See Diop, 1959.
13  Tall, 1993, 3.
14  Ripert, 2017, 160.
15  Malaquais and Vincent, 2016, 194–5.
16  See Snipe, 2003; M'Baye, 2017; Ficquet and Gallimardet, 2009, 140–1.
17  The conference proceedings have been published by Société africaine de culture, 1967 and 1971.
18  Vincent, 2016, 46.
19  Ficquet and Gallimardet, 2009, 140.
20  Greaves, 1996.
21  Harney, 2004, 76.

22 M'Baye, 2017, 142. For a detailed analysis of FESMAN, Dakar 1966, see Cooke, 1966; Murphy, 2016; Wane and Mbaye, 2020.
23 See Ratcliff, 2014.
24 Anderson, 2016.
25 Radcliffe, 2014, 87.
26 Société nationale d'édition et de diffusion (Algérie), 1969.
27 Jaji, 2016, 125.
28 See Anderson, 2016.
29 For an in-depth report on the organisation of the festival, as well as an examination of the recommendations suggested in the Pan-African Cultural Manifesto – a product of the festival's colloquium on the themes 'The Realities of African Culture', 'The Role of African Culture in National Liberation Struggles' and 'The Role of African Culture in Economic and Social Development of Africa' – see Meghelli, 2014.
30 Levi, 2017, 185.
31 See Apter, 2005.
32 See Apter, 2005.
33 Obasanjo, 1977.
34 From an organisational perspective, the main theme of the colloquium was divided into ten sub-themes and then divided among five working committees, with two sub-themes forming a work group, for example: 1.1 Black Civilisation and Arts, 1.2 Black Civilisation and Pedagogy; 2.3 Black Civilisation and Literature, 2.4 Black Civilisation and African Languages.
35 For an in-depth exploration of the proceedings and recommendations of the colloquium vis-à-vis the Lagos programme, see Amoda, 1978.
36 See Serra, 2018.
37 World Bank, 1990, 1.
38 Serra, 2018, 150.
39 Structural adjustment programmes promoted and placed emphasis on free trade, subsidy removal, privatisation, currency devaluation and public bureaucratic reforms. See Serra, 2018.
40 Apart from the general criticism that these interventions, rather than restructuring African economies, contributed to state delegitimisation, a lack of domestic policy autonomy and the vagaries of downsizing measures that precipitated brain-drain and development crises across the continent, it is widely held that the aggressive implementation of the programme ignored the human condition, especially the possibility of worsening the wellbeing of the most vulnerable, as well as the fact that the significant reductions it imposed across sectors such as education and primary healthcare could pose unmitigated risks to the continent's economic future. See Serra 2018, 161.
41 See Yankah, 2012; Schramm, 2010; Adutwumwah, 2020.
42 Adutwumwah, 2020.
43 CJAS, 2020, 128.
44 Pierre, 2013, 131.
45 McMahon, 2014, 13.
46 Schramm, 2010, 180.
47 Balme and Szymanski-Düll, 2017, 8. See also the introduction to this volume.
48 Huchard, 2010, 458.
49 Diallo, 2019.
50 Niang, 2012.
51 Kimmel, 2021, n.p.
52 See FESTAC '77, Reports and Summary of Accounts, 11.
53 Diawara, 1998, 8.

# References

Adutwumwah, Doreen Gyimah. 'The continuities within the Ghanaian festival scene: the performance of nation building and identity formation', *Senior Projects Spring 2020* 195 (2020). Accessed 7 June 2021 . https://digitalcommons.bard.edu/senproj_s2020/195.

Aka-Evy, L. 'Présence Africaine: de la société Africaine de culture à la communauté africaine de culture', *Présence Africaine* 175–7: 234–9 (2007). https://doi.org/10.3917/presa.175.0234.

Amoda, Moyibi. *Festac Colloquium and Black World Development*. Lagos: Nigerian Magazine Special Publications, 1978.

Anderson, Samuel. 'Negritude is Dead: performing the African revolution at the first Pan-African cultural festival (Algiers, 1969)'. In *The First World Festival of Negro Arts, Dakar 1966: Contexts and legacies*, edited by David Murphy, 133–50. Liverpool: Liverpool University Press, 2016.

Apter, Andrew. *The Pan-African Nation: Oil and the spectacle of culture in Nigeria*. Chicago: University of Chicago Press, 2005.

Apter, Andrew. 'Beyond négritude: black cultural citizenship and the Arab question in FESTAC 77', *Journal of African Cultural Studies* 28 (3) (2016): 313–26.

Balme, Christopher and Szymanski-Düll, Berenika. 'Introduction'. In *Theatre, Globalization and the Cold War*, edited by Christopher B. Balme and Berenika Szymanski-Düll, 1–22. Cham: Palgrave Macmillan, 2017.

CJAS. 'In conversation with Esi Sutherland', *Contemporary Journal of African Studies* 7 (1) (2020): 126–41.

Cooke, Paul. 'The art of Africa for the whole world: an account of the first world festival of negro arts', *Negro History Bulletin* 29 (8) (1966): 171–2, 185–6, 189.

Diallo, Mamadou. 'Is the Museum of Black Civilisations a place for today or the 1960s?', *The Sole Adventurer: Contemporary Art Magazine*. https://thesoleadventurer.com/is-the-museum-of-black-civilisations-a-place-for-today-or-the-1960s-by-mamadou-diallo/.

Diawara, Manthia. *In Search of Africa*. Cambridge, MA: Harvard University Press, 1998.

Diop, Alioune. 'Discours d'ouverture, Deuxième Congrès des Écrivains et Artistes Noirs (Rome: 26 mars – 1er avril 1959)', *Présence Africaine* (1959): 40–8.

*FESTAC '77: Report and Summary of Accounts*. Lagos: CBAAC.

Ficquet, Eloi. 'L'impact durable d'une action artistique: le festival mondial des arts nègres de Dakar en 1966', *Africultures* 73 (2008): 18–25.

Ficquet, Éloi and Gallimardet, Lorraine. '"On ne peut nier longtemps l'art nègre". Enjeux du colloque et de l'exposition du Premier Festival mondial des arts nègres de Dakar en 1966', *Gradhiva* 10 (2009): 134–55.

Greaves, William. *First World Festival of Negro Arts* (film). 1966.

Harney, Elizabeth. *In Senghor's Shadow: Art, politics, and the avant-garde in Senegal, 1960–1995*. Durham, NC: Duke University Press, 2004.

Harney, Elizabeth. 'FESMAN at 50: Pan-Africanism, visual modernism and the archive of the global contemporary'. In *The First World Festival of Negro Arts, Dakar 1966: Contexts and legacies*, edited by David Murphy, 180–93. Liverpool: Liverpool University Press, 2016.

Huchard, Ousmane Sow. *La culture, ses objets-témoins et l'action museéologique. Sémiotique et témoignage d'un objet-témoin: le masque kanaga des dogons de sanga*. Dakar: Éditions le Nègre International, 2010.

Jaji, Tsitsi Ella. 'The next best thing to being there: covering the 1966 Dakar festival and its legacy in Black popular magazines'. In *The First World Festival of Negro Arts, Dakar 1966: Contexts and legacies*, edited by David Murphy, 113–29. Liverpool: Liverpool University Press, 2016.

Kimmel, Anna Jayne. 'On remembering Le Premier Festival Culturel Panafricain d'Alger 1969: an assembled interview', *Lateral* 8 (1) (2021): 1–24. https://doi.org/10.25158/L10.1.6.

Kulla, Morgan. 'The politics of culture: the case of FESTAC', *Ufahamu: A Journal of African Studies* 7 (1) (1976): 166–92.

Levi, Ron. 'Zaire '74: politicising the sound event', *Social Dynamics* 43 (2) (2017): 184–98.

Levi, Ron. 'The musical diplomacy of a landless ambassador: Hugh Masekela between Monterey '67 and Zaire '74', *Interventions* 20 (7) (2018): 987–1002.

Malaquais, Dominique. 'Rumble in the jungle: boxe, festival et politique', *Africultures, Festivals et biennales d'Afrique: Machine ou Utopie?* 73 (2008): 43–59.

Malaquais, Dominique and Vincent, Cédric. 'PANAFEST: a festival complex revisited'. In *The First World Festival of Black Arts, Dakar 1966: Contexts and legacies,* edited by David Murphy, 194–202. Liverpool: Liverpool University Press, 2016.

M'Baye, Babacar. 'Pan-Africanism, transnationalism, and cosmopolitanism in Langston Hughes's involvement in the First World Festival of Black Arts', *South Atlantic Review, Special Issue: Black Transnationalism* 82 (4) (2017): 139–59.

Mbiti, John S. *Introduction to African Religion*. London: Heinemann, 1975.

McMahon, Christina S. *Recasting Transnationalism through Performances: Theatre festivals in Cape Verde, Mozambique and Brazil*. New York: Palgrave Macmillan, 2014.

Meghelli, Samir. 'A weapon in our struggle for liberation: black arts, black power, and the 1969 Pan-African cultural festival'. In *The Global Sixties in Sound and Visions*, edited by T. S. Brown and A. Lison, 167–84. New York: Palgrave Macmillan, 2014.

Murphy, David. 'Introduction. The performance of Pan-Africanism: staging the African renaissance at the first world festival of negro arts'. In *The First World Festival of Negro Arts, Dakar 1966: Contexts and legacies*, edited by David Murphy, 1–42. Liverpool: Liverpool University Press, 2016.

Niang, Amy. 'African renaissance between rhetoric and the aesthetics of extravagance: FESMAN 2010 – entrapped in textuality'. In *African Theatre 11: Festivals*, edited by M. Banham, J. Gibbs and F. Osofisan, 30–8. Woodbridge: Boydell & Brewer, 2012.

Obasanjo, Olusegun. 'Africans have Come of Age'. Speech at the opening ceremony of the Second World Black and African Festival of Arts and Culture (FESTAC), 15 January 1977, Lagos. CBAAC/FESTAC/IFC/1977/Col OS/03.

Pierre, Jemima. *The Predicament of Blackness: Postcolonial Ghana and the politics of race*. Chicago: University of Chicago Press, 2013.

Ratcliff, Anthony. 'When negritude was in vogue: critical reflections of the first world festival of negro arts and culture in 1966', *Journal of Pan-African Studies* 6 (7) (2014):167–83.

Ripert, Yohann. 'Rethinking Negritude: Aimé Césaire & Leopold Senghor and the imagination of a global postcolony'. PhD thesis. New York: Columbia University, 2017.

Schramm, Katharina. *African Homecoming: Pan-African ideology and contested heritage*. Walnut Creek, CA: Left-Coast Press, 2010.

Selberg, Torunn. 'Festivals as celebrations of place in modern society: two examples from Norway', *Folklore* 117 (3) (2006): 297–312.

Senghor, Léopold Sédar. 'Fonction et signification du Premier Festival Mondial des Arts Nègres'. In *Liberté 3: Négritude et civilisation de l'Universel*, 58–63. Paris: Éditions du Seuil, 1977 [1966].

Serra, Gerardo. 'Development indicators at the United Nations Economic Commission for Africa, 1980–1990', *Histoire & mesure*, 33–1 (2018): 149–72. https://journals.openedition.org/histoiremesure/6942.

Snipe, Tracy. 'Cultural politics in post-independence Senegal'. In *Afro-Optimism: Perspectives on African advances*, edited by Ebere Onwudiwe and Minabere Ibelema, 53–66. Westport, CT: Praeger, 2003.

Société africaine de culture. *Colloque sur l'Art nègre: Fonction et signification de l'art nègre dans la vie du peuple et pour le peuple (30 mars–8 avril 1966)*. 2 vols. Paris: Présence Africaine, 1967–71.

Société nationale d'édition et de diffusion (Algérie). *La Culture africaine: Le symposium d'Alger. 21 juillet–1er août 1969. 1. Festival culturel panafricain*. 1969.

Tall, Papa Ibra. *Curriculum Vitae*. Unpublished, 1993.

Vincent, Cédric. 'The real heart of the festival: the exhibition of *l'art nègre* at the Musée Dynamique'. In *The First World Festival of Negro Arts, Dakar 1966: Contexts and legacies*, edited by David Murphy, 45–63. Liverpool: Liverpool University Press, 2016.

Wane, Ibrahima and Mbaye, Saliou, eds. *Le 1er Festival Mondial des Arts Nègres: Mémoire et actualité*. Dakar: Harmattan Sénégal, 2020.

World Bank. *World Development Report 1990: Poverty*. Oxford: Oxford University Press, 1990.

Yankah, Victor K. 'The Pan-African Historical Theatre Festival (PANAFEST) in Ghana, 1992–2010: the vision and the reality'. In *African Theatre 11: Festivals*, edited by James Gibbs, 45–55. Woodbridge: Boydell & Brewer, 2012.

3
# Theatre for development (TfD) as an organisational field
Abdul Karim Hakib

## Introduction

Globally, the theatre for development (TfD) phenomenon has come to stay. It developed into an academic discipline from varied practices derived from different parts of the world, and at different times has been labelled community theatre, popular theatre and theatre for integrated rural development. Although the technique is employed widely and in different ways, there is still little scholarship about how this theatrical discipline developed institutional characteristics. This chapter delineates how these diverse practices evolved into an organisational field – a key term of neo-institutional theory that refers to sets of organisations marked by professionalisation, common goals and a high degree of isomorphism. It will trace the evolution of TfD and discuss how it was consolidated into an organisational field through a series of workshops, which became field-configuring events (FCEs) in the language of organisational and institutional theory (seminal among them the theatre for development workshop that took place in Murewa, Zimbabwe in 1983). Finally, this chapter will highlight the involvement of practitioners and scholars from many African countries, as well as the substantial support from various countries and international organisations such as the ITI and UNESCO. Although there exists a considerable body of literature by scholars, practitioners and researchers on TfD, little or nothing has been done to examine how the field became configured and subsequently diffused in Africa.[1] The perspective shared here contributes to an understanding of the multiplexity of power relations, the complex transnational engagements and the varied institutional (both local and international) interest of the many actors who transformed TfD into an organisational field. The first part of the chapter explores the beginnings of TfD and surveys its 'conferencisa-tion'. It is followed by an examination of the role the 1983 TfD workshop in Zimbabwe played in the consolidation of TfD as an organisational field with the support and influence of international organisations such as UNESCO and the ITI.

## History and glocal conferencisation

The journey of TfD in its varied forms and under various labels has been conditioned by the developmental and decolonial dilemma of African countries and scholars in the postcolonial era. This is evident in the debate over cognate terms before the eventual acceptance of 'theatre for development'. The Laedza Batanani project that started in Botswana in 1973 is often cited as the beginning of TfD in Africa,[2] but there had been a number of projects with similar characteristics long before then. Sandy Arkhurst argues that, several years before the Laedza Batanani project, Efua Sutherland in Ghana fully integrated culture, education and indigenous performance genres as a means of motivating individuals and communities to help themselves in confronting the challenge of 'poverty, environmental degradation, lack of sanitation and resources and the fading influence of indigenous cultural values'. In a different but related context, Christopher Kamlongera argues that TfD in Africa 'is as old as indigenous practices are on the continent on the one hand, and as old as colonialism on the other'. However, for the purposes of this chapter we will use the Botswana experiment as a starting point.

The practice started spreading in the Southern African region from 1978 after the first TfD workshop was held to celebrate the success of the Laedza Batanani project. Ross Kidd writes that it 'represented the culmination of four years of experimental work in Theatre for Development', and that 'it was organised to pass the experience and skills gained from the experimental work on to development workers from other regions in the country'.[3] The Laedza Batanani project aimed to develop local community development facilitators and non-formal education workers. The methodology was diffused across Botswana because participation was extended to community development officers from all parts of the country. Botswana's government wanted the methodology to be adapted and appropriated in other community and non-formal education projects. Therefore popular theatre, as it was then called, was incorporated into the integrated non-formal education campaign in Botswana.[4] This paved the way for sharing best practices with neighbouring countries, which kick-started the diffusion process in the Southern African region and eventually in the rest of Africa and the world.

The international workshops – what David Kerr calls 'the "conferencisation" of arts for development in Southern Africa', and by extension Africa – began in Chalimbana in 1979.[5] He argues that 'perhaps, the most influential workshop for launching the Theatre for Development movement was the one held at Chalimbana about 30 km east of Lusaka in Zambia in 1979'.[6] It is noteworthy that the primary purpose of the workshop was to 'develop the methodology initiated by the Laedza Batanani team', implying that participants from other countries were introduced to the concept as it was experimented with within Botswana.[7] It is not surprising that immediately after this workshop the methodology started spreading rapidly, with some degree of variation, throughout the Southern African region.[8] This diffusion was led mainly by those who participated in the workshop, indicating that the TfD methodology was mainly extended to other countries by people who participated in practical learning processes and national and international workshops. This phenomenon will continue throughout the life of the practice in Africa and beyond, and the workshop will eventually become a format, methodology and integral dissemination mechanism in the TfD milieu (see chapter 7).

## Contextualising TfD as an organisational field

The term 'organisational field' was developed as a 'critical unit bridging the organisational and societal levels in the study of social and community change'.[9] It provides a basis for understanding the recurrent and interdependent relationships between organisations, institutions and the need for social change, community cohesion and development. This is why Paul DiMaggio and Walter Powell argue that organisational fields are 'those organisations which, in the aggregate, constitute a recognised area of institutional life: key suppliers, resources and product consumers, regulatory agencies, and other organisations that produce similar services or products'[10] – in essence, organisations and actors with shared characteristics and sometimes varied aims coming together to coexist in an environment that constitutes a recognised area of institutional life. They constitute 'a community of organisations that partakes of a common meaning system and whose participants interact more frequently and fatefully with one another than with actors outside of the field'.[11]

Characterising TfD as an organisational field implies seeing it as a 'collection of organisations operating in the same domain, as identified by the similarity of their services, products or functions, together with those organisations that critically influence the performance of focal organisations'.[12] The interesting aspect of TfD's development into a formidable organisational field is that it evolved as a web of interchanges 'that emerge as structured and structuring environments for organisational and individual participants'.[13] It was largely achieved through the organisation of workshops, or what in institutional and organisational theory are called FCEs, the term being closely linked to organisational fields and denoting temporary gatherings that bring actors and organisations together to define a field. Alan Meyer, Vibha Gaba and Kenneth Colwell suggest that FCEs are 'settings where people from diverse social organisations assemble temporarily, with the conscious, collective intent to construct an organisational field'.[14] The coming together of diverse actors in the case of TfD was motivated by the practitioners' aspiration to develop and formalise an emerging praxis. Importantly, the field in question emerged 'out of a felicitous combination of resources, technical know-how, and supportive organisations' because '[popular theatre practitioners and scholars] clustering is rarely serendipitous – it is a socially structured process'.[15]

## The evolution of TfD as an organisational field

The Laedza Batanani project ran in Botswana from 1974 to 1978. After four years of local implementation, the project's success led to a two-week national TfD workshop that brought together extension workers and adult education workers from all over the country.[16] This was after an inter-agency committee was formed to promote the integration of drama, culture and the creative arts in non-formal education activities. The institute of adult education at the University of Botswana was charged with organising and leading the workshop.[17] The event set the stage for a series of further workshops in other countries that functioned as FCEs in the context of TfD. These FCEs provided a platform for continuous interaction between African and expatriate adult-education experts, theatre scholars, popular theatre enthusiasts and development practitioners.

In 1979 'the first major international Theatre for Development Workshop' was held in Chalimbana, Zambia,[18] beginning the TfD field-formation process in Africa and the rest of the world. Commenting on its significance, David Kerr noted that:

> Perhaps the most influential workshop for launching the Theatre for Development movement was held at Chalimbana about 30 km east of Lusaka in Zambia in 1979. This provided a venue for the marriage between two types of activist-adult educators and social workers on one side (particularly the Botswana-based Laedza Batanani team of Ross Kidd, Martin Byram and Martha Maplanka) and the university-based artists with their roots in travelling theatre (such as Mapopa Mtonga, Dickson Mwansa and myself from Zambia, the Zimbabwean Stephen Chifunyise, and Tanzanians Amandina Lihamba and Eberhard Chambulikazi).[19]

In essence, the workshop was a learning opportunity for the different actors who came together to form what would ultimately become an organisational field. Kerr confirms this when he says 'the workshop linked the mobilisation and social analysis skills of the adult educators to the drama and choreography skills of the theatre workers'. The justification for uniting people with different skills was to marry skills, share experience and learn from one another. Here, learning is conceptualised by Schüßler, Grabher and Müller-Seitz as a 'predominantly intentional undertaking of individuals, teams or organisations to acquire new or deepen existing knowledge or skills'.[20] The dynamics that accompany this kind of learning mean it is 'by no means only about the process of acquiring explicit knowledge; it also entails the exchange in the form of transferring and disseminating tacit knowledge to inform others, enable learning, exert power, and legitimise one's own actions'.[21] The formation, consolidation and structuration path of the field of TfD has always been that of learning and negotiation.

The role of actors and organisations in the field continuously shifts between transferring knowledge, testing methodologies, exerting power and legitimising experiments and actions. Fundamentally, the Chalimbana workshop was where the institutional logic of TfD as an organisational field took shape – that is 'the belief systems and associated practices that dominated the field'[22] began to be formed and negotiated. The guidelines that became the basis for all other FCEs were tested at this workshop, which was driven mainly by the practitioners and leaders of the Laedza Batanani project. Kerr confirms that 'the Chalimbana workshop's main achievement was to develop the methodology initiated by the Laedza Batanani team'.[23] This is in line with Penina

Muhando Mlama's claim that 'in the Chalimbana workshop, theatre and development workers came together to generate ideas on using theatre as a tool for development'.[24] This FCE thus opened doors for a cross-pollination of ideas that saw the introduction of other actors to the TfD discourse including university theatre professors, who ended up playing a pivotal role in the processes that ensured the consolidation of the field as an area of research and study in African higher education institutions.

After the Chalimbana workshop the TfD technique, with its numerous variations, started spreading throughout the continent. As a result, other national and international workshops were organised in many countries, including Nigeria (Maska, 1979; Borno, 1981; Benue, 1982–3, 1986), Malawi (Mbalachanda, 1981; Liwonde, 1987), Lesotho (Maseru, 1982), Zambia (1979, 1981), Zimbabwe (Murewa, 1983; Harare, 1993, 1997), Cameroon (Kumba, 1984), Swaziland (Mhlangano, 1981, 1982), Germany (Berlin, 1980), Bangladesh (Koitta, 1983), Ghana (Winneba, 1994), Sierra Leone (1979, 1983), Canada (Edmonton, 1987), Sweden (Stockholm, 1985) and Angola (Luanda, 1994).

The role played by the university community must be acknowledged here. Departments of extramural studies, adult education and theatre arts at several universities helped to nurture TfD as an organisational field, and the processes that led to the field becoming isomorphic involved actors in higher education institutions. The theatre and performing arts departments in most African countries became hubs for TfD training and research once the field became established. Of course the FCEs, throughout the history of TfD, should be regarded as the fundamental 'ubiquitous strategies of claim making that link[ed] diverse participants together into a collective performance'.[25] The FCEs brought practitioners together into an effective 'grid of discourse spaces created … by the most important vehicle of experimental coordination and integration'.[26] The TfD practitioners aimed to evolve an organisational field and ensure it became well established and recognised globally. It must also be emphasised that the Zambians were the first to add a new dimension to the practice by involving both theatre workers and development workers as actor-animateurs in the TfD processes.

By the 1980s actors and pioneers had succeeded in establishing TfD as an organisational field. It had become ubiquitous and legitimised by governments and higher education institutions in most African countries, and its methods and techniques became effective tools for social mobi-lisation, community development and development communication. Undoubtedly, the FCEs provided an ideological context that propelled the evolution and institutionalisation of TfD as an efficacious empowerment praxis that negotiated between international development programmes, NGO funding and universities.

A closer inspection of the workshops mentioned above indicates that while all FCEs may be roughly equal, some are more equal than others. Indeed, some define or configure a field rather than simply maintain it. For example, in the history of TfD and its attendant FCEs in Africa, the 1983 workshop in Zimbabwe truly defined and configured TfD as an organisational field. It established some of the foundational principles and consolidated the journey of TfD as a practical and theoretical methodology for rural and community development. It also alerted different but related constituents to common concerns and allowed them to share information, coordinate their actions, shape and subvert agendas, and mutually influence the structuration of the field.[27] In short, the 1983 workshop helped researchers and practitioners understand three things: first, the specific mode of learning and knowledge exchange the workshop generated as part of innovations in TfD; second, the type of innovation and learning outcomes that emerged at the FCE; and finally, the kind of platform for innovation and learning the FCE provided for actors in the field. What happened in the workshop helped clarify the questions Elke Schüßler, Gernot Grabher and Gordon Müller-Seitz asked in their article about how FCEs are arenas for field innovation and learning.

## Pan-African theatre for development workshop (Zimbabwe, 1983)

This African theatre for development workshop took place between 15 August and 1 September 1983. The workshop's planning started long before Zimbabwe was engaged to host it. At the 1982 Theatre of Nations festival in Sofia, Bulgaria the then secretary-general of the ITI, Lars af Malmborg, approached Professor Francis Imbuga of Kenyatta University College about the possibility of Kenya hosting the workshop. He followed this with a letter to the chairman of the Kenyan National Commission on Culture in July 1982. However, Kenya's political situation was not conducive to hosting the event, as 'in March 1982, Kenyan authorities banned for the second time a popular theatre performance created by a community organisation of peasants and workers, the Kamiriithu Community Educational and Cultural Centre (KCECC). The organisation was subsequently deregistered and the open-air theatre which the community had built was battered down'.[28] Following this event, the leaders of the KCECC were forced to flee the country. Ngugi wa Thiong'o escaped to Europe, and Ngugi wa Mirii and Kimani Gecau fled to Zimbabwe. In November 1982, when it became clear Kenya could not host the workshop, Lars af Malmborg contacted John Mapondera, then deputy chief of cultural affairs at the Ministry of Education and Culture in Zimbabwe, and offered Zimbabwe the opportunity to host the workshop.[29] Thus, the first Pan-African TfD workshop, initiated by UNESCO and the ITI, was hosted by the government of Zimbabwe. The International Popular Theatre Alliance (IPTA), acting as consultants on the project on behalf of the ITI, worked with the Zimbabwean government to organise the event, and more than a hundred participants took part, 43 from 17 African countries and 57 from the host nation.

This account is critical because prior to this particular FCE, all other workshops throughout Africa had taken place on either a sub-regional or country-specific basis. This was the first time a workshop had been organised at the Pan-African level and as a collaboration between several international and donor organisations. It was proof that TfD had developed into an organisational field and acquired global recognition. As noted by Kidd, one of UNESCO's consultants to the programme from the IPTA, 'the Zimbabwe workshop was the first occasion to bring popular theatre workers together on a pan-African basis. Theatre workers who had heard of each other's work but never met came together for the first time, shared and debated their ideas, and talked about ways of maintaining the exchange'.[30]

A number of factors contributed to the impact of this particular FCE in configuring the field. The event should be regarded as a significant occasion in which the field materialised and 'jelled in the form of agreed-upon categories of relevant artefacts, actors, relation-ships between them and the boundaries demarking the domain of the field'.[31] As a result, the actors navigated and legitimised the practice and entrenched its global efficacy. Furthermore, the workshop represented a forum akin to 'an active mechanism whereby any assemblage of hetero-geneous elements, humans and materials, becomes configured and reconfigured in real time'.[32] A strong argument in favour of this point can be extrapolated from the concept of translation, specifically the idea of translation as 'displacement, drive, invention, mediation, the creation of a link that did not exist before and that to some degree modifies two elements or agents'.[33] The 1983 FCE in Murewa, Zimbabwe, did just that, offering the perfect ground for such translation to occur. For the first time, different agents with different enthusiasms, who had engaged in different innovations in terms of methods and approaches, were brought together in a shared space that offered an opportunity for those approaches to be modified, configured and maintained. In other words, actors in the field were brought together in a communal environment that expanded their network and ignited the structuration and homogenisation of TfD's organisational field. One can also relate this to Comrade Dzingai Mutumbuka's call to the workshop participants (especially the Zimbabweans) to translate their experience into TfD praxis. According to Kidd, Mutumbuka said workshop participants should translate 'the liberation theatre experience into new strategies for conscientisation, mobilisation and community-building'.[34] This was indeed a point at which indigenous practice was fairly systematised and integrated into TfD praxis.

The workshop had three broad aims, agreed upon by all the actors, organisations and networks that collaborated to organise the event. At the continental level, the workshop's main focus was the consolidation and diffusion of TfD methodology and concepts to theatre workers and countries in Africa, which had not yet been exposed to this approach. For Zimbabwe, as organiser of the first international popular theatre workshop under the label of TfD, it was an opportunity to test out the ideas of TfD and adapt them to a local context. It was also hoped that the workshop would help Zimbabwe reassess its experiences of people's theatre during the liberation struggle, and train its development cadres in TfD skills and processes. The final aim was directed towards the aspirations of the ITI: the purpose of the workshop and the three-day conference that followed was to create an opportunity for exchange and dialogue among African theatre workers, with a significant focus on theatre as a tool for development.

The 1983 Zimbabwean workshop came about due to UNESCO and the ITI developing an interest in TfD. They were impressed with the efficacy of the TfD methodology and the experimentation that had taken place in many African countries, and wanted to support its diffusion to other African countries that had not experimented with the concept. The idea of organising the workshop was also in line with the ITI's desire to increase African participation in their organisation. Furthermore, the ITI supported the development of inter-African networking, cooperation and collaboration in the theatre field. The IPTA was brought on board as a consultant because its coordinator, Ross Kidd, had been actively involved in the TfD movement. Kidd was one of the pioneers of the movement, and had written extensively on TfD and popular theatre in Africa. He was also involved in training workshops in Botswana, Nigeria and Zambia.

In addition to UNESCO, the ITI and the Zimbabwean government, sponsors included the African Cultural Institute (Dakar), the ITI-Extra European Fund, the Canadian International Development Agency (CIDA), the Canadian University Service Overseas (CUSO), the Commonwealth Foundation (CF), the German Foundation for International Development (DSE), the French Agency for Cultural and Technical Cooperation (ACCA), NOVID (Netherlands) and the Swedish International Development Agency (SIDA). Some of the participants were also funded by the International Council for Adult Education. A report written by Kidd about the experience of one participating group was published by the Centre for the Study of Education in Developing Countries (CESO), which was based in the Hague and would go on to become a key organisation for popularising and institutionalising TfD among European funding bodies.

The workshop saw participation from both Francophone and Anglophone parts of Africa. The countries represented included Burundi, Cameroon, Congo, Ethiopia, Gabon, Ghana, Ivory Coast, Kenya, Malawi, Mali, Mauritius, Nigeria, Senegal, Sierra Leone, Somalia, Swaziland, Tanzania, Upper Volta (now Burkina Faso), Zaire and Zambia. There were a total of 53 participants from Zimbabwe, consisting of a mix of individual theatre workers and development cadres. Twenty 'resource persons' were drawn from experienced practitioners and countries with extensive practice, including Ethiopia, Ghana, Kenya, Mauritius, Nigeria, Swaziland, Tanzania, Zambia and Zimbabwe. Additionally, four resource persons with practical experience of TfD came from the UK, Canada, India and Sweden, respectively. There were also three observers: a representative of UNESCO from the Dakar office, a Canadian popular theatre worker and a German cultural researcher.

As far as the objectives of the workshop are concerned, it was for the organisers and participants from Zimbabwe an experimental venture, trying out the TfD approach and adapting it to the Zimbabwean cultural situation. In addition to aligning with the desire to transform the country after independence in 1980, the workshop was a training opportunity for development workers and theatre artists. Not only did the workshop launch a TfD programme in Murewa, it provided Zimbabwe with an opportunity to reassess its experience of people's theatre for conscientisation and mobilisation during the liberation struggle. The participants from different parts of Africa saw the gathering as an opportunity to evaluate the potential and operational requirements of TfD work in a practical manner. It was also a platform for learning the skills and processes involved in TfD work, especially for those new to it.

Additionally, the ITI used the workshop to network with theatre workers and TfD enthusiasts across Africa. Finally, for UNESCO, the ITI and the IPTA, the workshop was an avenue for diffusing TfD skills and experience to African countries with minimal or no experience in TfD. Particularly for the organisers, the aim of the workshop was to foster exchange and cooperation among theatre workers, and expand the TfD and ITI networks in Africa.

## UNESCO, the ITI and the impact of the 1983 workshop on TfD

The 1983 TfD workshop in Murewa, Zimbabwe, represented a watershed moment for the practice in both theoretical and practical terms. This particular FCE occupies a significant and unique position in the evolution of the discipline, and was field defining in several ways. First, it was a locus for essential developments and methodological innovation. Second, although experiments and projects had previously taken place in different parts of Africa, most were regional or, in some cases, national. The 1983 event represented the first time a TfD workshop had been organised at a Pan-African level, involving multiple local and international actors and organisations. Hence, when looking at TfD as an organisational field, the field was to a large extent configured and consolidated at this workshop. Third, the process of structuration and homogenisation began at this workshop. The conceptualisation (in terms of both theory and practice), organisation and implementation of the workshop drew on decades of accumulated practical and theoretical TfD experience, which likewise negotiated and found a way of integrating new and innovative approaches derived from the Zimbabwean experience of liberation theatre for conscientisation and mobilisation. The workshop further dealt with 'the micro- and macro-level processes that shaped individual and shared realities' of the local, national, regional and international actors who were present.

The workshop also created an indispensable condition that placed responsibility, paradoxically, on practitioners and researchers in their quest to lend the discipline structure and homogeneity. Given the context, it stands to reason that the workshop would create a platform that recognised the participants' agency to create and believe in their ideas and experiments, in order for them to make progress with their chosen approach and convince others to follow their lead. At the same time, both local and international participants were encouraged to 'also be ready to disbelieve their realities and be willing to embrace the emerging shared reality even if it does not match theirs'.[35] This was the exact situation that both new and experienced practitioners and actors at the workshop were confronted with, which is why there was a general understanding, implicit in the objectives of the workshop, that the gathering was a way of 'setting standards, defining practices, and codifying key vocabularies, as well as positioning the field relative to other fields and institutions'.[36] Given the plethora of actors in both the primary and ancillary fields of TfD who were part of the initiation, organisation and implementation of the workshop, it is clear why the workshop continues to occupy a key position in the historical memory and historiographical analysis of the discipline.

The 1983 workshop represents the first time in approximately three decades that actors in the field agreed to use TfD as an umbrella term for different socially engaged theatre experiments on the continent, after which the term became well established among various competing and cognate terms. In Joseph Lampel and Alan Meyer's estimation the workshop focused on 'expanding, refining, and solidifying beliefs and practices', as well as gauging and reinforcing TfD's field position 'relative to other fields and institutions'.[37] The term's social capital was established, and subsequent activities and projects reinforced it and what it encapsulated. What is more, TfD's legitimacy was concretised by the endorsement of several international organisations involved in the organisation and funding of the workshop, including UNESCO, the ITI, the Agence de coopération culturelle et technique, the Canadian International Development Agency, the Swedish International Development Cooperation Agency, Canadian University Service Overseas, the Commonwealth Foundation and the Deutsche Stiftung für internationale Entwicklung. They paved the way, through their funding, for other countries to participate in the workshop. In this context, such organisations must be deemed the leading 'institutional entrepreneurs' who had 'an overt field-building agenda'. Having funded earlier national and regional projects and FCEs, it seems that by the time of the 1983 workshop these entities agreed that TfD best described the grassroots approach to community and human development they believed was the way forward for development cooperation.

The ITI and UNESCO should be acknowledged as providing a platform and the necessary support for legitimising the field. The Chalimbana workshop that kick-started the field-formation process was organised by the Zambian branch of the ITI, which together with UNESCO initiated and organised the 1983 TfD workshop that configured and consolidated the field. Through their sponsorship, the two organisations ensured wider participation and the eventual diffusion of the praxis in Africa and the rest of the world.

## Conclusion

Tracing the evolution and eventual consolidation of the field of TfD is different from conducting a historiographical survey (for the latter, it is necessary to expand the process and context – see Hakib, 2020). However, as a field-configuring event consolidating and defining a movement, the 1983 workshop stands out. Significantly, the workshop provided both content (what TfD training and practice should involve) and context (when TfD methodologies should be employed), and established itself as the moment when the field was configured and the structuration process started. It is also the point at which the field's key institutional logics were developed. Thus, the 1983 workshop changed and advanced the organisational field of TfD for actors in the field, and in terms of the methods and approaches employed.

## Notes

1  See Hakib, 2022.
2  See Byam, 1999; Mda, 1993; Kidd, 1979; Kidd and Byam, 1978; Kamlongera, 1989.
3  Kidd, 1983, 33.
4  Kidd and Byam, 1978, 175.
5  Kerr, 1999, 79.
6  Kerr, 1999, 79.
7  Kerr, 1999, 80.
8  See Kerr, 1995 and Mda, 1993.
9  DiMaggio, 1986, 337.
10  DiMaggio and Powell, 1983, 148.
11  Scott, 1994, 20–8.
12  Scott, 1991, 117.
13  White, Owen-Smith, Moody and Powell, 2004, 97.
14  Meyer, Gaba and Colwell, 2005, 467.
15  Powell, 1999, 45.
16  See Kidd and Byram, 1978.
17  Byram and Kidd, 1978, 86.
18  Byam, 1999, 56.
19  Kerr, 1999, 79.
20  Schüßler, Grabher and Müller-Seitz, 2015, 166.
21  See also Nonaka and Takeuchi, 1995.
22  Oliver and Montgomery, 2008, 1147.
23  Kerr, 1999, 80.
24  Mlama, 1991, 72.
25  Rao, 2001, 266.
26  Knorr-Cetina, 1995, 131.

27  Anand and Jones, 2008, 1037.
28  Kidd, 1983, 18.
29  Letters from Lars af Marlmborg to Kenya and Zimbabwe in the ITI archives at UNESCO.
30  Kidd, 1984, 8.
31  Garud, 2008, 1062.
32  Garud, 2008, 1062.
33  Latour, 1994, 32.
34  Kidd, 1984, 13.
35  Garud and Rappa, 1994, 344.
36  Lampel and Meyer, 2008, 1029.
37  Lampel and Meyer, 2008, 1029.

# References

Anand, N. and Jones, B. C. 'Tournament rituals, category dynamics, and field configuration: the case of the Booker Prize', *Journal of Management Studies* 45 (6) (2008): 1036–60.

Arkhurst, Sandy. 'Kodzidan'. In *The Legacy of Efua Sutherland: Pan-African cultural activism*, edited by Anne V. Adams and Esi Sutherland-Addy, 165–74. London: Ayebia Clarke Publishing, 2007.

Balme, Christopher and Leonhardt, Nic. 'The Rockefeller connection: visualizing theatrical networks in the cultural Cold War', *Comparatio* 12 (2) (2020): 127–44.

Byam, Lee Dale. *Community in Motion: Theatre for development in Africa*. Westport, CT: Bergin and Garvey, 1999.

DiMaggio, Paul. 'Structural analysis of organizational fields: a blockmodel approach', *Research in Organizational Behavior* 8 (1986): 335–70.

DiMaggio, Paul and Powell, Walter W. 'The iron cage revisited: institutional isomorphism and collective rationality in organizational fields', *American Sociological Review* 48 (2) (1983): 147–60.

Garud, Raghu. 'Conferences as venues for the configuration of emerging organizational fields: the case of cochlear implants', *Journal of Management Studies* 45 (2008): 1061–88.

Garud, Raghu and Rappa, M. 'A socio-cognitive model of technology evolution', *Organization Science* 5 (3) (1994): 334–62.

Hakib, Abdul Karim. 'Towards historiographies of theatre for development', *Research in Drama Eduction: The Journal of Applied Theatre and Performance* 25 (4) (2020): 581–4. Accessed 25 September 2023. https://doi.org/10.1080/13569783.2020.1791695.

Kamlongera, Christopher. 'Theatre for development: the case of Malawi', *Theatre Research International* 7 (3) (1982): 207–22. https://doi.org/10.1017/S030788330000064X.

Kamlongera, Christopher. *Theatre for Development in Africa with Case Studies from Malawi and Zambia*. Bonn: German Foundation for International Development (DSE), 1989.

Kerr, David. *African Popular Theatre: From pre-colonial times to the present day*. London: James Currey, 1995.

Kerr, David. 'Art as tool, weapon or shield?'. In *African Theatre in Development*, edited by Martin Banham, James Gibbs and Femi Osofisan, 79–86. Oxford: James Currey, 1999.

Kidd, Ross. 'Folk theatre: one or two way communications?', *Development Communications Report* 28 (1) (1979): 5–7.

Kidd, Ross. 'From outside in to inside out: the Benue workshop on theatre for development', *Didactic Theatre* 6 (1) (1983): 33–42.

Kidd, Ross. *From People's Theatre for Revolution to Popular Theatre for Reconstruction: Diary of a Zimbabwean workshop*. The Hague: Centre for the Study of Education in Developing Countries (CESO), 1984.

Kidd, Ross and Byram, Martin. 'The performing arts and community education in Botswana', *Community Development Journal* 13 (3) (1978): 170–8.

Knorr-Cetina, K. 'How superorganisms change: consensus formation and the social ontology of high-energy physics experiments', *Social Studies of Science* 25 (1) (1995): 119–47.

Lampel, J. and Meyer, A. D. 'Field-configuring events as structuring mechanisms: how conferences, ceremonies, and trade shows constitute new technologies, industries, and markets', *Journal of Management Studies* 45 (6) (2008): 1025–35.

Latour, Bruno. 'On technical mediation: philosophy, sociology, genealogy', *Common Knowledge* 3 (2) (1994): 29–64.

Mda, Zakes. *When People Play People: Development communication through theatre.* London/New York: Zed Books, 1993.

Meyer, A. D., Gaba, V. and Colwell, K. 'Organizing far from the equilibrium: non-linear change in organizational fields', *Organization Science* 16 (2005): 456–73.

Mlama, Penina Muhando. *Culture and Development: The popular theatre approach in Africa.* Uppsala: Nordiska AfriKainstitutet (The Scandinavian Institute of African Studies), 1991.

Nonaka, I. and Takeuchi, K. *The Knowledge Creating Company.* New York: Oxford University Press, 1995.

Oliver, A. L. and Mongomery, K. 'Using field-configuring events for sense-making: a cognitive network approach', *Journal of Management Studies* 45 (2008): 1147–67.

Powell, W. W. 'The social construction of an organizational field: the case of biotechnology', *International Journal of Biotechnology* 1 (1) (1999): 42–66.

Rao, H. 'The power of public competition: promoting cognitive legitimacy through certification contests'. In *The Entrepreneurship Dynamic,* edited by C. B. Schoonhoven and E. Romanelli, 262–85. Redwood City, CA: Stanford University Press, 2001.

Schüßler, Elke, Grabher, Gernot and Müller-Seitz, Gordon. 'Field-configuring events: arenas for innovation and learning?', *Industry and Innovation* 22 (3) (2015): 165–72.

Scott, W. R. 'Unpacking institutional arguments'. In *The New Institutionalism in Organizational Analysis,* edited by W. W. Powell and P. J. DiMaggio, 164–82. London: University of Chicago Press, 1991.

Scott, W. R. 'Conceptualizing organizational fields: linking organizations and societal systems'. In *Systems Rationality and Partial Interests,* edited by U. Gerhardt, F. Scharpf and H. Derlien, 203–21. Baden: Nomos, 1994.

White, D. R., Owen-Smith, J., Moody, J. and Powell, W. W. 'Networks, fields and organizations: micro-dynamics, scale and cohesive embeddings', *Computational and Mathematical Organization Theory* 10 (1) (2004): 95–117.

# 4
# Theatre against development in the Occupied Palestinian Territories[1]
Rashna Darius Nicholson

The Oslo Accords, signed between the government of Israel and the Palestine Liberation Organisation in 1993, mark a significant turning point in the history of the Middle East, as they were assumed to herald Palestinian self-determination and regional stability. Since then the administrative, social and not least cultural environment of the Occupied Palestinian Territories has structurally transmogrified through international development-aid flows and neoliberal policies, even as Palestinians are no closer to realising these objectives. Consequently, several studies have argued that Euro-American development experts, who emerged after the post-Cold War termination of competing bilateral financial assistance, should be included in the assortment of powerful agents that economically and politically transmuted the region.[2]

The objective of this chapter, following the growing consensus on the negative repercussions of neoliberal state building and development, is to offer a critical evaluation of the impact of foreign aid on theatre in the Occupied Palestinian Territories (OPT). Despite an overwhelming body of governmental and non-governmental documentation on theatre in conflict zones, the institutional links between culture and conflict are seldom problematised. By first historicising the institutionalisation of Palestinian theatre and subsequently analysing its imbrication in the human-rights industry through the example of the Freedom Theatre, this chapter complicates the conception of development as a neutral, disinterested, technocratic exercise divorced from arts practice. As a corollary, it will also complicate the dominant narrative that theatre in conflict zones facilitates empowerment, decolonisation and cultural resistance. Although foreign aid provided the material conditions for the institutionalisation of Palestinian theatre, in accordance with broader geopolitical strategic goals it concurrently promoted a structural dependency that undercut Palestinian anticolonial agency. Just as Palestinian economic development has been described as skewed, stalled or impoverished, so also Palestinian cultural development has generated a phantom sovereignty directed towards international development experts. By historicising how the performing arts were subsumed within the aegis of development in the OPT in the aftermath of the Oslo Accords, this chapter argues that the resultant restructuring of theatre through its 'NGOisation' has jeopardised the objective of national liberation rather than advancing it.

## The beginnings of international funding to Palestinian theatre

In 1984 the Ford Foundation, the first international agency to fund theatre in the so-called developing world, granted US$416,000 to the El-Hakawati Theatre. As part of the US battle to win the Cold War, the foundation had by then established an advanced cultural-development model for soft-power activities in emerging countries. As I have argued elsewhere, American foundations, which were the first to recognise that 'there may be more to development than socio-economic considerations alone', facilitated the development of a trans-regional knowledge economy through the creation of networks of aid-dependent artists and cultural institutions.[3] While the foundation had several decades of experience in South Asian theatre, its foray into the arts of the Middle East in the 1980s was unprecedented.

In 1972 François Gaspar, known to the world as François Abu Salem, established the theatre troupe al-Balalin (the Balloons). Along with other troupes such as Dababis (Pins) and Sunduq al-'Ajab (the Wonder Box), al-Balalin marked a significant turning point in the Palestinian theatre movement. These companies performed plots from *One Thousand and One Nights* in the Palestinian vernacular rather than classical Arabic, using indirect allusions to contemporary events in order to avoid censorship.[4] But their productions, according to a Ford Foundation report, were amateurish. None had a regular budget, rehearsal hall or staff, and their actors worked full time in other jobs, rehearsing in the evenings and on weekends. Most of the groups had apparently died out by the 1980s, although one managed to continue: the El-Hakawati Theatre Company, established by Abu Salem in 1977 after the disbanding of al-Balalin and a second company he helped establish,

Bilaleen (Without Mercy).[5] It is with the founding of the El-Hakawati Theatre that the institutionalisation of Palestinian theatre commences, characterised by the establishment of playhouses, professional actor-training schools, and regional and international cultural networks, along with the creation of big-budget theatre productions.

By 1984 the troupe had produced at least five plays, its membership had grown from seven to fifteen persons, its tour schedule in Israel, the West Bank and Europe had tripled, and its annual operating budget was US$82,650 (including US$15,000 for rent and US$48,000 for the salaries of ten full-time technicians and actors).[6] Through savings and donations from wealthy Palestinians, the group managed to rent the previously burned-down Al-Nuzha movie theatre in Jerusalem in October 1983. Jackie Lubeck, a member of the troupe, initially approached the Ford Foundation for assistance with the theatre's renovation programme, but was directed by Ford's officers towards soliciting funding for the group's theatre programme as a whole.[7] At the time, Ford had only a fledgling arts programme in North Africa. After seeking advice from its geopolitically strategic India office, Ford's Cairo office decided to fund El-Hakawati in order to develop 'networks for training, support and management of the arts in different third world settings'.[8] After in-person meetings in Jerusalem in May 1984, it was agreed that core support of US$100,000 would be delivered over a two-year period for operational costs (including supporting productions and the salaries of full-time staff) and workshops for children and adults, thus putting in place a format for theatrical activity in the OPT and other conflict zones that survives to this day.[9]

As early as April 1984, Linn Cary, assistant programme officer and later assistant to the president of the Ford Foundation, asked 'what is the relation of the workshop programs to the overall objectives of the theatre? The workshops would certainly not serve to advance them as a professional theatre group.'[10] Despite these concerns, additional support of approximately US$300,000 was granted by Ford to both workshops, for activities such as poster and fabric design as well as theatre productions, in 1986, 1988 and 1990. In so doing, Ford facilitated the development of the institutionalised Palestinian theatre as both profes-sional and community focused, a dichotomy reflected in El-Hakawati's then-confused identity as both company and non-profit organisation.[11]

The growth of the theatre was nevertheless not 'entirely smooth'.[12] In 1989, during the First Intifada, the troupe distanced itself from the activities of the Al-Nuzha theatre. The playhouse had by then become a community arts and cultural centre, its board of directors having created a set of activities independent of those of the troupe.[13] This significant change transpired because El-Hakawati had 'rarely been in Palestine' due to its extensive touring schedule, and was therefore accused 'of catering primarily to a Western audience, leaving the Palestinian community in the Occupied Territories behind'.[14] As Abu Salem poignantly prophesied of the future Palestinian theatre:

> El-Hakawati is a moving project … it goes wherever it *can* go, wherever it can survive, in terms of its identity and in terms of its economical survival. We have hardly ever *chosen* being abroad. Strange. I think, that sounds like the essence of what it is like to be a Palestinian, a Palestinian refugee. [Emphasis in original.][15]

The 'fundamentally diverse' visions of the Al-Nuzha theatre – as a community centre for diverse groups and a rehearsal space for El-Hakawati – thus spelled the break up of the first 'professional' Palestinian theatre company.[16] Although Abu Salem relocated to Europe, the precedent he had set was swiftly followed. While the new Al-Masrah for Palestinian Culture and Arts, set up at the Al-Nuzha theatre, received funding from Ford to produce plays for children,[17] many of the erstwhile members of El-Hakawati set up a new company, the Jerusalem Ashtar for Theatre Training and Performing Arts, in 1992.

Having gained expertise in fundraising and theatre production at El-Hakawati, Edward Muallem and Iman Aoun approached Ford for US$40,000, further developing the children's workshop and professional-production model instituted by El-Hakawati.[18] Significantly, Ashtar's grant applications – which stipulated target audiences for its workshops; 'human', 'educational', 'artistic', 'cultural' and 'economic' aims; and the involvement of women in its activities – were more professional, reflecting an awareness of the changing philanthropic landscape of the OPT, and a considerable effort to make Palestinian theatre legible within a development optic.[19] Accordingly, Ashtar managed to procure funding from the Associazione Ricreativa e Culturale Italiana (ARCI), Caritas Switzerland and the Cassinelli Vogel Foundation, even as it was negotiating grants with the US consulate, the Rockefeller Foundation, the Swedish International Development Cooperation Agency (SIDA), the British Council and Pro Helvetia.[20] In the tempestuous period during the drafting and shortly after the signing of the Oslo Accords, many of these organisations established a physical presence in the OPT, thereby prompting a sudden spurt in cultural activity. While the Ford Foundation broadened its field of operation, European agencies including SIDA, the

Norwegian Agency for Development Cooperation (NORAD), the Swiss Agency for Development and Cooperation (SDC) and numerous other government representations began funding theatres – now reframed as non-governmental organisations (NGOs) – in the territory administered by the new Palestinian Authority (PA). With Palestinian organisations no longer subject to the Israeli two-tiered permit system to stage plays in the West Bank, the centre of gravity of Palestinian culture shifted from East Jerusalem to the West Bank. While Ashtar and the Al-Kasaba Theatre moved base to Ramallah, Lubeck founded Theatre Day Productions (TDP) in November 1995. Other centres followed, such as the Alrowwad Cultural and Theatre Training Center, founded in 1998 at the Aida refugee camp, Bethlehem; the Al-Harah Theater, established in 2005 in Beit Jala, Bethlehem; the Freedom Theatre, founded in 2006 at the Jenin refugee camp; and Yes Theatre, established in 2008 in Hebron. Moreover, with the shift in performing-arts funding, from self-funding and private funding to development aid, theatre NGOs began to operate on a professional scale, building or renting theatres, theatre schools and cultural centres; employing salaried staff members; and developing programmes, budgets and grant applications. What, however, does this short history of the institutionalisation of Palestinian theatre tell us about a new mode of Palestinian performance? What had cultural resistance to the Israeli occupation become, and who, above all, was the Palestinian theatre's audience?

## Human development

Criticisms of applied theatre are not new. The instrumentalisation of theatre by development experts in the service of 'social change', 'empowerment' and 'good governance', and the concomitant devastation of political language, socialisation of intellectual elites and normalisation of particular values, have been critiqued by scholars such as Tim Prentki, Christopher Odhiambo Joseph and Jane Plastow.[21] However, I would argue that theatre operating in the service of development assumes a distinct function in conflict zones, of which the Palestinian case is paradigmatic. In the 1990s critics lambasted structural-adjustment programmes (SAPs), a neutral, universal developmental force 'disembodied from culture',[22] as inimical to development. In response, the United Nations Development Programme's (UNDP) seminal first Human Development Report, in 1990, delineated 'the essential truth that people must be at the centre of all development'.[23] The report, as Toufic Haddad notes, spearheaded the disaggregation of the role of the state in development by Western donor governments, the United Nations and international financial institutions (IFIs).[24] Previously, social priorities such as basic education were part of a state-centred model of development informed by national economic policies and public social-welfare systems. Within the liberal-peace model, the delineation of these priorities as isolated problems disassociated from territorial conflict, political sovereignty and wider economic development allowed for numerous developmental agents to focus on them independently. Thus, development as conceived by the World Bank functions as an anti-politics machine involving recognition of topics associated with the political situation (for example, Israel's destruction of Palestinian agricultural industries) before endeavouring to insulate the economic dimensions from the political (separating lack of water and poor produce from the deliberate diversion of water, Israeli control of Palestinian markets, and so on). This is followed by efforts to solve the former rather than the latter (in this case through an emphasis on environmental issues).[25] By addressing the externalities of the conflict, the structural determinants of Palestinian underdevelopment – the expropriation of critical Palestinian resources, the progressive integration of the Palestinian economy with the Israeli market and restrictions on the development of national institutions – are disregarded, and settler-colonial reality is further entrenched.[26] The local or individual, rather than the national or communal, becomes the site for empowerment, good governance, and peace building and state building, providing legitimacy to international development intervention, the caretaker government of the PA, and NGOs working towards the fulfilment of human rights – even as human rights violations that could not be named as such gathered breakneck speed.[27] But what does this have to do with theatre and performance?

## Palestinian performance

The use of the language of performance in development literature on Palestine is of critical importance: the '"stagiest" approach to achieving Palestinian rights', the masking of reality by Fayyadism, the transformation of Palestinians into 'spectators to their own ongoing tragedy', and the 'shared charade' of human rights that 'was a pretence, a façade that everyone recognised as such but was feigning to keep up nevertheless'.[28] Imbricated in Palestinian notions of performance is the conceptual distinction between human rights (for example rights to freedom of movement and assembly) and the so-called 'human rights industry', described by Lori Allen as the complex of organisations and actions that operate under the name of human rights.[29] It is the human rights industry that predominantly conditions institutionalised Palestinian representational forms, from individual claims of Palestinian humanity and citizenship, to the performance of human rights and statehood by the proto-government of the PA. With Palestinians viewing the PA as complicit in the occupation, the NGOs as wilful players reliant on a steady cash flow, and the international donor community as incapable of stopping Israeli atrocities, their co-enactments of human rights are perceived as disciplinary mechanisms that normalise Palestinian subjects and supplant anti-colonial politics, thereby producing a bad-faith society that disbelieves these performances.[30] Paradoxically, therefore, while the language of human rights espoused by the PA, NGOs and donors makes Palestinian humanity globally legible, it draws local attention to the fragility of its claims due to its depoliticisation of the Palestinian struggle.

According to Allen, there are at stake two contesting moral economies, political imaginaries or forms of ideological claim-making, one directed inward and based on populist ideals and local legitimacy, and another directed outward and based on compliance with international human-rights law.[31] Despite often being critical of the NGOisation of Palestinian culture, theatre practitioners are, due to their reliance on funding, largely compelled to demonstrate adherence to the second, humanitarian frame. A 1998 report by Ashtar states that 'theatre groups nowadays are mostly concerned with raising certain existential topics like Democracy, Human Rights ... by presenting them as they surface in the social, political and economic issues of daily life'.[32] By adhering to the criteria of normality set by Western-dominated IFIs, individual Palestinians – the target of artistic interventions – assume the burden of finding solutions to the social ruin caused by settler colonialism. Accordingly, a train of development experts – from the World Bank's technocrats, through representatives of donor networks, to grant writers and arts managers – ensure that Palestinian theatres like the PA, which they typically despise, mutually work towards the building of a neoliberal Palestinian state. Simultaneously, the arts are increasingly divorced from pre-existing political attempts to address the structural domination of Palestinians by both the Israeli occupation and a suppressive neoliberal regime.

## Phantom state, phantom resistance

The Freedom Theatre is in many ways prototypical of the post-Oslo predicament of Palestinian theatre. It was established in 2006 by Jonatan Stanczak, Zakaria Zubeidi and Juliano Mer-Khamis, the latter the son of a Jewish mother and Palestinian father who received international acclaim as an actor and director. The Freedom Theatre was built on foundations laid by Mer-Khamis's mother Arna, who established the Care and Learning Project at the Jenin refugee camp, and subsequently the Stone Theatre (named after the stones children would volley at Israeli armed vehicles). A culture of both peace and *sumud* (steadfastness) was implicit in the agenda of the Care and Learning Project, which not only functioned as a refuge for children through games and cultural activities, but also helped disseminate prohibited resistance pamphlets. After her centre was bulldozed in 2002 with the Israeli invasion of the Jenin camp, many of Arna's children became leaders in armed struggle and, by the end of the Second Intifada, martyrs.[33]

The Freedom Theatre was thrown into the spotlight when Juliano Mer-Khamis was assassinated on 4 April 2011. As the murderer was never identified, Mer-Khamis's death has become the focus of speculation, with potential perpetrators including a killer contracted by discontented, influential figures in Israel or the PA, angered upholders of Islamic tradition and an assassin with a motive of personal vengeance. Meanwhile, the response to the murder from the Jenin camp was muted. Mer-Khamis's killer, who absconded in broad daylight from the middle of the camp, was not apparently seen by any of its 16,000 residents. Moreover, his murder was not marked by any public acts of mourning, such as those that typically follow the deaths of martyrs in Jenin, marked by processions of hundreds carrying pictures of the dead.[34] The question is not who killed Mer-Khamis, but rather why the Jenin camp, the people for whom the Freedom Theatre was ostensibly built, neither mourned him nor cooperated with the investigation.

Although the Freedom Theatre has been associated with militant terms such as 'cultural intifada' and 'cultural resistance', and although it often emphasises that its founders did 'not attempt to replace other forms of resistance', the messages it conveyed to donors, volunteers, and spectators were mixed.[35] As Mer-Khamis argued in a BBC interview, 'we are fighting a lot of fundamentalists that see what we are doing as a disgrace … We are fighting a lot of enemies, before, before we get to the Israeli soldiers.'[36] Similarly, at the Kunst.Kultur.Konflikt conference in Bonn in 2011, Christa Meindersma, director of the Prince Claus Fund, quoted a Freedom Theatre student: 'The theatre has given me the chance to become an actor instead of a martyr.'[37] The influence and success of art in a crisis could hardly be expressed more clearly, the conference report concluded.[38]

Perhaps Mer-Khamis, his teachers and his students merely mouthed the words development experts and government heads such as Meindersma wanted to hear – a conscious self-ventriloquism. Perhaps above all else they desired a world-class, professional theatre, and used all available means to realise that ambitious goal. Or perhaps they truly believed they needed to 'liberate the minds first and then liberate the land'.[39] However, the idea of cultural resistance subsuming violent conflict by means of a 'universal' freedom that would 'achieve liberation from all the elements of the occupation, including the internal social oppression' was a precarious one in a place that was proud of its militant past.[40] Although the theatre was vociferous in its critique of the PA and the Israeli occupation,[41] its primary focus on the individual and local – the 'occupation from within' as the site of cultural resistance – echoed the discursive and performative elements of Fayyadism that highlighted the role of the individual in ensuring the smooth development of a flourishing consumer economy.[42] The seemingly activist orientation of creating change agents, civic imagination and leadership, effecting empowerment, and decolonising the mind to build credible partners for peace, typifies the human-development model where the externalities of the conflict are cyclically addressed. The language of the human-rights industry and its attendant moral economy thus reconfigures the language of resistance, such that the redressal of underdevelopment is aimed at one's own supposedly oppressive culture rather than at a systemic imbalance of power. Depoliticised phantom state building, in line with the neoliberal aims and ambitions of the World Bank, thus augurs a soft phantom resistance directed at proving the modernity – that is, the humanity – of Palestinians and their capacity to sustain the Oslo peace process before the international community. When directed inward, weaponised terms such as 'internal occupation' and 'internal siege' become flaccid, emptying the theatre of emancipatory potential and undermining cultural resistance such that its purchase on the external Israeli occupation is mitigated. Foreign aid places the emphasis of resistance on liberation from an intolerant, backward society, generating a spectral cultural resistance for the audience of the inter-national community. By appropriating the global language of human rights, national non-recognition becomes embedded in its apparent converse, the performance of emancipation, and a bad-faith society of to-be-reformed peoples disbelieving in the theatre's progressive mission is further entrenched.

Nowhere is this clearer than in the gender focus of the Freedom Theatre. Nearly all donor bodies, following the development agenda of the post-Washington consensus, emphasise 'the promotion of **gender-aware** dialogue' (emphasis in original), a policy that has had a significant impact on Palestinian theatre, which has increasingly developed programmes 'to promote social change with regards to gender-related stereotypes and prejudices'.[43] According to Hala Al-Yamani and Abdelfattah Abusrour, Mer-Khamis believed that 'the struggle against the occupier must be accompanied with our struggle for liberating women'. In his own words: 'How can I be liberated of Israeli occupation when I oppress my sister or my wife?'[44] In textual and video interviews in English, female students of the theatre's acting school often note how resistance for them entails fighting societal 'norms and traditions'.[45] Similarly, the website of the Millennium Development Goals Achievement Fund (MDG-F), under the poignant heading 'Palestinian Identity Unfolds on Two Stages', describes the theatre's *Waiting for Godot* thus:

> As the West Bank Palestinian leadership was preparing for its September statehood bid at the United Nations General Assembly, 20-year-old Mariam Abu Khaled was getting ready for a different drama … 'On stage, I can do whatever I want,' says Mariam, who came of age in the decade following the second Palestinian Intifada … Not only was the fabric of Palestinian cultural life shattered, but Palestinian society, always skeptical about girls' involvement in theatre, had become increasingly conservative … 'Art has the power to make girls feel better inside,' says Miriam. She says it encourages her to take risks and to challenge the status quo that perpetuates the Palestinians' political stalemate and that limits women's rights and equality. Her friend Batool agrees: 'Today I have two struggles; to free myself as a Palestinian from Israeli occupation and to free myself as a woman in my society.'[46]

The juxtaposition of the Palestinian bid for statehood with the ostensible achievement of the normative goals of the MDG-F through theatre implies that the figure of the Palestinian woman was, first and foremost, a locus for demonstrating the capacity of Palestinians to reform their despotic culture and subsequently administer their own state. It is the modernisation of women through the theatre that will 'challenge the status quo that perpetuates the Palestinians' political stalemate', bringing to fruition the project of peace building and state building. As in the nineteenth-century colonial 'women's question', the indigenous woman here becomes the sign of an inherently oppressive tradition and the site for its reconfiguration. Suzanne Bergeron notes, in the context of the World Bank's appropriation of feminist discourse, that the developmental target category of 'women' is founded on a 'colonial effect', a formulaic account of Third-World women as helpless, marginal and deprived – and consequently requiring expert humanitarian assistance.[47] By taking the freethinking, progressive Western woman as the norm against which the Palestinian woman is evaluated, development discourse abjures a comprehensive understanding of empowerment and liberation, which encompasses a dialogue on the circumstances in which Palestinians can assume operative political power to effect policy change. Modernisation theory is repetitively enacted: 'human rights are considered modern and non-Western cultures are hastily equated with inequality, patriarchy and religious fundamentalism', even as local publics retreat further into alternative forms of social cohesion.[48]

Mer-Khamis was not unaware of the risks involved in trying to emancipate Palestinian women through theatre. His chastising of female international volunteers who sunbathed on the theatre roof in full view of the adjacent mosque, his rules prohibiting female staff members from socialising in public after sunset in the aftermath of the contentious *Animal Farm* (2009), and the videotaped premonitions of his death indicate that he recognised the danger, if not the intractable contradictions in using development and peace-building aid to set up a professional, world-class acting school in the conservative Jenin camp.[49] Shortly before his next production, an adaptation of *Alice in Wonderland* (2011), he said:

> … now we are going to do our next scandal which is *Alice in Wonderland*, but our Alice is not a stupid girl who finds out that there is a caterpillar, our Alice is going to rebel. Tradition, religion, schools, papa and mamma, she is going to say, give me a break guys, I have my own way. That's dangerous.[50]

Thus, Alice, the only woman not wearing a hijab, escapes her engagement party and arranged marriage, symbols of a tyrannical tradition that oppresses women. On reaching Wonderland, she is declared leader of a subjugated people, yet she must persuade them she is not their true leader. Eventually, the White Queen, the true messiah, emerges, and Alice returns to her real life to tell her betrothed she will not marry him:

'her engagement ring freed Wonderland, and Wonderland freed her from the ring'.[51] 'Are the oppressors', Samer Al-Saber asks, 'the Israeli occupiers, the camp's traditionalists, or both?'[52] Shortly before the play's first performance on 23 January 2011, the student Mariam Abu Khaled, dressed as the Red Queen, advertised the production by shouting through a megaphone from the roof of Mer-Khamis's car. She was told by onlookers not to show her face in the area again.[53] A few weeks later, the familiar refrain of 'the suspicious theatre … whose only goal is to spread corruption and Western culture' was echoed in pamphlets drafted by unknown militant groups.[54] A week after the last performance, Mer-Khamis was no more.

## Conclusion

If Mer-Khamis's ambition was to create an outstanding professional Palestinian theatre school, he succeeded. Many of his pupils, the future leaders of a future Palestinian state, now pursue remarkable professional careers in theatres in Germany, the UK and the Middle East. Few have continued their work in Jenin, in contrast to Arna Mer-Khamis's students. Read against a narrative of rupture and exile, the theatrical notion of the cultural intifada or cultural resistance, 'a movement that harnesses the force of creativity and artistic expression in the quest for freedom, justice and equality', becomes an oxymoron.[55] As Abu Salem prophesied, the Palestinian theatre 'goes wherever it *can* go, wherever it can survive, in terms of its identity and in terms of its economical survival. We have hardly ever *chosen* being abroad'.[56] Operating both as utopia and as heterotopia, depending on who is doing the observing, the Palestinian theatre appears mirror-like where resistance and statehood manifest as real and unreal – apparitions refracting reality while existing outside it. Not unsurprisingly, Palestinian recipients of EU cultural funding assert: 'You want us to look the same as you'.[57] By relocating a core local constituency of intellectuals from the origins of the conflict to the externalities, liquid capital smooths over the impenetrability of borders, global humanity is standardised, resistance is fetishised and culture is subsumed within a larger ecosystem of funding, normalisation and bio-political governmentality. 'To be free is to be able to criticise, to be free is to be able to express yourself freely, to be free is to be free first of all of the chains of tradition, religion, nationalism, then you can start for yourself', Juliano Mer-Khamis once said.[58] Who was he speaking to? Who was his audience? And who was he? Was he, as he was often made out to be, a wilful '*infant terrible*' (sic) desiring an unalloyed, absolute freedom from the PA, Israel, Islamic tradition and all societal norms,[59] or a scapegoat in the complex clockwork of Euro-American soft power at the dawn of the Arab Spring? If the latter, isn't everyone in the parasitic network of the human-rights industry who derived social and economic capital from parachuting into Palestinian lives, winning for them chimerical rights and freedom – heads of government representations, global-development experts, international theatre scholars and ex volunteers – to a degree complicit in his death?

'I think it is extraordinary that we live in a world where a foundation like yours can help a group like El-Hakawati', Abu Salem wrote.[60] He spoke only too soon.

## Notes

1   A longer version of this chapter was published in *Theatre Research International*, 2021.
2   Taghdisi-Rad, 2011; Haddad, 2016; Khalidi and Samour, 2011.
3   Nicholson, 2020; Sommer, 1973, 1.
4   Carmichael, 1984, 5.
5   Carmichael, 1984, 5.
6   'Letter of Introduction', 1994; Carmichael, 1984, 7, 9.
7   Carmichael, 9.
8   Mayleas, 1984; Cary, 1984.
9   Lesch, 1984.
10  Cary and Mayleas, 1984.
11  Lubeck, 1984–94.
12  Gerhart, 1990.
13  Gerhart, 1990.
14  'Theatre in Occupied Palestine', 1992.
15  Salem, 1991 and 1992.
16  Barsalou, 1986.
17  Ghosheh, 1991.
18  Davies, 1993, 2, 6.
19  'Ashtar for Theatre and Performing Arts, Educational Project, Year II, 1993', 3.
20  'Ashtar for Theatre and Performing Arts, Educational Project, Year II, 1993', 15.
21  Prentki, 1998; Joseph, 2005; Plastow, 2014.
22  Zein-Elabdin, 28.
23  United Nations Development Programme, *Human Development Report 1990*, iii.
24  Haddad, *Palestine LTD.*, 21–2.
25  Haddad, *Palestine LTD.*, 58.
26  Roy, 1999, 66.
27  Hanieh, 2016, 34.
28  Haddad, 2016, 47; Tartir, 2015, 485; Khalidi, 2016, 11; Allen, 2013, 2.
29  Allen, 2013, 4.
30  Allen, 2013, 69.
31  Allen, 2013, 10–12.
32  Ashtar Studio, 1998.
33  Mer-Khamis, 2004.
34  Shatz, 2013.
35  Johansson and Wallin, 2018a, 19, 22.
36  Jecks, 2009.

37  goethe.de.
38  goethe.de.
39  Johansson and Wallin, 2018b, 126.
40  Wallin and Stanczak, 2018a, 37.
41  The Freedom Theatre's *Animal Farm* depicted a thinly veiled portrait of the PA as collaborators with Israel.
42  Wallin and Stanczak, 2018b, 91; Tartir, 2015.
43  'The EU Cultural Programme 2012'.
44  Bathaish, 2011; Al-Yamani and Abusrour, 2012, 79.
45  thefreedomtheatre.org.
46  'MDG Joint Programme: culture and development in the Occupied Palestinian Territory: final report'.
47  Bergeron,  2003.
48  Kapoor, 35.
49  MiddleEastNewsWatch, 2011.
50  Videopeacereporter, 2011.
51  Mee, 2012, 169–70.
52  Al-Saber, 2023.
53  Shatz, 2013.
54  Journeyman Pictures, 2011.
55  thefreedomtheatre.org.
56  Salem, 1991 and 1992.
57  Schneider, 2014, 16.
58  Jecks, 2009.
59  Johansson and Wallin, 2018c, 55.
60  Salem, 1991 and 1992.

# References

## Archival sources

Al-Saber, Samer. 'Alice in Dangerland'. Accessed 24 September 2023. https://www.thefreedomthe atre.org/news/alice-in-dangerland.

'Ashtar for Theatre and Performing Arts, Educational Project, Year II, 1993', *The Jerusalem 'Ashtar' for Theatre Training and Performing Arts: support for development of a theater school* 1 July 1993–1 July 1994: 3. Reel R6572 (microform), Rockefeller Archive Center.

Barsalou, Judy. 'Re: el-Hakawati, Inter-office Memorandum', *The Jerusalem El-Hakawati for Theatre and Visual Arts* 1 August 1984–31 March 1994 (1986). Reel R6746 (microform), Rockefeller Archive Center.

Carmichael, William D. 'Recommendation for Grant Action', *The Jerusalem El-Hakawati for Theatre and Visual Arts: support for operating costs and workshops to strengthen theatre arts and cultural expression (Jerusalem)* 1 August 1984–31 March 1994 (1984): 5. Reel R6746 (microform), Rockefeller Archive Center.

Cary, Linn. 'Hakawati Theatre, Inter-office Memorandum' to Ann Lesch, *The Jerusalem El-Hakawati for Theatre and Visual Arts* 1 August 1984–31 March 1994 (1984). Reel R6746 (microform), Rockefeller Archive Center.

Cary, Linn and Mayleas, Ruth. 'El Hakawati, Inter-office Memorandum', *The Jerusalem El-Hakawati for Theatre and Visual Arts* 1 August 1984–31 March 1994 (1984). Reel R6746 (microform), Rockefeller Archive Center.

Davies, Kristina. 'Delegated Authority Grant to Ashtar $40,000 Inter-office Memorandum', *The Jerusalem 'Ashtar' for Theatre Training and Performing Arts: support for development of a theater school* 1 July 1993–1 July 1994 (1993): 2, 6. Reel R6572 (microform), Rockefeller Archive Center.

Gerhart, John D. 'Recommendation for Grant/FAP Action', *The Jerusalem El-Hakawati for Theatre and Visual Arts* 1 August 1984–31 March 1994 (1990). Reel R6746 (microform), Rockefeller Archive Center.

Ghosheh, Jamal. 'A Progress Report to the Ford Foundation March 1991: Al-Masrah for Palestinian culture and arts', *The Jerusalem El-Hakawati for Theatre and Visual Arts* 1 August 1984–31 March 1994 (1991). Reel R6746 (microform), Rockefeller Archive Center.

Jecks, Nikki. 'Animal Farm Rankles the West Bank', *BBC News*, 28 March 2009. Accessed 24 September 2023. http://news.bbc.co.uk/2/hi/middle_east/7968812.stm.

Journeyman Pictures. 'Deadly Drama – Israel/Palestine', *YouTube*, 18 July 2011. Accessed 24 September 2023. https://www.youtube.com/watch?v=fkuneA6nIGA&t=859s&app=desktop.

'Konferenz Kunst.Kultur.Konflikt. 17–18 May 2011 Dokumentation', *Goethe Institut*, 2011. Accessed 25 September 2023. https://web.archive.org/web/20200504111642/www.goethe.de/ges/prj/kue/bil/kkk/pro/Dokumentation_KunstKulturKonflikt.pdf.

Lesch, Ann. 'Grant Negotiations: El-Hakawati theatre group', *The Jerusalem El-Hakawati for Theatre and Visual Arts* 1 August 1984–31 March 1994 (1984). Reel R6746 (microform), Rockefeller Archive Center.

'Letter of Introduction', *The Jerusalem El-Hakawati for Theatre and Visual Arts* 1 August 1984–31 March 1994. Reel R6746 (microform), Rockefeller Archive Center.

Lubeck, Jackie. 'Introduction to the Workshop Proposals', *The Jerusalem El-Hakawati for Theatre and Visual Arts* 1 August 1984–31 March 1994. Reel R6746 (microform), Rockefeller Archive Center.

Mayleas, Ruth. 'Visit to Jerusalem – El Hakawati Theatre Company, Inter-office Memorandum', *The Jerusalem El-Hakawati for Theatre and Visual Arts*, 1 August 1984–31 March 1994 (1984). Reel R6746 (microform), Rockefeller Archive Center.

MDG Achievement Fund. 'MDG Joint Programme: culture and development in the Occupied Palestinian Territory: final report', March 2013. Accessed 24 September 2023. http://mdgfund.org/sites/default/files/Palestinian%20Territory%20-%20Culture%20-%20Final%20Narrative%20Report.pdf.

MiddleEastNewsWatch. 'Juliano Mer-Khamis predicted his own murder by Palestinians', *YouTube*, 7 April 2011. Accessed 10 March 2020. https://www.youtube.com/watch?v=fSPUxYMoKRs.

Sommer, John G. 'Culture and the Ford Foundation in India: a note for discussion'. Report 006455, Box 290, FA739C (1973): 1. Catalogued reports, Ford Foundation Records, Rockefeller Archive Center.

Salem, François A. 'Letter to David Nygard', Paris, 10 November 1991 and New York, 8 May 1992, *The Jerusalem El-Hakawati for Theatre and Visual Arts* 1 August 1984–31 March 1994. Reel R6746 (microform), Rockefeller Archive Center.

'Seminar Report, "Teaching Acting": methods and techniques, Ashtar Studio, 9–11 January 1998', *Ramallah: Ashtar, for Theatre Production and Training* (1998): 21.

'The EU Cultural Programme 2012', *European Union External Action*. Accessed 24 September 2023. https://eeas.europa.eu/archives/delegations/westbank/documents/news/2013/20130211_cultureprogrammesummary_en.pdf.

The Freedom Theatre, 16 November 2015. Accessed 23 March 2020. https://www.thefreedomtheatre.org.

'Theatre in Occupied Palestine', *The Jerusalem 'Ashtar' for Theatre Training and Performing Arts: support for development of a theater school* 1 July 1993–1 July 1994 (1992). Reel R6572 (microform), Rockefeller Archive Center.

Videopeacereporter. 'Intervista a Juliano Mer Khamis, direttore del Freedom theatre di Jenin', *YouTube*, 8 April 2011. Accessed 2 March 2020. https://www.youtube.com/watch?v=PNWsyqftD9I.

## Published sources

Allen, Lori. *The Rise and Fall of Human Rights: Cynicism and politics in occupied Palestine*. Stanford, CA: Stanford University Press, 2013.

Al-Yamani, Hala and Abusrour, Abdelfattah. 'Juliano Khamis: martyr of freedom and culture', *Research in Drama Education: The Journal of Applied Theatre and Performance* 17 (1) (2012): 73–81.

Bathaish, F. 'Alice in the Wonderland: Jasmine's rebellion in Jenin', *Trevizion* 472 (2011): 26–30.

Bergeron, Suzanne. 'The Post-Washington consensus and economic representations of women in development at the World Bank', *International Feminist Journal of Politics* 5 (3) (2003): 397–419.

Haddad, Toufic. *Palestine LTD.: Neoliberalism and nationalism in the occupied territory*. London: I. B. Tauris, 2016.

Hanieh, Adam. 'Development as struggle: confronting the reality of power in Palestine', *Journal of Palestine Studies* 45 (4) (2016): 32–47.

Johansson, Ola and Wallin, Johanna, eds. *The Freedom Theatre: Performing cultural resistance in Palestine*. New Delhi: LeftWord Books, 2018a.

Johansson, Ola and Wallin, Johanna. 'A conversation about cultural resistance: the Freedom Theatre school alumni'. In *The Freedom Theatre*, edited by Ola Johansson and Johanna Wallin, 123–30. New Delhi: LeftWord Books, 2018b.

Johansson, Ola and Wallin, Johanna. 'Juliano Mer-Khamis'. In *The Freedom Theatre*, edited by Ola Johansson and Johanna Wallin, 53–61. New Delhi: LeftWord Books, 2018c.

Joseph, Christopher Odhiambo. 'Theatre for development in Kenya: interrogating the ethics of practice', *Research in Drama Education: The Journal of Applied Theatre and Performance* 10 (2) (2005): 189–99.

Kapoor, Ilan. *The Postcolonial Politics of Development*. New York: Routledge, 2008.

Khalidi, Raja. 'Twenty-first century Palestinian development studies', *Journal of Palestine Studies* 45 (5) (2016): 7–15.

Khalidi, Raja and Samour, Sobhi. 'Neoliberalism as liberation: the statehood program and the remaking of the Palestinian national movement', *Journal of Palestine Studies* 40 (2) (2011): 6–25.

Mee, Erin B. 'The cultural Intifada: Palestinian theatre in the West Bank', *TDR/The Drama Review* 56 (3) (2012): 167–77.

Nicholson, Rashna Darius. 'Canonising impulses, cartographic desires, and the legibility of history: why speak of/for "Indian" theatrical pasts?'. In *The Routledge Companion to Theatre and Performance Historiography*, edited by Tracy C. Davis and Peter W. Marx, 186–205. London: Routledge, 2020.

Nicholson, Rashna Darius. 'On the (im)possibilities of a free theatre: theatre against development in Palestine', *Theatre Research International* 46 (1) (2021): 4–22.

Plastow, Jane. 'Domestication or transformation? The ideology of theatre for development in Africa', *Applied Theatre Research* 2 (2) (2014): 107–18.

Prentki, Tim. 'Must the show go on? The case for theatre for development', *Development in Practice* 8 (4) (1998): 419–29.

Roy, Sara. 'De-development revisited: Palestinian economy and society since Oslo', *Journal of Palestine Studies* 28 (3) (1999): 64–82.

Schneider, Mirjam. 'Palestine country report: culture in EU external relations', 26 February 2014. Accessed 24 September 2023. https://ec.europa.eu/assets/eac/culture/policy/international-cooperation/documents/country-reports/palestine_en.pdf.

Shatz, Adam. 'The life and death of Juliano Mer-Khamis', *London Review of Books* 35 (22) (2013): 3–11. https://www.lrb.co.uk/the-paper/v35/n22/adam-shatz/the-life-and-death-of-juliano-mer-khamis.

Taghdisi-Rad, Sahar. *The Political Economy of Aid in Palestine*. London: Routledge, 2011.

Tartir, Alaa. 'Securitised development and Palestinian authoritarianism under Fayyadism', *Conflict, Security & Development* 15 (5) (2015): 479–502.

United Nations Development Programme. *Human Development Report 1990*. Oxford: Oxford University Press, 1990.

Wallin, Johanna and Stanczak, Jonatan. 'The beginning'. In *The Freedom Theatre*, edited by Ola Johansson and Johanna Wallin, 29–45. New Delhi: LeftWord Books, 2018a.

Wallin, Johanna and Stanczak, Jonatan. 'The Freedom Theatre's cultural resistance'. In *The Freedom Theatre*, edited by Ola Johansson and Johanna Wallin, 83–99. New Delhi: LeftWord Books, 2018b.

Zein-Elabdin, Eiman O. 'Articulating the postcolonial (with economics in mind)'. In *Postcolonialism Meets Economics*, edited by Eiman O. Zein-Elabdin and S. Charusheela, 21–39. London: Routledge, 2004.

# Part II
## Technopolitics

# 5
# Instituting national theatres in Africa[1]
Christopher B. Balme

National theatres have been a feature of the urban landscape for at least 250 years, and perhaps even longer if we take the Comédie-Française as the first exemplar, a national theatre in all but name. A national theatre is defined usually as a purpose-built structure designed to represent the nation and supported by state subventions of some kind. Metonymically it stands in for the state and nation in cultural matters.[2] In Germany, Gotthold Ephraim Lessing and Friedrich Schiller provided the theoretical underpinnings for the concept, but never managed to establish a permanent national theatre in the current German territories, where there are today, depending on the definition, either none or several. The first national theatres outside of France and Germany were founded in Eastern Europe in the nineteenth century, often in countries which had not even achieved full political independence. For emerging peoples such as the Czechs, Slovaks, Poles, Hungarians and Serbs, national theatres were erected rapidly in current or future capital cities, where they occupied pride of place in the urban landscape. Today these countries tend to have several national theatres (Croatia has five) – the smaller the country the greater the number. It took the British over a century of prolonged debate to grudgingly apportion public funds to the building of a national theatre, which finally opened, temporarily, at the Old Vic in 1962 before the current purpose-built structure opened on the South Bank in 1976.

If we turn to the African continent we can identify strategies that follow the East European model, where an emergent or emerging nation-state erects a national theatre to mark its newly won statehood. In sub-Saharan Africa we find, in rough order of construction, the Kenya National Theatre in Nairobi (1952), the Ethiopian National Theatre in

Addis Ababa (1955), the National Theatre of Uganda in Kampala (1959), the National Theatre of Somalia in Mogadishu (1967), the National Arts Theatre in Lagos, Nigeria (1977), and the National Theatre of Ghana in Accra (1992). The oldest national theatre on the African continent is located in Nairobi, and opened in 1952 on the initiative of British and Indian settlers.[3] It was followed by the theatre in Uganda, which was largely a project of the colonial authorities. The national theatre in Somalia was built by the Chinese in 1967, and damaged in the 1990s during the civil war.[4] The national theatre in Nigeria, built for the Second World Black and African Festival of Arts and Culture and based on the design of the Bulgarian Palace of Culture and Sports, was at the time arguably the largest cultural edifice on the African continent. The national theatre in Ghana was designed and erected by the Chinese in 1992 on the site of Efua Sutherland's Drama Studio. It opened in 1960 and was, in the words of David Donkor 'in looks and deeds if not in name, very much a national theatre'.[5] South Africa occupies a somewhat anomalous position in this history because under the apartheid regime the country set up several regional theatres, known as Performing Arts Councils (PACs), after the German model of generously subsidised municipal and regional theatres complete with drama, opera and ballet companies, which performed for largely white audiences.[6]

These buildings, still standing, bear the often literal scars of African history in the age of post-colony. While each theatre has its own particular history, they share certain common experiences that together can be read as an allegory of postcolonial cultural history. This narrative is bracketed by the seemingly contradictory terms 'modular modernity' and 'cultural heritage' – modernity with its promise of the clean slate and forward-looking innovation, cultural heritage with its ideology of preservation and cultural memory. While apparently oppositional these terms are in fact two points on a continuum of Western influence on the African continent (and elsewhere). There is a direct through-line connecting modular modernity with cultural heritage – a connection, I shall argue, that has enabled most of these buildings, despite weak institutional support structures, to survive, and in most cases avoid the almost-inevitable fate of conversion into shopping centres or car parks. My main example is the Uganda National Cultural Centre (UNCC), popularly known as the National Theatre. Built in 1959 under the auspices of the British colonial administration, this parting gesture from a well-meaning official embodied the 'progressive' style of modernist tropical architecture. Sixty years later it was earmarked for demolition as its central location in downtown Kampala promised more profitable use as a multistorey shopping centre. Its rescue, after vociferous protests, came down to its status as a cultural-heritage building. The narrative and argument of this chapter will extend beyond the temporal framework of the Cold War proper and into the present, as both modular modernity and cultural heritage represent *longue durée* global discourses that act on nations and cultures across the globe over prolonged periods.

## Modular modernity

National theatres are outgrowths of nationalism and the formation of nation-states. The concept of modular modernity proposed here is heavily influenced by historiographical concepts of nationalism, especially those of Benedict Anderson and Ernest Gellner, who both employ the notion of modularity or modular thinking to explain the rapid diffusion of nationalism around the globe. Here modularity functions as a cultural prerequisite for the importation and adaptation of a very European ideology forged in the eighteenth and nineteenth centuries. The aim of this chapter is to bring together, through the concept of modularity, previously separate strands of thinking about theatre for postcolonial nations in the 1950s and 1960s. The concept and practice of modularity can accommodate both aesthetic and institutional dimensions of theatre that are normally dealt with separately, dimensions that coalesce most notably in the architecture of national theatres but are by no means restricted to it. The modular is transportable and potentially transferrable to diverse cultural contexts.

A more specific application of the term modularity to the processes of decolonialisation can be found in theories of nationalism. Benedict Anderson defined his famous concept of imagined communities in terms of cultural artefacts that could be easily transported in 'modular' form to highly disparate cultural contexts:

> My point of departure is that nationality, or … nation-ness, as well as nationalism, are cultural artefacts of a particular kind … I will be trying to argue that the creation of these artefacts towards the end of the eighteenth century was the spontaneous distillation of a complex 'crossing' of discrete historical forces; but that, once created, they became 'modular', capable of being transplanted, with varying degrees of self-consciousness, to a great variety of social terrains, to merge and be merged with a correspondingly wide variety of political and ideological constellations.[7]

Ernest Gellner, perhaps the other most prominent and influential postwar theorist of nationalism, also sees in the concept of modularity a defining characteristic of nationalism. He follows a binary model of 'traditional' societies wedded to 'non-modularity' and more 'modern' ones that embrace nationalism via modular thinking. Non-modularity, where humans are embedded in tight networks with a social life regulated by highly 'dramatic' rituals, is the norm of existence: 'A traditional wedding involves two entire clans, great expense, much sound and fury; it is modern man who can get married in a quick sober procedure with a couple of witnesses and yet incur legally and socially serious consequences.' For Gellner the norm of non-modularity is rooted politically in nativised structures of tightly observed kinship networks, the 'rule of cousins' as opposed to the centralised 'tyranny of kings'.[8]

The theatrical discourse of the postcolonial world in the 1950s and 1960s mirrored Western debates and trends while adding a specific decolonial component, namely the integration of indigenous performance culture and traditions. This move corresponds to Anderson's concept of merging with local constellations, and has been extensively analysed in aesthetic terms under concepts such as syncretic, hybrid and intercultural theatre. My argument is that modern Western theatre in the twentieth century provided an example of a practice based on modular principles, in the sense that it comprised forms and elements that could be selected, assembled and recombined at will. This sets it aside from and in opposition to culturally matrixed performance forms, which integrate aesthetics, belief systems and specific cultural contexts. We find such forms in all cultures, but they are especially prevalent in indigenous performance traditions. In performance forms that are culturally matrixed to a high degree it is hard to detach individual modules and transport them across cultures. When this is attempted the result is usually folkloric, even exoticist entertainment.

## (Tropical) architecture and national theatres

National theatres are first and foremost architectural structures that evince the concept of modularity. These structures were mostly erected in the 1950s and 1960s, and paralleled political decolonisation. Although Anderson does not deal specifically with theatre (he focuses instead on museums), there is little doubt that national theatres are examples of transportable, modular cultural artefacts, insofar as they embody ideas as well as functions. The architectural movement most closely associated with modularity is Bauhaus (and its various extensions and adaptations), including Le Corbusier's International Style. These movements had a colonial and, in particular, decolonial extension in the projects of the 1950s, 1960s and 1970s known as tropical architecture. The term encompasses a relatively close-knit network of architects, a number of whom were German exiles such as Ernst May and Otto Königsberger, who began formulating and practising modern architectural principles in colonial contexts across the globe. In 1953 they gave organisational form to the movement following a conference in London.[9]

In the field of theatre, one of the most influential examples of modularity was the so-called theatre-in-the-round or arena theatre (see also chapter 9 in this volume). We find several projects that propagated and installed theatre-in-the-round in non-European contexts, usually in a spirit of cultural adaptation to pre-existing autochthonous forms. The programmatic model was, however, a publication by the Texas-based American theatre director Margo Jones, *Theatre-in-the-Round* (1951). A regular recipient of funding from the Rockefeller Foundation, Jones was an indefatigable promotor of professional, non-profit regional theatre in the US, and a theatrical modernist in both the aesthetic and institutional senses.

Although Jones linked a specific architectural form (arena staging) to the non-profit model, the non-profit model is an institutional form not wedded to a particular kind of building. The widespread adoption of non-profit theatre signals the 'sacralisation' of theatre as an art form, its inclusion in the canon of 'high culture', as Paul DiMaggio has argued in the context of the US.[10] There it was closely connected to demands for a national theatre, a project that gained support during the Cold War, although it ultimately came to nothing.[11] While this shift from commercial enterprise to high-culture status took place at different times in different countries, by the mid-twentieth century it had been widely achieved in the Global North.

The foundational years of the US non-profit modernist model – the 1950s and 1960s – run parallel to the establishment of theatre in postcolonial nations. There is little to no time lapse, no period of catch up or perpetual belatedness, so often characteristic of postcolonial discourse. We can speak indeed of a theatrical coevality. The repertory Jones extolled – a combination of new playwriting and classics, with an emphasis on the former – was also exported largely intact. The classical repertoire comprised the Greeks, Shakespeare, Molière and an emerging modernist canon including writers such as Ibsen, Chekhov, George Bernard Shaw, Eugene O'Neill and later, and more controversially,

Brecht. All postcolonial theatre agreed on the necessity of encouraging new writers to give voice to the new national identity. The modernist modular theatre repertoire comprised a bedrock of classics that was largely the same wherever theatre was performed, from Cape Town to Port-of-Spain. The variation lay in the field of indigenous playwriting, where repertoire remained highly specific, and indeed site specific, with very few plays or writers transferring to other locales.

Theatre-in-the-round – or arena staging, as it was often termed – was frequently promoted in the postcolonial world as an alternative to Western-style proscenium stages, with their confrontational structure emphasising the separation of spectators and performers. Sutherland's Drama Studio, built in 1962, was constructed as a theatre-in-the-round, based on the housing compounds of the Akan people of Ghana.[12] It received funding from the Rockefeller Foundation, which funded a number of similar projects: the Seoul Drama Center in South Korea,[13] Severino Montano's Arena Theatre in the Philippines (chapter 9) and the Arena Theatre in Sao Paulo, Brazil, established in 1953.[14] These were all national theatre projects in terms of spirit and ambition even if in the end they did not attain this status. National theatres were always institutional as much as architectural projects, state support being equally as significant as the actual physical foundations on which the many buildings rested, if not more so.

The importance of the US in promoting modernist, modular theatre is indissolubly linked to the involvement of US philanthropic organisations, most prominently the Rockefeller and Ford foundations but also the CIA-funded Congress for Cultural Freedom (see introduction, and chapters 10 and 14). The close imbrication of philanthropy, US foreign policy and the promotion of a seemingly apolitical modernist aesthetic, of which modular architecture appeared the perfect proof, provides the background to understanding national theatre projects in Africa.

## National theatre in Uganda

The idea for a Ugandan national theatre was first proposed in 1952 by the governor of the protectorate, Andrew Cohen. Of Jewish-Russian descent and Cambridge educated, Cohen joined the colonial service before the Second World War and by 1947 had risen to head of the African division in the Colonial Office. He was a dedicated proponent of decolonisation, especially in Africa, and under the Labour government he found a sympathetic supporter in the minister for the colonies, Arthur

Creech Jones. After Jones left the colonial office with the fall of the Labour government, Cohen was 'exiled' (as he put it) to Uganda, where he was appointed governor. There he began to negotiate with local rulers to prepare the country for self-rule and eventually independence.[15]

Cohen envisaged a cultural centre or institute housing a theatre and providing various culturally active, amateur theatrical societies with a headquarters, a place where European, African and Indian communities could meet and mix. The new building was therefore predominantly a theatre, but included spaces for rehearsals, meetings and social events. The theatre was established by an Act of Parliament of 1959, the Uganda National Cultural Centre Act, which specified that the UNCC was a semi-autonomous body to be run as a trust and not directly by government. About GB£30,000 was raised by bodies most closely connected with the project, and the balance of GB£90,000 was approved by the government. The choice of a trust as the form of governance is typical of the British approach to the relationship between government and arts adminis-tration, which can only be described as arm's-length. It reflects the non-profit model that had gained widespread support in the US during the New Deal years. The act itself specifies the trust's central function to be the administering of the 'trust property' (i.e. the centre), but also more broadly:

> (a) to provide and establish theatres and cultural centres; (b) to encourage and develop cultural and artistic activities; and (c) subject to such directions as may be given to it by the Minister from time to time, to provide accommodation for societies, institutions or organisations of a cultural, artistic, academic, philanthropic or educational nature.[16]

The first provision mentions theatres and cultural centres in the plural, and clearly Cohen envisaged a more regional approach in the long-term. Paragraph 13 of the act specifically provided for the establishment of district arts committees 'for the purpose of encouraging and developing artistic and cultural activities in its area'.[17] Direct government influence was exercised through the appointment of a board of trustees, who were entrusted in turn to appoint an executive committee to oversee the day-to-day running of the centre. Despite Uganda's violent postcolonial history, particularly in the Idi Amin years, the act remains in force to this day.[18]

The design and building of the UNCC was executed by the Kampala-based architectural firm Peatfield & Bodgener, established in London in

1952 by two ex-RAF servicemen. They established a permanent office in Kampala that is still active today, and have been placed in the context of tropical architecture.[19]

The modernist building has a reinforced concrete frame faced with terrazzo slabs and round *brise soleil* grilles incorporating East African white marble chips (figure 5.1). Behind the grilles, the window walls have local cedar framing. The auditorium has no doors, and the individual seat rows are accessed directly from side passageways. The building has a passive ventilation system, with large louvers and roof vents. The exterior is quite typical of buildings in the tropical architectural style, such as the library at the University of Ibadan in Nigeria designed by Maxwell Fry and Jane Drew, often considered emblematic of the movement. It is also aesthetically sympathetic to other modernist buildings of the period, including the Ugandan parliament building (also designed by Peatfield & Bodgener) and Ernst May's Ugandan Museum (1954).[20]

The floor plan of the UNCC (figure 5.2) shows a conventional proscenium-style stage, dressing rooms, a green room, a box office and a manager's office. The community room indicates where various organisations – the offices and library of the British Council, the clubroom of the Uganda Society, the studio of the Parinal Art Academy, the Red Cross, the Kampala youth league and others – were accommodated.

At its opening in 1959 the theatre was arguably the best equipped theatre building of its kind in sub-Saharan Africa, and from a modernist, tropical-architectural perspective the most innovative. Despite its

**Figure 5.1**   Exterior of the Uganda National Cultural Centre, 1960.
Credit: Peatfield & Bodgener Architects, Kampala.

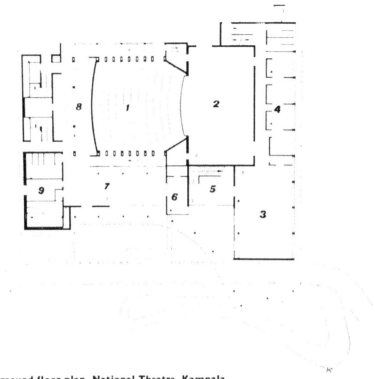

**ground floor plan, National Theatre, Kampala**

**key** 1, auditorium. 2, stage. 3, green room. 4, dressing rooms. 5, office entrance hall. 6, box office. 7, entrance foyer. 8, bar foyer. 9, manager's office.

**Figure 5.2** Floor plan of the Uganda National Cultural Centre. Credit: Peatfield & Bodgener Architects, Kampala.

eye-catching features, however, a British drama judge, Peter Carpenter, who visited Kampala just after its opening, asked:

> But what of the theatre? What is it for? Who will use it? What will be presented on its stage? How can a new and well-equipped theatre, with its own professional director and staff, prosper in the heart of Equatorial Africa, amid a population consisting of 5 1/2 million Africans, 55,000 Indians, and less than 9000 Europeans?[21]

With more than a hint of condescension, Carpenter poses the institutional question, perhaps the most difficult component of modular theatrical modernity to get right: how can long-term sustainability be achieved? His implication is that the theatre lacked the necessary quotient of

European supporters. It quickly transpired, however, that they were not needed.

When Wole Soyinka visited the theatre in 1962, he was underwhelmed: 'What we found was a doll's-house, twin-brother to our own National Museum … it was disconcerting to find a miniature replica of a British provincial theatre, fully closed in – another advantage this, extraneous noise at least was eliminated.'[22]

It is little wonder the theatre appeared as 'replica of a British provincial theatre' when one considers the job description of the theatre manager. The advertisement for the position, published in the London-based trade paper *The Stage*, was framed explicitly as a colonial tour of duty for a British professional. The advertisement sought 'a man of all-round ability responsible for the day-to-day management of the Theatre, the engagement of theatrical companies from overseas, assistance with the production of plays, dramatic education, and the general encouragement of amateur drama in Uganda'.[23] The salary range of GB£1,200–£1,650 per annum was generous for the theatre profession, as was the allowance of fully paid leave. The emolument was very much seen as compensation for a tropical tour of duty.

The theatre's first manager was an Englishman, Maxwell Jackson, whose tenure was rather short. He attempted to realise Cohen's vision of a multi-ethnic meeting place for Africans, Europeans and Asians, but unfortunately the expatriate community immediately asserted control of the theatre, marginalising other ethnic groups. According to the Ugandan writer Charles Mulekwa: 'the first director of the theatre G. Maxwell Jackson was apparently sacked and deported by the colonial authorities in the early 1960s because he insisted on making the creative space at the theatre available to African Ugandans'.[24]

Despite Jackson's removal, after independence in 1962 the theatre did indeed become a focal point for African artists, actors, dramatists and directors. From the mid-1960s onwards a succession of prominent East African theatre makers – including Robert Serumaga, Byron Kawadwa (who was murdered by Idi Amin), Rose Mbowa and John Ruganda – launched their careers from the UNCC. The venue also saw the premiere of Ngugi wa Thiong'o's *The Black Hermit* in 1962, the first full-length play in English by an East African writer, and two years later Wycliffe Kiyingi-Kagwe's *Gwosussa Emwani* (1964) in the Luganda language. The theatre became part of an organisational field including Makerere University, which produced all the dramatists mentioned above, and for some years the Rockefeller Foundation, which funded an experimental training programme at the UNCC in the mid-1960s.

Despite these auspicious beginnings the UNCC gradually declined, starved of government funding and forced to operate at a profit during Idi Amin's dictatorship and the subsequent austerity of structural-adjustment programmes. Nevertheless, it continued to hold an attraction for fledgling theatre makers, for whom a performance at the theatre represented artistic fulfilment and recognition.

By 2016 the UNCC had become dilapidated after almost sixty years of continuous use with little maintenance. Other, larger venues had become available, and the theatre's main source of revenue was the adjacent car park. Because many national theatres date from the colonial and early independence period, they often occupy prime urban plots while offering little return on investment in terms of square metres. Plans were drawn up to demolish the building and erect in its stead a 36-storey, multi-purpose retail centre complete with art gallery and cinema – but without a theatre. At the time the UNCC generated half a million US$ in revenue from rents, while the new retail centre was projected to earn US$14 million.[25]

The plans were made public in June 2017, prompting vociferous protest from the theatre community. Those opposed to the plans cited the notion of heritage, and even a certain nostalgia for the building, although parts of the theatre community had moved elsewhere.[26] The protests were successful and the demolition plan was replaced with a renovation and preservation programme (the theatre was needed as a venue for the biannual East African Community Arts and Culture Festival, which Uganda had agreed to host).

A similar fate threatened the Kenya National Theatre in Nairobi, but this was averted after the Kenyan government recognised it as part of the city's and nation's cultural heritage. The theatre's deed of title had not been registered on handover at independence, and prior to 2014 the building had not received any government support, relying entirely on box office takings and charges from the adjacent car park. A combination of private sponsorship and government funds finally led to a major renovation, with an exhibition documenting the theatre's colonial and postcolonial history.[27]

What may have helped save the UNCC and its sibling in Kenya is the fact that both were instituted by Acts of Parliament, meaning they received symbolic if not fiscal support from the state. This may distinguish the East African theatres from others on the continent, but also links them with the South African provincial theatres that enjoyed direct state support.

## The paradox of colonial cultural heritage

The UNCC has been placed on a list of 59 cultural-heritage buildings constructed before 1969 deemed to have significant cultural value. We find similar cases in Kenya and Nigeria, and even in war-torn Somalia. National theatres, even those associated with a colonial past, have mutated from being icons of modular modernity to symbols of cultural heritage – currently the dominant signifier of Western provenience. The transformation of the UNCC from a dilapidated remnant of a colonial past to a proud example of iconic architecture appears somewhat paradoxical, and is difficult to grasp without an understanding of cultural heritage as an international movement with a discursive and, ultimately, political power similar to that of the modular modernity that preceded it.

The concept of cultural heritage is fundamentally paradoxical, as Spanish sociologist and anthropologist Gil-Manuel Hernàndez i Martí has argued:

> … the concept of cultural heritage is itself a product of modern Western culture and, like the nationalist ideology to which it is closely linked, it has not stopped globalizing since the 19th century, which has generated a mimesis in the colonial territories that gained independence in the processes of decolonization in the 20th century.[28]

He suggests that the modern idea of cultural heritage implies a high degree of hybridisation, at odds with its essentialist claims. It mixes elements rescued from the past with elements generated in the present for its continued endurance, so that cultural heritage can be transmitted from generation to generation. Cultural heritage is paradoxical because, while it appears to be predicated on a 'tragic and nostalgic awareness of the … past', it creates its objects out of the needs of the present. His conclusion therefore: 'cultural heritage appears before us as a *zombie* or a living dead'.[29]

The view of cultural heritage as a zombie extracting blood is perhaps hyperbolic, but not entirely inaccurate if extraction means having the discursive power to mobilise and exert political influence. Ever since UNESCO adopted the Convention Concerning the Protection of the World Cultural and Natural Heritage in 1972 it has steadily expanded its influence by identifying World Heritage sites both natural and man-made, and more recently by introducing the notion of Intangible Cultural Heritage, encompassing cultural practices and performance forms.[30] Both programmes are explicitly internationalist in outlook, and competitive in the sense that nation-states compete for inclusion in UNESCO's influential lists. The effect on tourism, both positive and negative, is now undisputed, as UNESCO itself has recognised.[31]

Although originating with UNESCO, cultural heritage has long featured on the funding agendas of philanthropic organisations and national and international bodies. The involvement of international funding organisations has had a direct impact in many countries in the Global South. In Uganda, the European Union via its External Action Service (EEAS) initiated a project to 'document, establish an inventory, raise awareness and advocate for the protection of the many beautiful buildings located in the three targeted cities, and eventually for their restoration/rehabilitation',[32] the three cities being Kampala, Entebbe and Jinja. The project involved a three-day workshop to train twenty partici-pants, including photographers, historians, architects and researchers, as well as officers of the local authorities. At the opening of the workshop, the EU ambassador to Uganda, Attilio Pacifici, emphasised in his address the 'European' heritage of cultural heritage, and that the *limited awareness of the importance of cultural heritage* [italics mine], coupled with demand for "modern" structures and facilities, the rural–urban migration and rapid population growth, cultural heritage preservation has become a vital and urgent issue'.[33] The 'limited awareness' was implicitly on the part of the audience, i.e. the Ugandans, who needed to understand that their demand for 'modern' structures and facilities should not lead to a neglect of buildings bequeathed to them by the colonial past. Although this is perhaps an extreme example of development aid being perceived as an extension of the neocolonial white man's burden, it highlights how cultural-heritage discourse has become globalised.

## Conclusion

While government funds are available to renovate the buildings, the international community is also prepared to preserve them for posterity. The real challenge for the future will be institutional sustainability. Will governments commit to long-term support for national theatres as institutions and not just as examples of iconic heritage architecture? Or conversely, will international donors commit resources to institu-tional and not just architectural conservation? Probably not. National theatres are very much of the nation and for the nation, whereas present-day global philanthropy supports either concrete structures (often of the colonial era) or Theatre for Development projects. The challenge will be to reconcile these not-always congruent agendas. While modular modernity excited colonial administrations, African nationalists and American philanthropic organisations with a promise of futurity, cultural heritage remains a global discourse caught up in an uneasy tension between showcasing a problematic colonial past and curtailing possible new architectural initiatives. Although cultural heritage may be slowly taking root in government agendas, it is primarily focused on the materiality of the inherited structures and not on the enacted organisational networks theatres need. These are constituted by the artists, technicians and administrators who quite literally embody the institution, and who provide the institutional sustainability national theatres need to flourish.

## Notes

1   This chapter was written as part of the European Research Council project 'Developing theatre: building expert networks for theatre in emerging countries after 1945', funding ID-694559.
2   Wilmer, 2004.
3   https://buildesign.co.ke/kenyanationaltheatre/.
4   Plastow, 2020, 81.
5   Donkor, 2017, 47.
6   For example, the Natal Performing Arts Council (NAPAC) in Durban grew to be the second-largest performing arts council in South Africa, with 700 employees in the 1980s and a production programme of drama, musicals, symphony concerts, opera, ballet and school tours. It was severely reduced in size in the post-apartheid period. See Kruger, 1999, 100–1, and https://esat.sun.ac.za/index.php/Performing_Arts_Councils.
7   Anderson, 4.
8   Gellner, 1995, 41.
9   See Le Roux, 2003.
10  See DiMaggio, 1992.
11  See Canning, 2009.
12  Donkor, 2017, 35.
13  Creutzenberg, 2019.
14  Rockefeller Foundation 1960, 189–90.
15  Cohen, 1959.
16  Uganda National Cultural Centre Act 1959. https://old.ulii.org/ug/legislation/consolidated-act/50.
17  Uganda National Cultural Centre Act 1959. https://old.ulii.org/ug/legislation/consolidated-act/50.
18  https://www.gou.go.ug/topics/uganda-national-cultural-centre-uncc.
19  Flatman, 2017.
20  Hughes, 1960.
21  Carpenter, 1959, 6.
22  Soyinka, 1963, 21–2.
23  'National theatre Uganda', 1959, 9.
24  Mulekwa, 2011, 49.
25  Kiganda, 2017.
26  Kasadah, 2017.
27  Makokha, 2018.
28  Hernàndez i Martí, 2006, 97.

29  Hernàndez i Martí compares the heritage zombie to the replicants from the movie *Blade Runner* in whom artificial memories have been implanted: 'They are not personal memories, but memories that have been implanted and incorporated through the institutional process of patrimonialization.' Hernàndez i Martí, 2006, 103–4.
30  See https://www.unesco.org/culture/ich/index.php?lg=en&pg=00002.
31  UNESCO, 1972.
32  European Union External Action, 2018.
33  Pacifici, 2018, 2.


# References

Anderson, Benedict. *Imagined Communities: Reflections on the origin and spread of nationalism*. London: Verso, 1983.
Asiedu, Awo Mana. 'China in Ghana: an interview with Mohammed Ben Abdallah about the national theatre built in Accra by the Chinese government'. In *African Theatre: China, India and the Eastern world*, edited by James Gibbs and Femi Osofisan, 3–27. Woodbridge: James Currey, 2016.
Balme, Christopher B. *Decolonizing the Stage: Theatrical syncretism and post-colonial drama*. Oxford: Clarendon Press, 1999.
Barber, Karin, Collins, John and Ricard, Alain. *West African Popular Theatre*. Bloomington: Indiana University Press; Oxford: James Currey, 1997.
Becker, Howard. *Art Worlds*. Berkeley: University of California Press, 1982.
Blair, John G. *Modular America: Cross-cultural perspectives on the emergence of an American way*. Westport, CT: Greenwood Press, 1988.
Canning, Charlotte. '"In the interest of the state": a Cold War national theatre for the United States', *Theatre Journal* 61 (2009): 407–20.
Carpenter, Peter. 'A national theatre in Uganda', *The Guardian* 3 December (1959): 6.
Cohen, Andrew. *British Policy in Changing Africa*. London: Routledge & Kegan Paul, 1959.
Cole, Catherine M. *Ghana's Concert Party Theatre*. Bloomington: Indiana University Press, 2001.
Creutzenberg, Jan. 'Dreaming of a new theatre in Cold War South Korea: Yu Chi-jin, the Rockefeller Foundation and the Seoul Drama Center', *Journal of Global Theatre History* 3 (2) (2019): 34–53. https://doi.org/10.5282/gthj/5118.
Crow, Brian and Banfield, Chris. *An Introduction to Post-Colonial Theatre*. Cambridge and New York: Cambridge University Press, 1996.
De Readt, Kim. 'Tracing the history of socially engaged architecture: school building as development aid in Sub-Saharan Africa'. In *The Routledge Companion to Architecture and Social Engagement*, edited by Karim Farhan, 71–86. London: Routledge, 2018.
DiMaggio, Paul. 'Cultural boundaries and structural change: the extension of the high culture model to theater, opera, and the dance, 1900–1940'. In *Cultivating Differences: Symbolic boundaries and the making of inequality*, edited by Michèle Lamont and Marcel Fournier, 21–57. Chicago: University of Chicago Press, 1992.
Donkor, David Afriye. 'Making space for performance: theatrical-architectural nationalism in postindependence Ghana', *Theatre History Studies* 36 (2017): 29–56. https://doi.org/10.1353/ths.2017.0002.
Eisenstadt, Shmuel N. 'Multiple modernities', *Daedalus* 129 (1) (2000): 1–29.
European Union External Action. 'EU funded project to protect historical buildings in Uganda kicks off', *European Union External Action*, 31 August 2018. Accessed 22 December 2021. https://eeas.europa.eu/delegations/uganda/49938/eu-funded-project-protect-historical-buildings-uganda-kicks_en.
Fischer-Lichte, Erika, Riley, Josephine and Gissenweher, Michael. *The Dramatic Touch of Difference: Theatre, own and foreign*. Tübingen: Narr, 1990.
Flatman, Ben. 'An architect's guide to surviving the rule of Idi Amin', *Building Design Online*, 7 July 2017. Accessed 22 December 2021. https://www.bdonline.co.uk/comment/an-architects-guide-to-surviving-the-rule-of-idi-amin/5088622.article.
Fry, Maxwell and Drew, Jane. *Tropical Architecture in the Humid Zone*. London: Batsford, 1956.
Gellner, Ernest. 'The importance of being modular'. In *Civil Society: Theory, history and comparison*, edited by J. A. Hall, 32–55. Cambridge: Polity Press, 1995.

Gellner, Ernest. *Language and Solitude: Wittgenstein, Malinowski and the Habsburg dilemma*. Cambridge: Cambridge University Press, 1998.

Gilbert, Helen and Tompkins, Joanne. *Post-Colonial Drama: Theory, practice, politics*. London and New York: Routledge, 1996.

Graf, Rüdiger and Jarusch, Konrad H. '"Crisis" in contemporary history and historiography', *Docupedia-Zeitgeschichte*, 27 March 2017. Accessed 22 December 2021. https://docupedia. de/zg/Graf_jarausch_crisis_en_2017.

Hernàndez i Martí, Gil-Manuel. 'The deterritorialization of cultural heritage in a globalized modernity', *Transfer: Journal of Contemporary Culture* 1 (2006): 92–107. https://www.llull. cat/rec_transfer/webt1/transfer01_foc04.pdf.

Herschel, John Frederick William. *Two Letters to the Editor of the Athenæum, on a British Modular Standard of Length*. London: Wertheimer & Co., 1863.

Hughes, Richard. 'East Africa', *The Architectural Review* 1 July (1960): 21–30.

Jones, Margo. *Theatre-in-the-Round*. New York: Rinehard & Co., 1951.

July, Robert W. African diary, 1961. Robert W. July collection, New York Public Library. Sc MG 748, b. 1 f. 6–7.

Kasadah, Badru. 'Ugandans protest demolition of national theatre', *Eagle Online*, 14 June 2017. Accessed 2 November 2022. https://eagle.co.ug/2017/06/14/ugandans-protest-demolition-of-national-theatre.

Kiganda, Antony. 'Uganda to construct shopping mall in place of national theatre', *Constructionreview*, 21 June 2017. Accessed 2 November 2022. https://constructionreviewon line.com/2017/06/uganda-to-construct-shopping-mall-in-place-of-national-theatre.

Koenigsberger, O. H., Ingersoll, T. G., Mayhew, Alan and Szokolay, S. V. *Manual of Tropical Housing and Building, Part One: Climatic design*. London: Longman Group, 1974.

Kruger, Loren. *The National Stage: Theatre and cultural legitimation in England, France, and America*. Chicago: University of Chicago Press, 1992.

Kruger, Loren. *The Drama of South Africa: Plays, pageants and publics since 1910*. London and New York: Routledge, 1999.

Leonhardt, Nic. 'The Rockefeller roundabout of funding: Severino Montano and the development of theatre in the Philippines in the 1950s', *Journal of Global Theatre History* 3 (2) (2019): 19–33. https://doi.org/10.5282/gthj/5117.

Le Roux, Hannah. 'The networks of tropical architecture', *Journal of Architecture* 8 (3) (2003): 337–54. https://doi.org/10.1080/1360236032000134835.

Makokha, Kwamchetsi. 'Theatre facelift secures state apology, land title and money', *Nation*, 18 September 2018 (updated 5 July 2020). Accessed 2 November 2022. https://nation.africa/ lifestyle/weekend/Kenya-National-Theatre-facelift-State-apology/1220-2875986-anh9tv/ index.html.

Mulekwa, Charles. 'Theatre, war and peace in Uganda'. In *Acting Together I: Performance and the creative transformation of conflict*, edited by Cynthia Cohen, Roberto Gutiérrez Varea and Polly O. Walker, 45–71. Oakland, CA: New Village Press, 2011.

'National theatre Uganda' (advertisement), *The Stage* 26 February (1959): 9.

Pacifici, Attilio. 'Opening of the training on historical buildings documentation', *European Union External Action*, 27 August 2018. Accessed 22 December 2011. https://eeas.europa.eu/sites/ eeas/files/speech_hod_opening_training_ccfu.pdf.

Pavis, Patrice. *Theatre at the Crossroads of Culture*. London and New York: Routledge, 1992.

Phillips, Christopher J. *The New Math: A political history*. Chicago: Chicago University Press, 2014.

Plastow, Jane. *A History of East African Theatre, Volume 1: Horn of Africa*. London: Palgrave Macmillan, 2020.

Rockefeller Foundation. *On the Arena Theatre in Washington DC*. New York: Rockefeller Foundation, 1960.

Soyinka, Wole. 'Towards a true theatre', *Transition* 8 (March) (1963): 21–2.

Stanek, Łukasz. *Architecture in Global Socialism: Eastern Europe, West Africa and the Middle East in the Cold War*. New Jersey: Princeton University Press, 2020.

UNESCO. 'Convention concerning the protection of the world cultural and natural heritage', *World Heritage Convention*, 25 July 2010. Accessed 22 December 2021. https://whc.unesco.org/ archive/2010/whc10-34com-inf5F3.pdf.

Wilmer, S. E., ed. *Writing and Rewriting National Theatre Histories*. Iowa City: University of Iowa Press, 2004.

# 6
# Divided Europe in Damascus: the Higher Institute of Dramatic Arts in Damascus between Eastern European dictatorship and Western European intellectualism

Ziad Adwan

## Introduction

I taught at the Higher Institute of Dramatic Arts (HIDA) in Damascus between 2009 and 2013. One of the classes I took at the theatre studies department, where I studied between 1994 and 1998, was called theatre laboratory. Although the class occupied a significant portion of the student's weekly schedule, and had a considerable impact on the student's final grade, tutors were given the freedom to teach according to their interests. When I taught it I taught 'systems of rehearsal', focusing on Stanislavsky, Keith Johnstone and Augusto Boal. Tutors also enjoyed the freedom to teach what they wanted in the 'subject related to theatre' class; I taught masks in theatre and an introduction to performance studies. In these two semi-free classes, I used to ask first-year students what brought them to the institute and what their plans were after graduation. Some were interested in theatre and wanted to organise their reading, but most of the answers were variations of 'we are here because we want to study cinema, but since Syria does not have a cinema academy, we study theatre'. Some female students revealed they joined the theatre studies department because they could not study acting due to social restrictions. I also recall students who studied at the institute secretly so as not to upset their parents. HIDA also attracted many university students who found the social and intellectual environment of Syrian universities unsatisfactory.

In the acting department, the answers I received were more predictable. Most of the acting students wanted to become actors, and with the rising popularity of Syrian television series, involvement in such projects was considered the most prestigious type of work. For Syrian acting students, and within artistic and literary circles in general, the word work meant employment in a Syrian television production, which attracted film directors, novelists, playwrights, satellite channels, businessmen and political leaders.[1]

The acting students' desire to extend their ambitions beyond theatre is not unique to Syria, especially given the allure of film acting. Students and academics at theatre studies departments in other countries also find their departments scrutinised, beset with uncertainty regarding their disciplines, interdisciplinary approaches, and their technical and liberal efficiency,[2] as well as the foundational question of the department's demarcation from literature faculties[3] and its role in producing theatre performances.[4] However, the students' shifting interests did not prevent HIDA from becoming the most prominent theatre academy in the Middle East and the Gulf region. At the academic level it has provided the Arab theatre scene with influential artists, academics and cultural administrators, while at the commercial level its alumni became prominent stars in the television industry. Coinciding with the decline of the theatre scene in Lebanon because of the Lebanese Civil War (1975–90), and in Iraq because of the Iran–Iraq War (1980–8), HIDA became a destination for many Arab students, theatre professionals and academics.

HIDA also gained credibility as one of the few Syrian educational institutions not affected by corruption and arbitrary rule in a socialist, totalitarian state, and for maintaining a certain level of freedom of speech and individual liberty in a conservative country. Thus, in a country that controls and monitors its sectors and citizens, blocks sources of information, interferes in academic curricula and imprisons its opponents, HIDA suffered least from this repression, and was given the freedom to be influenced by both socialist ideology and Western-European thought. However, the institute's intellectual image was compromised at the national level, and this led to controversies inside the institute itself. The acting department and the theatre studies department adopted opposing positions in their interpretation of intellectualism, and clashed over which could claim this prestigious description – the theatre studies department with its dedication to the pursuit of pure knowledge, or the acting department devoted to professional training.

In this chapter I examine the foundation of HIDA, and read its development in relation to the markets in which its alumni operate and the changing interpretation of the intellectual, based on literature on intellectualism from the Eastern bloc. I argue that while HIDA adopted the intellectual label from a heavily compromised Damascus University, the institute became a place where the significance of intellectualism was distorted and subsequently remanufactured as a caricature to adapt to life under dictatorship.

## History, influences and the oasis of knowledge

Although HIDA is subordinated to the Ministry of Culture, it grants its students an internationally acknowledged BA certificate. When it was established in 1977, HIDA consisted of only an acting department offering a four-year course. Later, in 1984, the theatre studies department opened, and its associated degree course, also running for four years, was launched. The strong bond between Syria and former socialist countries facilitated invitations to Russian instructors, who served as experts in the acting department for decades. Also, through European cultural centres in Damascus, the institute invited many European theatre makers to give workshops. Additionally, HIDA signed cultural agreements with several European academies and institutions, and provided its alumni with scholarships for postgraduate study in East and West Europe.

HIDA was initially located in the suburbs of Damascus, and it remained there for 13 years. In 1990 it moved to the opera-house complex at Umayyad Square, a place of considerable political signifi-cance, which is surrounded by the General Organisation of Radio and TV (main target of the military coups), the Al-Assad National Library, the General Staff Command Building of the Syrian Armed Forces and the Sheraton Damascus Hotel. Gigantic statues of Hafez al-Assad can be found at all these locations except the hotel. The building complex (figure 6.1) placed HIDA alongside the Higher Institute of Music and the ballet school, emphasising the institute's artistic and civilised image. Later, in the 2000s, the scenography, dance and technical theatre departments opened.

Challenged by social and religious prohibitions, political restric-tions and economic limitations, theatre was considered problematic in Syria, not only socially and politically, but also economically and academically, and HIDA received few applications when it first opened. Even when it became popular and applications increased, the number of students in each class remained below fifteen. HIDA students have the right to live on the Damascus University campus and are provided

**Figure 6.1**   The building complex housing HIDA and the Higher Institute of Music, Damascus. Credit: private collection.

with books and training clothes, and some are given a monthly stipend if they can demonstrate a need for it. The relationship between teachers and students is to an extent informal, and the institute organises a yearly football match between students and teachers. There have also been instances of students changing teachers, where the teacher's approach was incompatible with the student's ambitions.

The institute's first dean was the writer Adib Al-Lujami, who also served as the assistant minister of culture. In 1982 Al-Lujami was succeeded by theatre academic Ghassan Al-Maleh, a regional editor of *The World Encyclopaedia of Contemporary Theatre (The Arab World)*. When the institute moved to its new premises, Iraqi musician Solhi Al-Wadi became the dean of both HIDA and the Higher Institute of Music. All three deans had a strong connection with Najah Al-Attar, who served as minister of culture for 24 years before being appointed vice president of Syria in 2006.

From its inception, HIDA attempted to gather, integrate and synthesise various European influences. Its founders had studied mainly at the faculty of literature at Damascus University before continuing their education in Europe. Nabil Haffar, who served as head of the theatre studies department between 1990 and 2005, studied english literature and then philosophy at Damascus University before taking his PhD in theatre studies at Leipzig University in the German Democratic Republic. Mari Elias and Hanan Kasab Hassan (the latter served as the dean of the institute between 2006 and 2008) both studied French literature at Damascus University before obtaining their doctorates at the Sorbonne. Saadallah Wannous, one of the institute's founders, studied journalism in Cairo and later took a research trip to Paris so he could familiarise himself with the French theatre scene. Naila Al-Atrash, who served as head of the acting department, studied at the National Academy for Theatre and Film Arts in Bulgaria. Fawaz Al-Sajer and Nadeem Mu'alla took their doctorates at the Russian Institute of Theatre Arts in Moscow. Through the ties Syria established with the former Eastern bloc, many acting teachers studied in Bulgaria and Poland before returning to Syria to occupy positions at HIDA. The institute also maintained ties with Western Europe by offering its alumni the opportunity to undertake post-graduate studies at various universities there.

The rise of HIDA in the 1980s coincided with the decline of Damascus University, as educational sectors slipped into corruption and came under the control of the socialist Ba'ath Party (other cultural sectors were also subjected to arbitrary control, and vulnerable to corruption). In *Ambiguities of Domination*, Lisa Wedeen analyzes how the al-Assad regime, after seizing power in 1970, in addition to the atrocities it committed, controlled slogans and spoken and written metaphors. She says that 'Assad is powerful because his regime can compel people to say the ridiculous and to avow the absurd'.[5] The value of scientific research declined, and the relationship to knowledge at universities became ambivalent.[6] University faculties were controlled by Ba'ath unions that monitored students and staff, and supervised state-organised 'spontaneous marches' to glorify al-Assad.[7]

HIDA demonstrated a resilience to these issues, however. While novelists were marginalised, filmmakers criminalised, the faculty of literature ridiculed and intellectuals arrested or exiled, HIDA remained to some extent immune to corruption and the intimidating gaze of the secret police. The cafeteria at the institute was a centre for intellectual discussion, knowledge exchange and criticism of the state – activities that were systematically stamped out in other Syrian cultural venues as the regime prevented renovations and closed cafes, arguably to prevent interaction between intellectuals.

Over the past century, the word *mothaqaf* ('مثقف, literally 'intel-lectual'), derived from *thaqafa* ('ثقافة, literally 'culture'), has undergone a nuanced evolution in terms of its connotations. Initially associated with writers and academics, it has broadened to encompass actors, artists, directors and musicians. Furthermore, *tathqeef* (تثقيف, literally 'to educate') has expanded the semantic boundaries of *mothaqaf* to encompass not only writers, artists and thinkers but also educators and the educated, emphasising the integral role of education in defining intellectualism. Beginning with the early 1920s' theorisations of the modern state of Syria, these associations gained currency via commercial plays that labelled a university student a *mothaqaf*. Under the socialist dictatorship, a *mothaqaf* was reinterpreted as a dissident, and several Syrian groups initiated oppositional actions conjoined with *mothaqaf*, such as the Statement of the Intellectuals and The Demonstration of the Intellectuals.[8] In Syrian television series, the intellectual (*mothaqaf*) is reduced, simply, to someone who reads newspapers and books.

HIDA combined these images in a place of unrestricted education, freedom of expression and personal liberty, where people read not only world drama but also translations of Western European philosophy and literature. The curricula at HIDA, reflecting international models, 'insist on unexamined discourses of high art elitism, as they prepare students to enter what is described monolithically as "the profession"',[9] to use Jill Dolan's words from her discussion of the identity of theatre studies and its academic location. Following Lawrence W. Levine, who explains in *Highbrow/Lowbrow* the transition of Shakespeare's plays from popular to high culture, language and style were used to inculcate values and express ideas and attitudes that were hard to sell to average members of the community.[10] HIDA developed an esoteric language, ideology and practice, and to some extent created a sense of 'we-ness' inside its building. Consequently, the institute was looked at as a place of high culture and professional knowledge, and was commonly called 'the place of the intellectuals'.

## Intellectuals outside the safe zone

In *Representation of the Intellectual*, Edward Said argues that whatever one does is done according to an idea or representation one has of oneself.[11] Teachers at HIDA were able to integrate their critical vocabularies and ideologies into their classes, reflecting either a communist sensibility, which was associated with the opposition, or a Ba'athist sensibility, which was associated with the socialist regime. Whether they inclined to communism or to Ba'ath, both positions embodied Brecht's famous saying, adapting Marx, that it is not 'the purpose of theatre to understand the world but to change it'.[12] This mission was a challenge for the HIDA intellectuals, especially when students and teachers were aware of the challenges and dangers involved in trying to enact change in a country that proposed 'taboos rather than models'.[13] Polish sociologist Marian Kempny suggests that intellectuals are normally associated with missions or responsibilities arising from the 'position of guardians of lasting and universal values … spokesmen for national society, a position which is still connected with their self-image of bearers of a solemn historical mission, or their special accountability for the whole nation'.[14]

In December 1998, students at HIDA staged a sit-in protest in front of the US embassy in Damascus to condemn American airstrikes against Iraq (code-named Operation Desert Fox). An air of uncertainty surrounded the embassy, which stands between Hafez al-Assad's home and his office, because police forces did not know what to do with the protestors, of whom I was one. The protest was in line with state slogans condemning the airstrikes, but Damascus was the only Arab capital that did not denounce the airstrikes publicly because Syrians had stopped demonstrating when al-Assad seized power.

That the secret police were wrongfooted by a small number of students can be attributed to the special position HIDA has held under the al-Assad regime. Totalitarian regimes compel individuals to self-censor and learn their limits. Oppositional discourse, like many practices under dictatorships, is usually conducted orally, as we did in the institute cafeteria. In his essay 'Intellectual life under dictatorship', Andrei Plesu, who served as minister of culture, and as minister of foreign affairs after the Romanian Revolution in 1989, seeks to answer the question of intellectual survival under socialist dictatorship. Although he ends his piece by wondering if intellectuals really did survive under Ceaușescu, he asserts that 'the need for culture springs from a primary instinct for survival and … from the exigency of individual "salvation" in an environment interested only in collectivistic solutions'.[15]

Underlining Plesu's observation, to survive under a dictatorship, people should live as if a change of regime is almost unthinkable. In these conditions, compromises must be made between intellectuals and official platforms of expression. Plesu argues, however, that in addition to humour and hope, which are concomitant with the horror, evil cannot have a homogenous texture and be perfectly compact. This imperfection, he adds, is a 'strictly necessary condition for the adaptation to evil, with its unavoidable benefits and risks. [Therefore, to make intellectual life possible, intellectuals must] profit from all the cracks of the system.'[16]

In both Syria and Romania, censorship was frequently modified, especially when the two countries moved from glorifying socialist ideology to worshipping Al-Asad and Ceauşescu – both referred to as 'father' in their respective countries. Plesu tells us that dictators 'distinguish themselves by the surprising interstices in which rules are suspended. The law can suddenly become lax for no apparent reason.'[17] Despite the many similarities between the Ceauşescu and al-Assad regimes, Syria differed from Romania and other socialist countries, not only because al-Assad remained in power and could pass power to his son when the Eastern bloc collapsed, but because of the relationship between Syria and Western theatre. On the one hand, theatre was a novel art in Syria, circulated among only a small number of people, and the majority of Syrians did not know about HIDA. Eventually, the institute solidified its professional reputation in the 1980s, at a time when the idea of it posing a threat to the Syrian regime was unthinkable. On the other hand, theatre is perceived as a European refinement and high culture, and for a new state like Syria it is a practice that can reflect the 'Syrian civilised face', as the state media terms it. Thus, at HIDA civilised practices remain in its civilised building.

Polish historian Jerzy Jedlicki argues that one becomes an intellectual when one crosses the boundaries of one's speciality and tries to influence the minds and consciences of one's fellow citizens, or, quoting Sartre, when one 'meddles in other people's affairs'.[18] Edward Said adds another characteristic for developing-nation intellectuals, who live in 'triumphalist' nations that are 'always exacting loyalty and subservience rather than intellectual investigation and re-examination'.[19] On the one hand, intellectuals are 'unusually responsive to innovation and experiment rather than the authoritatively given status quo',[20] on the other, the masses expect them to commit 'to the public mood for reasons of solidarity, primordial loyalty, or national patriotism'.[21]

In addition to their ideological responsibilities, students and teachers at HIDA had obligations towards their profession. While they aimed to elevate the status of theatre, as well as television, they shared an ambition to make a living from their profession. In her diary-like piece 'Theatre training Moscow style', published just a few months before the collapse of the Soviet Union, Joanna Rotté describes her meeting with Oleg Tabakov, chancellor of the Moscow Art Theatre School:

> Tabakov explains that when admitting students, the school looks not only for talent but also for intelligence, the kind of intelligence that enables a person to think about people less fortunate than,

and different from, oneself. He says they want their students to become desirous of changing the world for the better through the profession. At the same time, he is worrying that, with governmental support dwindling and theatres becoming part of a market economy, the school somehow must insure that their graduates will be able to 'earn bread from this profession'.[22]

By 1991, the alumni of HIDA could not only earn a living but had become one of the wealthiest groups in the country, due to Gulf satellite channels' receptivity to Syrian television series. By contrast with Syrian thinkers, writers and artists, they were celebrated in state media, invited to demonstrate their knowledge, and given licence to involve themselves in social and political affairs, and express a degree of criticism towards the Syrian regime through their television series. It was not until the 1998 protest at the American embassy that the institute's intellectuals really crossed their professional boundaries and involved themselves in state affairs. The protest could claim to have posed a challenge to the regime by harnessing the intellectuals' network of power, which is normally systematically weakened by the arbitrariness of state power.[23]

Building on the protest, many students organised similar protests against the staff brought in under Bashar al-Assad in 2000. Gradually, the situation at the institute deteriorated. Students and tutors were interrogated by the secret police, and the authorities also began to interfere in the curricula, compelling many teachers to resign, including some of the institute's founders. These oppressive actions influenced not only educational quality at the institute, but also the objectives and meanings of intellectualism inside the institute and, consequently, across Syria.

## Curricula and the inner enmity

Since HIDA's acting department had a stable curriculum and was celebrated for its success in providing actors for television series, interference was focused on the theatre studies department, which was blamed for the protests. The department came under attack from the Ministry of Culture, the media and the acting department. Consequently, suggestions that the theatre studies department be eliminated or moved to Damascus University came to represent a real threat.

A tension that had been latent since the theatre studies department was founded resurfaced. Originally, the department had been called the criticism and theatre literature department, but the academics who had studied in Western Europe, influenced by European theatre movements, rejected the word 'criticism' and changed the department name to 'theatre studies' in 1996. The department continued to be referred to as the criticism department, despite major changes to the curriculum. It was expected that its graduates would become critics for daily newspapers, and most alumni in the 1980s eventually did. Conflict arose when the acting students and teachers came to feel they were being viewed critically by their intellectual peers. The perceived imbalance of knowledge was compounded by the fact that the acting students were in their early twenties, while the students of the criticism department were older, and most had completed a university degree before studying at HIDA.

HIDA placed knowledge of European theatre at the centre of its curriculum, and the theatre studies department took a historical approach to the subject. Ancient Greek drama and performance were taught in the first year; in the second year students studied Roman theatre, the Middle Ages and the Renaissance; in the third year they read classicism, romanticism and realism; twentieth-century text and performance were taught in the fourth year. Consequently, while students had a good knowledge of theatre developments and classical texts, they were disconnected from contemporary theatre movements and the practical side of theatre (Meyerhold, Brook, Boal, improvisation, choreography, etc.). Along with an emphasis on the classics, students read philosophy, psychology, art history, sociology and literature. Living under a dictatorship and being acclimated to excessive censorship, this openness to Europe was an attraction in its own right. Plesu describes this desire as a form of subversion:

> The obstacles – the interdiction against a number of ideas and methods characteristic of the spirit of the age (such as structuralism or psychoanalysis), labelled by Marxist criticism as 'formalistic', 'reactionary', and 'bourgeois' – intensified intellectual curiosity and gave the more or less conspiratorial 'transgressions' the prestige of political risk, the charm of unconventional options. To be a structuralist became exciting.[24]

The openness of the theatre studies department to European drama, literature and philosophy, combined with uncertainties about the curriculum and frequent staff changes, led to numerous adjustments to the department's academic plan. At times there was an inclination to enhance students' understanding of European philosophy and literature.

At others the focus turned to semiotics. At other points the emphasis shifted towards reading performance, and occasionally it aligned with the acting department, resulting in collaboration with acting students.

The curriculum of the acting department remained steady, and foregrounded Stanislavsky in its training. In their first two years, students rehearsed silent scenes and worked on stereotypes. In their third year, they presented full-length plays to the public, typically Shakespeare and American Realism plays. In the fourth year, students had fewer classes and worked on bigger productions, which were sometimes staged at the national theatre. The curriculum also provided basic knowledge of European theatre and philosophy, but as with many international acting institutes, students spent most of their time in their studios rehearsing. The curriculum of the acting department remains almost the same to this day.

The professional success of the acting alumni challenged the elitism of the theatre studies department, which acquired second-class status. Jill Dolan suggests that the reason for this fall in status is that theatre studies departments choose to seal themselves off from interdisciplinary invasions.[25] Thus, when the acting department became commercialised, the theatre studies department felt a need to safeguard its intellectual qualities, which it saw as a virtue.

Arguably, the only place that did not celebrate the stardom of the acting alumni was HIDA itself, and the theatre studies department in particular. It was believed that the students' knowledge should not be affected by practice – either allowed by the regime or conditioned by the market – to the extent that watching any play was perceived as practice that disturbed the pure knowledge derived from books. HIDA's approach placed theatre within an epistemological context that obliged students to prove their knowledge rather than apply it. In a country where the act of reading was viewed with suspicion, theatre studies alumni were doomed to an ambiguous future. Institutionally, their status was also ambiguous: they could not enrol in the artists' union because they were not artists, and they could not enrol in the journalists' union because they were not journalists, and thus remained without a union.

With the collapse of the Eastern bloc in the 1990s, the concept of intellectualism came under critical scrutiny. It was not only the view that 'being an intellectual is not itself a profession':[26] European ideologies, which the theatre studies department considered a cultural extension, started to decry intellectualism. Jedlicki describes how Polish cultural critics did not wait long before offering their diagnosis of the new national and global situation, following Europe and America in the production of eulogies for the intelligentsia as a class. Jedlicki traces how the intellectuals, who were supposedly striving mafia-like for power, heralded the true end of the age of ideology.[27]

In theatrical terms, this funereal attitude reflected in a trend for pronouncing the death of the author, the text, the character and ideology. A nihilist reading of life and art was set against a celebration of commercialism and changing definitions of success, profession, opposition, loyalty and intellectualism. Television stars were invited into the spectrum of those 'with a vocation for the art of representing, whether that is talking, writing, teaching, appearing on television'.[28] Through constant appearances on television and at prestigious public events, acting alumni were not only given the right to voice their opinions, but were also found 'suitable for representing the best thought culture itself – and making it prevail'.[29] Television stars were given permission to criticise certain aspects of Syrian political and social life, while intellectuals were censored or withdrew to the realm of their 'oral acrobatics'.[30] Alumni of the theatre studies department were seen as offering opposition for opposition's sake, 'always … beset and remorselessly challenged by the problem of loyalty'.[31] With no ideology, power or profession, or a union with which to defend themselves, they were also accused of disloyalty, and the image of the intellectual, which typified the department, gradually transformed into a caricature of the nihilist intellectual.

The gap between the theatre studies department and acting department intensified, resulting in physical altercations, which sometimes involved teachers, and open disputes in local and regional media. A campaign was launched by a number of acting teachers to close the theatre studies department or move it to Damascus University, but although the campaign reached the president, it ultimately failed. In addition to the bureaucratic complications, none of the students or teachers in the theatre studies department wanted to move to the university because of its infamous reputation. It was necessary for the theatre studies department to fight for autonomy from literature departments and claim distinctiveness, even at the expense of becoming somewhat insular and hermetic.

Tension was prevalent within many, if not all, sectors. Patrick Seale describes in *Asad* how intelligence sectors were turned against one another so the presidency remained untouched. Internal enmity infected the army, security forces and the Ba'ath Party: 'these largely closed worlds were not monolithic. Inside them ambitious men jockeyed for influence and intrigued against each other … although all looked to the president to arbitrate between them'.[32] Culturally, this antagonism, which encompassed physical fights and threats of incarceration, was also found between the Arab Writers Union and the Ministry of Culture, the national theatre and the theatre houses, artists and the Artists Union, and inside HIDA.

In *Political Performance in Syria*, Edward Ziter refers to the enemy as a primary concern in theatrical practice in Syria. Syria's defeat in the Six-Day War in 1967 intensified the desire to face the enemy again, and to triumph. Ziter lists plays that bravely discussed the defeat with remarkable self-criticism. Later, in 1973, the Yom Kippur War was framed as having restored Syrian dignity, a perspective propagated by commercial theatre. Syria subsequently spent decades in a no-war-no-peace state, and the enemy remained unrecognisable, 'acknowledged in [slogans] without reference to specific events and policy decisions'.[33] Ziter also refers to this exceptional approach to the enemy in Syria when he notes that 'war has been transformed into an abstraction'.[34] The absence of a clear strategy with which to defeat this invisible enemy turned enmity from external threats to internal potential dangers. The Arab Writers Union states in its rules of procedure, which are common in most Syrian institutions, that its aims include 'discovering and mobilising new Syrian talents … intensifying the Arabs' resistance spirit, fighting internal spoiled cultural currents that call for decadence and confronting occupation, imperialism and Zionism'.[35]

Although HIDA was given special treatment and the freedom to be influenced by European philosophy – which eventually became nihilistic – the acting and theatre studies departments resembled other Syrian sectors in the way they developed antagonistic standpoints. The mission became one of fighting the enemy within the institution and the profession, accusing antagonists of backwardness, hypocrisy and serving the enemy's agenda. The antagonistic climate seemed to serve Hafez al-Assad's aim of involving the various factions in internal fights while keeping his position untouchable. When Bashar al-Assad inherited power he also inherited the practice of intensifying inner enmity, until the revolution of 2011, with bombs falling on HIDA and across the whole country.

## Conclusion

From the time of its founding, HIDA possessed aspects of intellectualism under a socialist dictatorship. As a place of uncensored knowledge and professional training, the institute could reject monolithic discourses and practices. The institute's two main departments placed European knowledge at the centre of their curricula, but disagreed on many topics including the interpretation of intellectualism. Encapsulating the intellectual image, HIDA facilitated the processes of destroying intellectualism's significance and then reproducing it in an obedient manner. While alumni of the acting department were celebrated by the authorities and the public, theatre studies alumni faced the threat of their department being closed or moved to Damascus University. Many factors prevented this from happening, however, including the resistance of the teachers, alumni and students, and arguably the desire of the dictator to maintain a static image of Syrian institutions, keeping them in constant inner enmity.

## Notes

1  In his travelogue *Under More than One Sky*, Jordanian poet Amjad Nasser describes how Syrian writers and artists use the word 'work' (عمل) to refer only to television series.
2  Berkeley, 2004.
3  Bentley, 1948.
4  Dolan, 1993.
5  Wedeen, 1999, 12.
6  Wedeen, 1999, 105.
7  Lisa Wedeen translates مسيرات عفوية as 'spontaneous demonstrations', but I suggest translating it as 'spontaneous marches' (Weeden, 1999, 68).
8  In 2000, 99 'intellectuals' signed a statement calling for an end to the state of emergency. Although titled the Statement of 99, it is commonly known as the Statement of the Intellectuals. During the 2011 protests, many artists, journalists, students and alumni of HIDA organised a demonstration that they called the Demonstration of the Intellectuals.
9  Dolan, 1993, 424.
10  Levine, 1998, 32.
11  Said, 1994, xv.
12  Al-Zubaidi, 1978, 5.
13  Plesu, 1995, 61.
14  Kempny, 1996, 299.
15  Plesu, 1995, 62.
16  Plesu, 1995, 63.
17  Plesu, 1995, 64.
18  Jedlicki, 1994, 102.
19  Said, 1994, 36.
20  Said, 1994, 63–4.
21  Said, 1994, 32.
22  Rotté, 1992, 83.
23  Plesu, 1995, 64.
24  Plesu, 1995, 62.
25  Dolan, 1993, 424.
26  Jedlicki, 1994, 101.
27  Jedlicki, 1994, 103.
28  Said, 1994, 12–13.
29  Said, 1994, 29.

30  Plesu, 1995, 69.
31  Said, 1994, 40.
32  Seal, 1988, 178.
33  Ziter, 2015, 57.
34  Ziter, 2015, 57.
35  Arab Writers Union, 1969.

# References

Al-Zubaidi, Kais. *Theatre of Change: Essays on Brecht's artistic method*. Beirut: Ibn Rushd Publishing House, 1978.

Arab Writers Union. 'Legislative decree no. 72 and its amendments establishing the "Arab Writers Union" organization', 1969. Accessed 2 October 2023. https://awu.sy/72-رقم-التشريعي-المرسوم/ (in Arabic).

Bentley, Eric. 'Education and the literary heritage', *Journal of Higher Education* 19 (2) (1948): 67–74.

Berkeley, Anne. 'Changing views of knowledge and the struggle for undergraduate theatre curriculum, 1900–1980'. In *Teaching Theatre Today: Pedagogical views of theatre in higher education*, edited by A. L. Fliotsos and G. S. Medford, 7–31. New York: Palgrave Macmillan, 2004.

Dolan, Jill. 'Geographies of learning: theatre studies, performance, and the "performative"', *Theatre Journal* 45 (4) (1993): 417–41.

Fliotsos, Anne L. and Medford, Gail S. *Teaching Theatre Today*. New York: Palgrave Macmillan, 2004.

Jedlicki, Jerzy. 'What's the use of intellectuals?', *Polish Sociological Review* 106 (1994): 101–10.

Kempny, Marian. 'Between politics and culture: is a convergence between the East-European intelligentsia and Western intellectuals possible?', *Polish Sociological Review* 116 (1996): 297–305.

Levine, Lawrence W. *Highbrow/Lowbrow: The emergence of cultural hierarchy in America*. Cambridge, MA: Harvard University Press, 1998.

Plesu, Andrei. 'Intellectual life under dictatorship', *Representations* 49 (1995): 61–71.

Rotté, Joanna. 'Theatre training Moscow style', *TDR* (1988–), 36 (2) (1992): 81–96.

Said, Edward. *Representations of the Intellectual*. New York: Vintage Books, 1994.

Seal, Patrick. *Asad*. London: I. B. Tauris & Co., 1988.

Wedeen, Lisa. *The Ambiguities of Domination*. Chicago: University of Chicago Press, 1999.

Ziter, Edward. *Political Performance in Syria*. Houndmills: Palgrave Macmillan, 2015.

7

# From North to South: the workshop as a global epistemic format

Christopher B. Balme and Nic Leonhardt

## Introduction

It is highly likely that readers of this chapter have participated in a workshop during their student or professional life. They may have workshopped a play or other text in a collaborative mode, or imparted or received some kind of specialist knowledge within a temporal framework ranging from two hours to several days. In 1978 Ron Argelander, writing in *TDR*, referred to the workshop as 'one of the most frequently encountered words in the avant-garde theatre community'.[1] At that time the workshop was the only format where budding artists could receive any kind of training outside membership in one of the many groups that self-identified under that label. While Argelander logically linked workshop and theatre, today the connection is largely forgotten. Workshops are ubiquitous, and workshopping as a format for sharing knowledge is applicable to any sphere of activity outside structured curricula. Despite this ubiquity, the term 'workshop' has strong historical connections with the theatre, and indeed in its contemporary understanding can be directly linked to what used to be called avant-garde or experimental theatre. The history and dissemination of the term and practice can be traced to a particular conjunction of factors within US higher education and philanthropy, which supported the rise of modernist theatre and the theatrical epistemic community. This led in turn to a global distribution of workshop thinking and practice as a form of techno-political intervention. In this way the particular format developed by and associated with non-conventional theatre forms permeated contemporary thinking and pedagogical practice. This chapter explores the word's evolution from a noun denoting pre-industrial labour, to a catchword for various forms of experimental theatre practice, to a verb meaning to improve or develop something by the workshop format. The first section looks at the word's etymology before focusing on the early twentieth century in the US, where the semantic shift from shop floor to university seminar took place. From there we follow its trajectory to American philanthropy of the 1950s and 1960s, when the big foundations such as Rockefeller and Ford actively promoted modernist, non-profit theatre for which the workshop became a signal – despite its somewhat Marxist overtones – best encapsulated in Joan Littlewood's decidedly left-leaning Theatre Workshop, established in 1945. The two following sections examine the dissemination of workshop practices in developing nations, especially the theatre for development (TfD) movement, which spread through the workshop format. The chapter concludes with a discussion of Richard Sennett's concept of the workshop and its relationship to authority.

## Etymology

According to the *Oxford English Dictionary* the word 'workshop' originates in the sixteenth century, when it usually referred to a small room for the artisanal manufacture of goods. Often implied is the sale of the goods at the same place, hence the combination 'work-shop', which appears to derive from the Latin *officina*, a place of work and sale. In his book *The Craftsman* Richard Sennett traces the changes in the meaning of the word from a cultural-historical perspective. While in the Middle Ages the workshop was still a social institution, a place 'where labor and life mixed face-to-face', this changed during the Enlightenment and accelerated in the nineteenth century with the reorganisation of work during industrialisation.[2] By 1900 English law distinguished between factories and workshops, the latter being 'any premises, room or place, not being a factory, in which … any manual labour is exercised'.[3]

With the help of data mining, the usage frequency of a word or phrase can be determined over a (theoretically indefinite) period of time. The Google Ngram Viewer, for example, can search for words or sentences in digitally captured corpora from previous centuries and provide information about their use and economic cycles. Figure 7.1 shows a Google Ngram for the word 'workshop' between 1800 and 2000, clearly indicating the increasing use of the term over the past 200 years.

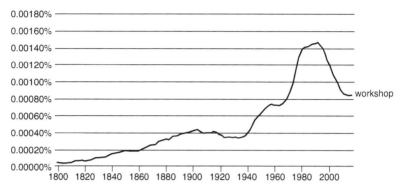

**Figure 7.1** Google Ngram for the word 'workshop' as a percentage of all words in a corpus published between 1800 and 2000. Source: Google Ngram Viewer.

The DWDS online dictionary records word clusters and the frequency of word usage in the German language over a period of 500 years – basically since the invention of book printing. The corpus of sources, from which the frequency is calculated, consists of printed products such as monographs, newspapers, world literature and periodicals. A query of the word 'workshop' results in a graph showing that use of the word is virtually non-existent in printed books before 1830 (figure 7.2). The frequency increases slightly over the course of the nineteenth century, and from the 1940s onwards a clear swing is visibile, indicating an increasing usage of the word and concept.

**Figure 7.2** Graph generated by DWDS showing the frequency of the word 'workshop' (in English) in German corpora since the eighteenth century. Source: DWDS-Referenzkorpora (1600–1999).

In a figurative sense Disraeli's famous description of England as the 'workshop of the world' referred to England's increasing reliance on manufacturing industry, especially cotton.[4] For Karl Marx the workshop was a site of the division of labour and its attendant alienation, and thereby a precursor to the modern industrial factory.[5] Given this connection with manual labour and incipient industrial manufacturing, it may appear surprising that the first semantic transferral (as opposed to figurative usage) of workshop occurs in the context of the field of theatre and drama as a university discipline.

## Theatre workshops and laboratories

In 1912 *The Writer*, a Boston-based monthly magazine dedicated to helping 'all literary workers', devoted a feature to George Pierce Baker, Harvard professor of English literature, and his playwriting course, which was designed to give students with literary ambitions the necessary skills and craft to further their dramatic ambitions:

> … it is now his hope to see at Harvard in the next few years a theatrical laboratory, so to speak – a combination workshop and theatre, where plays written by students can be produced, and where the young playwright can obtain a practical knowledge of the staging of plays through personal contact with the things that make the theatrical wheels go 'round.[6]

This is probably the first conjunction of the disparate terms laboratory and workshop in such a context, although they would go on to form a natural alliance in the twentieth century. The idea of a theatre laboratory almost certainly originates with Stanislavski's theatre-studio (laboratory's cognate term), which he established with Vsevolod Meyerhold in 1904 at the Moscow Art Theatre, 'a laboratory for more or less mature actors'.[7]

Baker's playwriting seminar, known as English 47 after its course number, was redubbed 47 Workshop – an 'engineering-like label' in the words of Shannon Jackson – that emphasised programmatically the idea of skill and practical knowledge over poetic inspiration for the budding dramatist.[8] Under this label Baker also began publishing selected products from the workshop. The 47 Workshop quickly established itself as a model for what came to be known as laboratory theatres, university-based experimental stages whose work, according to Constance Mackay, the first surveyor of the Little Theatre Movement, was 'of the present; their productions have contemporary interests; they appeal to the general public – not to an archaeological public'.[9] Apart from Harvard, she lists Dartmouth Laboratory Theatre, the Laboratory of the Carnegie Institute at Pittsburgh and, as the only professional, non-student laboratory theatre, Grace Griswold's Theatre Workshop in New York (figure 7.3). Griswold, a professional actress, undertook an ambitious effort in late 1916 to harness the energies of New York's many unemployed theatre artists and put them to artistically high-minded use, drawing inspiration from the European art theatre movement. The undertaking received enthusiastic support from Sheldon Cheney's *Theatre Arts Magazine*, the US mouthpiece of theatrical modernism.[10]

Although Griswold's Theatre Workshop only seems to have lasted until the end of the First World War, it marked the first tentative movement of the university-based laboratory theatre towards the professional stage. By the 1920s the 47 Workshop had expanded beyond playwriting to include the central areas of theatrical production, and as Baker emphasised in his first anthology of one-act plays: 'This is a "Workshop" because anyone who believes he has the ability in any of the arts connected with the theatre – acting, scene or costume designing, lighting, directing, or playwriting – may here prove his quality.'[11]

**Figure 7.3**   George Arliss conducting a workshop rehearsal on the stage of the Knickerbocker Theatre for Grace Griswold's Theatre Workshop, New York, 1917. Source: *Theatre Arts Magazine*, January 1918.

By the 1930s the terms workshop and laboratory had become twin, almost synonymous, concepts embodying a processual approach to theatre making both inside and outside the academy, and the term theatre workshop began to attach itself to mainly left-leaning, non-profit theatre groups. In 1936 it provided the title for a magazine founded by the New Theatre League, which was founded in 1935 as a left-wing federation of small theatres and amateur-theatrical groups, and which ran a theatre workshop that trained actors, directors, playwrights and stage managers.[12] Although a short-lived publication, *Theatre Workshop*'s editorial board boasted an impressive line-up of figures associated with the Group Theatre collective, including Lee Strasberg, Mordecai Gorelik and Joseph Losey. Its editorial policy emphasised 'craftsmanship' and a commitment to providing 'every serious *theatre worker* with a quarterly magazine which he can call his own' (italics mine), adding that 'the contemporary theatre looks to Moscow today for artistic leadership'.[13] By the mid-1930s the appellation 'theatre workshop' had moved away from the apolitical arts theatre of Sheldon Cheney and Grace Griswold and re-established its leftist credentials, as exemplified by the fact that the Federal Theatre Workshop was one of many projects funded by the WPA Federal Theatre Project.

With the founding of Joan Littlewood's Theatre Workshop in 1945, the two semantic streams merged. The Marxist-inflected site of labour, solidarity and the shop floor conjoined with the largely apolitical, modernist laboratory/studio, where new forms might be explored outside the constraints of conventional theatre production:

> The new name, Theatre Workshop, signalled Littlewood's increasing emphasis on the processes inherent in making theatre … this meant committing to a regular study and training regime encompassing impassioned lectures on theatre history, theatre and communism and theories of acting, and physical training encompassing relaxation, voice and movement exercises.[14]

While 'impassioned lectures' on theatre and communism remained somewhat specific to Littlewood's enterprise (she and her then partner Ewan MacColl were both members of the British Communist Party), the processual elements of theatre making, such as voice and movement exercises, were to become part and parcel of workshop vocabulary. Process rather than product became, and remains, the foundational principle of the theatre workshop.

## Workshops, philanthropy and modernisation

The immediate postwar period saw the rise of the workshop as an emblematic format for progressive artistic techniques. It became synonymous with experimentation, and was soon adopted by US philanthropic organisations (which could hardly be accused of leftist inclinations) during their period of energetic support for media and the arts outside the commercial realm in the late 1940s. In 1952 the Ford Foundation established the Television-Radio Workshop to foster experimental work in the new broadcast media. Why it chose the term 'workshop' to describe its new funding stream is not entirely clear, but was probably a conscious reference to the Columbia Workshop established in 1936 by CBS, and directed from 1939 by Norman Corwin, to provide an outlet for experimental radio drama. The Columbia Workshop had no predetermined format, and hosted contributions from, among others, Orson Welles, Archibald MacLeish and Corwin himself.[15] According to media scholar Paul Saettler, a radio workshop founded at New York University in 1936 in collaboration with the US Office of Education, a precursor to the Columbia Workshop, established the term 'workshop' in modern parlance.[16]

By the early 1950s the word 'workshop' evidently connoted a realm that privileged art above mass-market entertainment. The most famous product of the Ford Foundation's Television-Radio Workshop was the Omnibus series for the CBS network, dedicated to bringing television audiences an eclectic selection of highbrow offerings, such as a made-for-television version of *King Lear* directed by Peter Brook, starring Orson Welles as Lear and Brook's wife Natasha Parry as Cordelia, and with music by Virgil Thomson to round off its modernist credentials. Featured artists included Leonard Bernstein, who hosted educational programmes on music; the improvisational comedy duo Mike Nichols and Elaine May; and the choreographer Agnes de Mille and Eartha Kitt in a version of Oscar Wilde's *Salome*.[17] Just as it had in radio before the war, the term 'workshop', whether it referred to a programme or funding initiative, signalled a modernist openness to formal innovation, albeit one that required substantial philanthropic support to reach its audience.

In the theatre, the 1950s saw a plethora of theatre companies incorporating 'workshop' into their name: the Actor's Workshop, founded by Herb Blau and Jules Irving in San Francisco in 1952, established itself as an avant-garde theatre company; Anna Halprin set up the San Francisco Dancers' Workshop in 1955; and Derek Walcott began his ambitious Trinidad Theatre Workshop in 1959, an attempt to establish the Caribbean's first ensemble-based repertory theatre. As in broadcast media, the term signalled an approach that departed from established, usually commercially oriented rehearsal and production procedures. Again, the process rather than the product was primary, and informal, project-based approaches, conceived as a counter-model to the rigid rehearsal procedures of commercial or state-funded theatre (in Europe), began to dominate the theatre avant-garde.

Probably the most famous expression of the workshop approach was the Theatre of Cruelty season at the Royal Shakespeare Company (RSC) in 1963–4 directed by Peter Brook and Charles Marowitz. Their improvisations around the writings of Antonin Artaud could not be called rehearsals, although they were intended as preparations for a production of Jean Genet's *The Screens*; rather, the process was called an 'experimental workshop', and consisted largely of exercises centred on sound and movement rather than on the text of the play. The group was labelled the Royal Shakespeare Experimental Group.[18] Brook bemoaned the lack of experimental and avant-garde theatre while recapitulating the latter's standard mantra: 'In order to face new audiences with creative formulas, we must first be able to face empty seats.'[19]

A commitment to experimentation was not possible without either state support (in the case of the RSC) or private sponsorship. As we have seen in the case of television, US philanthropy was committed to supporting if not radical artistic experimentation then at least a fair amount of modernist programming, predominantly in the US but also abroad. In its 1961–2 financial year the Ford Foundation supported the Actor's Workshop with a grant of US$197,000 under its development of artistic institutions initiative 'to provide partial operating support while the group is financing a permanent theater building',[20] which enabled the company to continue paying professional salaries in the absence of a venue. In a similar vein the Rockefeller Foundation provided support throughout the 1960s for the Trinidad Theatre Workshop, which for the first years of its existence exclusively conducted workshops, staging no public performances until 1963. In 1967 the Rockefeller Foundation provided US$25,000 for the New Lafayette Theatre in New York 'toward costs of establishing a permanent theatre company and workshop in Harlem'.[21]

By the early 1960s workshop thinking permeated philanthropic policy, and not only in the realms of theatre and the arts. The Ford Foundation's annual report in 1962 contains numerous references to workshops, with funds allocated to 'workshops for television teachers and production personnel', 'summer research workshops' on research techniques in business education, staff-management workshops in Nigeria and Ghana, and a 'workshop on elementary-science teaching' in the same region. By the early 1960s the workshop process, although originating in the theatre, had established itself as the format of choice for funding initiatives outside established educational structures.

In both the Ford and Rockefeller foundations we find a clear commitment to experimentation in the arts for which the term 'workshop' functioned as a marker. The Ford Foundation established a funding line in the 1960s called 'experiments and demonstrations' that was mainly directed at the visual arts but also included theatre funding. The latter was organised under the subheading 'demonstrations in resident repertory theater', and recipients included the Actor's Workshop, the Arena Stage in Washington DC and Theatre, Inc. at the Phoenix Theatre in New York. A resident repertory theatre company in an otherwise commercially driven theatre culture was an experiment in itself, at least in the US. Grants in the repertory theatre stream totalled US$6.1 million, 'to strengthen the repertory theater as a significant cultural resource and as a major outlet for the professional dramatist, director, and actor'.[22] The Rockefeller Foundation also diverted funds in a programmatically experimental direction, funding an Institute for Advanced Studies in the Theatre Arts, a three-year international fellowship programme based in New York. While focused principally on developed nations, the programme's participants also came from developing nations. Its artistic ideology was made clear in its annual report from 1962: 'Commendation for the institute has been vigorous from those who favor *conscious theatrical style and deliberate rationality* in drama; less warm from proponents of naturalism in acting' (italics mine).[23] 'Conscious theatrical style' and 'deliberate rationality' are shorthand for an anti-naturalistic, high-modernist approach with perhaps a Brechtian inflection, which regarded naturalism as an outdated, nineteenth-century convention that limited the medium's artistic possibilities.

The terms 'workshop', 'laboratory' and 'experimental' had acquired considerable cachet, and outside the US a new generation of theatre makers eagerly attached them to their undertakings.[24] As well as the Trinidad Theatre Workshop, Rockefeller allocated funds to Ateneo Puertorriqueño in San Juan, Puerto Rico towards equipment for its experimental theatre in 1953; over US$9,000 in support of the experimental Ghana Drama Studio directed by Efua Sutherland in 1960; and a smaller sum towards an 'experimental training program' at the National Theatre of Uganda in 1964. Across the world we see that Rockefeller (and, in other countries, the Ford Foundation) was funding theatre activities that were not just artistically but experimentally focused. In India in 1992 the Ford Foundation established an initiative called forum for laboratory theatres, designed to help theatre groups become influential centres of research and creativity in their respective regions, and after a competitive selection process 12 'laboratories' were set up across the country. In 1996 the initiative was folded into the theatre development fund (TDF), administered by the India Foundation for the Arts but funded by Ford until 2005. The move to create such laboratories in different regions in India reflects a move on the part of the Ford Foundation in the 1980s towards decentralisation, especially of its cultural policy.

## Workshops and theatre for development

If Ford and Rockefeller were motivated by the idea of supporting artistic institutions in developing nations throughout the 1950s and 1960s – with an emphasis on institutions over individual artists – this began to change during the 1980s. The emergence of theatre for development (TfD) in the 1980s, especially in sub-Saharan Africa, challenged old-school institution building with its grassroots approach to theatre making. Originally a loose umbrella term for an assortment of practices that went by other names – often community theatre or popular theatre – it came to denote its own specific form of practice (see chapter 4). Whatever the moniker, TfD originated in the mid-1970s and came to full fruition in the 1980s when it slowly shed its radical origins, and often forged alliances with governmental, international and, later, nongovernmental development programmes. Through a symbiotic connection with the academy and theatre practice, a whole generation of theatre students were trained to go out into the community, carry out projects using theatrical means – ranging from building latrines to popularising the use of fertiliser – and write up the results. Here too the workshop proved to be the format of choice for the dissemination of ideas and techniques. As Kees Epskamp notes in his brief history of TfD: 'The didactic format was the workshop.'[25] Workshops can come in all shapes and sizes, however. In September 1983 an international African workshop on theatre for development followed by a three-day conference took place in Harare, Zimbabwe, sponsored by UNESCO, the International Theatre

Institute (ITI) and the Zimbabwean government, with support from the International Popular Theatre Alliance (IPTA). It involved 100 participants, 43 of whom came from other African countries and 57 from Zimbabwe. Through its size and conscious intent 'to support its popularisation and extension to other African countries', the workshop had more of the status of a field-configuring event (FCE).[26] The term 'workshop' served here a double function: it defined the overall framework of the event, and described the smaller, practical, didactic constituent workshops where particular techniques or tools (the word of choice) were demonstrated.

The terms 'tool' and 'development tool' recur throughout Ross Kidd and Remmelt Hummelen's report on the workshop. Its recurrence marks a semantic return, albeit indirectly, to the ideological world of the shop floor, organised labour and the engineering-like label of the 47 Workshop. Politically the space between Littlewood's Theatre Workshop and the early phase of theatre for development is not large: pioneers of TfD such as Ross Kidd, Ngugi wa Mirii and Michael Etherton certainly saw themselves harnessing theatre for the improvement of the masses. Indeed the historiography of TfD identifies the nationalist independence movements of the 1950s and 1960s and their use of dance, song and poetry as one of the streams into which TfD tapped.[27]

The TfD workshop belongs to the realm of adult education, staff training and upskilling, as evidenced by the Ford Foundation's grants for Nigeria and Ghana in the early 1960s, but it is also strongly defined by a Marxist or at least socialist understanding of the theatre as a medium for the masses. The workshop's origins were modernist yet also vocational, a place where the budding dramatist learnt their craft and the tools of the trade. By the mid-1970s the workshop had become the medium of choice for avant-garde theatre, and all forms of dance theatre except classical ballet (here the workshop could not displace hard grind at the bar).

## Workshops and expertise

Sennett defines a workshop as 'a productive space in which people deal face-to-face with issues of authority … In a workshop, the skills of the master can earn him or her the right to command, and learning from and absorbing those skills can dignify the apprentice or journeyman's obedience.'[28] This definition resonates with the conception of theatre workshops from the early-twentieth century onwards. Workshops as places for knowledge transfer presuppose a knowledge gap and a hierarchy: the workshop leader is notionally superior to the participants in terms of knowledge and experience; as an instructor, the leader is someone who 'furnishes, prepares' (latin *instruere,* to construct, build up), and is thus also someone who possesses influential power. Sennett reminds us that in artists' workshops the masters sketch out their works, which the students then carry out; the originality of the work is that of the artist; the pupils imitate the master's style. This presupposes that originality can be passed on, that extraordinary techniques can be learned. In the academies of art and music there are still 'master' classes in which renowned artists instruct select students.

A further term emerges from the workshops of the 1940s and 1950s, that of the 'expert'. Workshop leaders like Sennett's masters are experts: they have significant experience, know their field well and are often invited, in artistic or scientific contexts, to share their expertise through interviews and workshops. This may also involve imparting a specific doctrine (*Lehrmeinung*) or ideology.

One such expert is the Filipino director, playwright, educator and theatre manager Severino Montano, who taught drama at the Philippine Normal College in Manila at the beginning of the 1950s (chapter 9 of this volume deals with Montano's work in more detail). He serves as a representative example of a theatre expert who applied the concept and format of the workshop to pass on knowledge to teachers and actors in Manila and neighbouring rural areas; his students were mainly teachers with little or no theatrical experience. Photographs of Montano at work often show him at the centre of a circular arrangement surrounded by his students. The hierarchy of knowledge transfer is clear: Montano is the master, his disciples the unexperienced learners.

Severino, born 1915 in the Philippines, went to the US at a young age to study and teach playwriting, directing and economics, and to work for the Government of the Commonwealth of the Philippines in exile in Washington DC. He took part in the 47 Workshop at Yale, and subsequently delivered courses and workshops on rhetoric, drama and communication at the American University in Washington. He was approached by the Rockefeller Foundation in 1951 at a time when the development and financial support of theatre was high on their agenda, having been recommended to them as an expert on the development of drama in the Philippines. After 12 years abroad he returned to the Philippines with a Rockefeller scholarship and began to implement his mission through workshops for teachers at Philippine Normal College in the form of an arena theatre or theatre-in-the-round. Montano was a threefold expert: he had expertise in the field of theatre, community theatre and management; he enjoyed a solid Anglo-American education; and he possessed local knowledge of his place of work. This qualified him to guide – to instruct – and to circulate the idea of theatre development for the masses. His students would become multipliers of this idea.

If one considers the factors of format and organisation, social institution, expertise, knowledge gaps and knowledge transfer as essential constituents of workshops as a format, it might be argued that it is precisely this structure that makes workshops the preferred means of knowledge transfer (and influence) in the period after the Second World War, and that prompted philanthropic institutions that promoted culture to subsidise workshops. It can also be argued that the workshop, with its balance of expert instruction and informality, provided the ideal format for imparting knowledge – theatrical in the first instance, but later of any kind – especially in situations where there seemed to be a great distance between experts and learners. It certainly brought experimental thinking in the theatre and the arts into the mainstream of late modernity, and has become the format of choice for theatrical epistemic communities.

Sennett calls workshops 'social institutions', and the social aspect of this form of work deserves attention. Workshops are characterised by their limited duration, specific location, didactic and learning goals, and common learning rituals (group work, pauses, exchanges of experience, feedback, etc.). 'Workshops present and past have glued people together through work rituals, whether these be a shared cup of tea or the urban parade; through mentoring, whether the formal surrogate parenting of medieval times or informal advising on the worksite; through face-to-face sharing of information', says Sennett.[29] Therefore, it seems banal to conclude that workshops only *work* if we adhere to the duality of authority and obedience, teaching and willingness to learn, master and student. A workshop is an agreement between two parties, an arrangement that bears a resemblance to the 'theatrical contract'. In Sennett's terms:

> In the archaic theater there was relatively little divide between spectator and performer, seeing and doing; people danced and spoke, they retired to a stone seat to watch others dance and declaim. By the time of Aristotle, actors and dancers had become

a caste with special skills of costuming, speaking and moving. Audiences stayed offstage, and so developed their own skills of interpretation as spectators. As critics, the audience sought to speculate then about what the stage-characters did not understand about themselves … The classicist Myles Burnyeat believes that here, in the classical theater, lies the origin of the phrase 'seeing with the mind's eye'. Which is to say, understanding separated from doing, the 'Mind's eye' that of an observer rather than of a maker.[30]

In a workshop there are observers and performers, experts and learners, the knowledgeable and the not-yet knowledgeable. The eyes are on one person: the expert. From them the students learn to understand the 'how' that they can apply after the workshop, and thus become multipliers of a doctrine, of acquired knowledge and newly acquired skills. In contemporary workshops the hierarchy is flattened; there are still experts who lead workshops and guide participants, but the latter are not passive recipients, and can be experts themselves according to the situation.

In recent years the epistemic format of the workshop has also undergone a transformation due to increasing digitisation and the impact of the COVID-19 pandemic. How digital-learning environments and technologies such as artificial intelligence will impact workshop design and conceptualisation is something to explore in the coming years.

## Notes

1   Argelander, 1978, 3.
2   Sennett, 2008, 53.
3   UK Government, 1901. See also the *Oxford English Dictionary*.
4   See Disraeli, 1846.
5   Marx, 1971, 130–5.
6   Ranck, 1912, 21.
7   Brown, 2019, 4.
8   Jackson, 2004, 69.
9   Mackay, 1917, 181.
10  Cheney, 1917, 135.
11  Baker, 1921, vii.
12  The first issue was devoted entirely to theories of acting. For more information on the New Theatre League, see the archival holdings at the New York Public Library: https://archives.nypl.org/mss/2133#c180652.
13  Anon., 1936, 79–80.
14  Holdsworth, 2011, 12.
15  See the entry on Norman Corwin in Sterling, 2011, 70.

16  Saettler, 2004, 215. There is a direct through-line to the Children's Television Workshop and its innovative series *Sesame Street*, which changed educational television for children; see Saettler, 2004, 430.
17  Hawes, 2002, 17–18.
18  For the term 'experimental workshop' see Helfer and Loney, 1998, 127–8.
19  Brook, 1987, 57.
20  Ford Foundation, 1962, 24.
21  Rockefeller Foundation, 1967, 141.
22  Rockefeller Foundation, 1962, 23.
23  Rockefeller Foundation, 1962, 81.
24  By the end of the 1960s the term 'theatre laboratory' had come to be associated with Grotowski's theatre in Poland, but as we have seen its usage goes back at least as far as George Baker's 47 Workshop.
25  Epskamp, 2006, 14.
26  Kidd and Hummelen, 1983, 6.
27  Kidd and Hummelen, 1983, 3.
28  Sennett, 2008, 54.
29  Sennett, 2008, 73.
30  Sennett, 2008, 124.

# References

Anon. 'Theatre workshop: a prospect', *Theatre Workshop* 1 October (1936): 79–81.
Argelander, Ron. 'Performance workshops: three types', *TDR: The Drama Review* 22 (4) (1978): 3–18.
Baker, George P. 'Introduction'. In *Plays of the 47 Workshop: First series*, edited by George P. Baker and Kenneth Raisbeck, vii–xxiii. New York: Brentanos, 1921.
Barnouw, Eric, ed. *Radio Drama in Action: Twenty-five plays of a changing world*. New York: Rinehart & Co., 1945.
Brook, Peter. *The Shifting Point: Forty years of theatrical exploration 1946 to 1987*. London: Methuen, 1987.
Brown, Bryan. *A History of the Theatre Laboratory*. Abingdon: Routledge, 2019.
Bruce, Harold, ed. *Plays of the University of California Little Theatre Workshop*. Berkeley: University of California Little Theatre, 1922.
Cheney, Sheldon. 'Editorial comment', *Theatre Arts Magazine* 2 (1917): 134–8.
Disraeli, Benjamin. Speech on the third reading of the bill for the repeal of the Corn Laws. Hansard, 15 May 1846, 3/86, cols. 665–79.
Epskamp, Kees. *Theatre for Development: An introduction to context, applications and training*. London: Zed Books, 2006.
Ford Foundation. *Annual Report*. New York: Ford Foundation, 1962.
Hawes, William. *Filmed Television Drama, 1952–1958*. New York: McFarland, 2002.
Helfer, Richard and Loney, Glenn, eds. *Peter Brook: Oxford to Orghast*. London: Routledge, 1998.
Holdsworth, Nadine. *Joan Littlewood's Theatre*. Cambridge: Cambridge University Press, 2011.
Jackson, Shannon. *Professing Performance: Theatre in the academy from philology to performativity*. Cambridge: Cambridge University Press, 2004.
Kidd, Ross and Hummelen, Remmelt. 'African workshop on theatre for development: a report on an international workshop held in Zimbabwe'. Paris: ITI/UNESCO, 1983.
Mackay, Constance D'Arcy. *The Little Theatre in the United States*. New York: Henry Holt and Company, 1917.
Marx, Karl. *Capital: A critique of political economy*. Moscow: Progress Publishers, 1971.
Montano, Severino. 'The arena theatre of the Philippines, Philippine Normal College: progress report, 1955'. Manila: Arena Theatre, 1955.
Ranck, Edwin Carty. 'Teaching playwriting at Harvard', *The Writer: A Monthly Magazine to Interest and Help All Literary Workers* 24 (2) (1912): 17–21. https://archive.org/details/sim_writer_1912-02_24_2.

Rockefeller Foundation. *Annual Report*. New York: Rockefeller Foundation, 1962.

Rockefeller Foundation. *Annual Report*. New York: Rockefeller Foundation, 1967.

Saettler, Paul. *The Evolution of American Educational Technology*. Greenwich, CT: Information Age Publishing, 2004.

Sennett, Richard. *The Craftsman*. New Haven, CT: Yale University Press, 2008.

Sterling, Christopher H., ed. *The Biographical Encyclopedia of American Radio*. New York and London: Routledge, 2011.

UK Government. Factory and Workshop Act, 1901. https://archive.org/details/b22416365/page/81.

# 8
# Musical theatre routes: West End, Broadway and the Brazil of *Lei Rouanet*

Gustavo Guenzburger and Bernardo Fonseca Machado

In this chapter we analyse the global routes of musical theatre that emerged in the final decades of the twentieth century. We characterise these routes as transnational movements encompassing actors, ideologies and economies. To reflect the transnational nature of the subject, we have structured the chapter into three sections that follow the flow of strategies and musical-theatre productions around the world, from north to south, tracing the journey from the places where these works were created to where they were adopted and adapted. Our intention is not to represent a system in its entirety, but rather to investigate the pathways, connections and juxtapositions between people, theatrical practices and aesthetic references.

In the first section we outline the theatrical technopolitics that enabled the UK and the US to export Broadway and West End shows, models and modes of production to other countries. To illustrate the fabrication of these technopolitics we use the career of British producer Cameron Mackintosh. We then track the application of these technopolitics in the New York theatre market, where they were driven by urban policies and the arrival of large entertainment corporations.

In the second section we examine the contradictions surrounding the export (and subsequent adaptation) of such formulae to Brazil, a process made possible by the creation of specific legislation for cultural funding, the Rouanet Law (*Lei Rouanet*). To contextualise this discussion, we provide a brief historical summary of Brazilian musical theatre, tracing its rise in the nineteenth century and its decline in the twentieth. We then analyse the processes that led to musical theatre's recent renaissance, which essentially occurred in transnational terms.

In the third section we explore the relationship between the Brazilian legislation and the London production models, which assumed distinct forms in New York before arriving in São Paulo and Rio de Janeiro in the early 2000s. The ultimate consolidation of this process was contingent on the aspirations of numerous individuals who were invested in staging musical productions from the Global North on other continents.

In this chapter our objective is to elucidate how theatrical repertoires from diverse contexts can be relocated and redefined in new locations. This essay strives to trace the crucial factors, considering data from various locations (London, New York, Rio de Janeiro and São Paulo), that led to the actualisation of these repertoires on stages in the Global South.

## Musical technopolitics[1]

Up to the 1980s, the idea of an industrial model for producing and distributing musicals was not settled. A decade later, important agents in this field, such as composer and producer Andrew Lloyd Webber, still opposed it: 'Musicals are not produced by formula. There are big-buck companies now coming into the theatre, either through exploiting properties proven in other fields, or by regarding theatre simply as a business, but these guys don't really understand what it's all about.'[2]

Lloyd Webber was born in London in 1948, the son of a musician and a piano teacher. In the 1970s and 1980s he became known for successful shows in the UK and other countries, including *Jesus Christ Superstar* (1970), *Evita* (1978), *Cats* (1981) and *The Phantom of the Opera* (1986). Rather than arguing for or against Lloyd Webber's assertion that musicals are not produced by formula, it is more interesting to consider why he rejects the concept of a formula. In the late 1980s and early 1990s, the process of producing big-budget musical shows changed, revealing the construction of a particular technopolitics that enabled the expansion of plays across the globe, and attracted, as Lloyd Webber affirms, the interest of large corporations.

In this section we focus on aspects that impacted the transit of these musicals, which originated in the UK and New York, across the globe. The trajectory of producer Cameron Mackintosh is illustrative for this discussion, since his actions were central to the development of strategies that enabled shows like *Cats*, *Les Misérables* and others to expand their scope and be presented – following the original production precisely – in dozens of towns, cities and countries.

Mackintosh was born in 1946, the son of Ian Mackintosh, a jazz trumpeter, and Diana Mackintosh, a housewife of Maltese and French descent. In 1964, at the age of 17, having not achieved the grades necessary to enter universities that offered degrees in theatre – Manchester and Bristol – he entered the stage-management course at the Central School of Speech and Drama in London. When he graduated he worked behind the scenes at London theatres as a stage manager.[3]

To pay the bills, Mackintosh became a touring manager, specialising in taking shows fresh from London's theatre district – the West End – to regional UK theatres. During this period, in the early 1970s, he familiarised himself with the strategies of the business, including which theatres were suitable for which type of show, which yielded the best financial returns and which were able to mount technically complex productions.

In 1976 Mackintosh staged the musical *Side by Side with Sondheim* – a musical revue featuring songs by American composer Stephen Sondheim – in the UK. The production was successful and guaranteed a profit for over two years in theatres, resulting in considerable respect for the producer.[4] Recognition materialised in an invitation to produce the prestigious awards ceremony for the Society of West End Theatre. The following year Mackintosh produced a revival of *Oliver!*, a musical based on *Oliver Twist* by Charles Dickens with lyrics and music by Lionel Bart. Familiar with performing outside London, Mackintosh considered it pertinent to choose another city for the premiere: Leicester. At the time, it was unusual for plays outside London to receive large productions, with costumes, scenery and performers from the capital, but the decision proved to be the right one and the show began to tour throughout the country, achieving public success. The West End premiere the following year was eagerly awaited, and the acclaim guaranteed a two-and-a-half-year run.

This was also a period during which regional theatres in the UK were undergoing revitalisation using government resources under James Callaghan's administration (1976–9). The then finance director of the Arts Council of Great Britain (the UK agency for creative and cultural development) Tony Field[5] proposed that Mackintosh put on grandiose shows to promote new theatre buildings. After a period of negotiation they decided to produce the musical *My Fair Lady*, a work by Alan Jay Lerner adapted from *Pygmalion* by George Bernard Shaw. The production travelled to dozens of towns and cities, and delighted the British public. In 1979 the Arts Council wished to repeat the feat, so Mackintosh produced the American classic *Oklahoma!* by Rodgers and Hammerstein, again with public funds.

At the onset of the 1980s, Mackintosh, aged 34, was acquiring capital – economic, social and symbolic – like few other producers. He received a call from composer Andrew Lloyd Webber, who suggested he get involved in a new project, a stage adaptation of T. S. Eliot's 1939 poetry collection *Old Possum's Book of Practical Cats*. The play would be called, simply, *Cats*.

Drawing on his experience, Mackintosh devised a merchandising strategy. He believed the show should have an immediately recognizable visual identity – a logo that could be used on any type of product, anywhere in the world. The team hired the Dewynters advertising agency, which designed feline eyes with dancers in the pupils.[6] With success guaranteed following the premiere, the production began to sell badges, baseball caps, key chains, T-shirts, mugs and watches in the theatre lobby, as well as recordings of the show's songs. All the products were printed with the cat-eye design.

Following the London premiere, the objective became to win over the American public. British musicals had been sold to Broadway in previous decades, but playwrights and composers typically sold the rights to their songs and text to American producers, allowing buyers to control the production (direction, choreography, casting, costumes and scenery) and shoulder the financial risks. In the case of *Cats*, production company the Shubert Organization decided to pay the royalties and ask the British production to reproduce the London staging in New York,[7] which was an immediate success.

Soon, producers from countries including Japan, Hungary, Austria, Canada, Australia, Norway and Finland expressed interest in buying the show. According to Mackintosh, after *Cats*, foreign theatre producers did not want to perform a version of the play – 'they asked for the original'. Mackintosh stated that 'usually you would send the script and if they paid £3,000 you would send them the scenario plans and they would create their own version. But this time they said, "We want to do *Cats* in Vienna, or *Cats* in Denmark, but we want *your* production"'.[8] Although the demand for facsimile productions is an old practice – such as the musical comedies of the late-Victorian and Edwardian eras[9] – Mackintosh considered his productions something new and extraordinary.

To meet this demand and ensure quality, Mackintosh's team set up offices in America and Asia, maintaining London as a headquarters responsible for managing the brand's leadership. In addition, Mackintosh innovated by training directors and choreographers from other countries, tasking them with reassembling the original productions in foreign territories while maintaining the quality of the plays.

In the years that followed, Mackintosh applied the same strategy to three other shows: *Les Misérables* (1985), *The Phantom of the Opera* (1986) and *Miss Saigon* (1989), building a portfolio of musicals that could be sold in various corners of the world. His technopolitical strategies, forged during his years on the road in the UK and partly financed by the government (using Arts Council incentives), allowed him to come to the US with his productions under competitive conditions in a market that had been in trouble for years.

In New York, conditions for theatrical production were difficult. During the 1970s and 1980s, many stages in the theatre district had closed or began putting on sexually explicit shows, and the area was full of pornographic bookstores and cinemas, sex shops and massage parlours.

Several factors contributed to the theatre district's decline: the 1973 oil crisis; increased international competition; the devaluation of the dollar; the 1975 New York fiscal crisis; the expansion of budget deficits; and the city's brush with bankruptcy.[10] Investors ceased to financially support plays, which led to the interruption of numerous theatrical productions. In the 1980s, the number of shows dropped precipitously, and Broadway openings reached much lower numbers compared with previous years.

Given this difficult environment, public and private agents developed strategies to address the economic, social and political problems impacting the city. After two failed urban-reform proposals, a third aligned the interests of the city, the state, the private market and the theatre sector. The agenda focused on entertainment and tourism and aimed to present New York as a multicultural metropolis.

In the 1980s, in parallel with this urban reform, the investment model for Broadway shows underwent a transformation, with a decline in the relevance of small, independent investors and an increased prevalence of large corporations. One of the larger producers at the time was the Shubert Organization. Founded in 1900 by brothers Sam, Lee and Jacob J. Shubert, the organisation is the oldest professional theatre company in the United States.[11] The company weathered the difficult 1970s and 1980s to become one of the city's leading producers, owning 17 theatre buildings and the capital to invest in new shows.

In 1982 the Shubert Organization identified a business opportunity: by buying the copyright for an established UK show it could save money on the production, and reduce the risks of obtaining a musical that could fail at the end of a long development process. Buying *Cats* from Mackintosh saved Shubert time and resources while ensuring a certain

British prestige for the American stage. The wisdom of this decision and the success of the musical had an important impact on the theatrical-production model in the following years.

In Larry Stempel's book *Showtime: A history of the Broadway musical theater*, Mackintosh states:

> I think that extraordinary sequence of British shows, starting with *Cats* and then *Les Miz*, *Phantom*, followed by *Saigon*, completely rebuilt the road … [These shows] helped Broadway become this huge financial machine. Before Andrew [Lloyd Webber] and I had these kinds of worldwide successes, companies like Disney weren't interested in coming into the theater. Disney thought the theater was small beer, but then suddenly people said, 'These shows made how much?'.[12]

The technopolitics outlined by Mackintosh served as a competitive stimulus for other players in the market, such as the Disney conglomerate. To diversify its strategies and ensure growth over the following decade, the company decided to explore the theatre market. The stage production of *Beauty and the Beast*, which began previews at the Palace Theatre in 1994, inaugurated a new era for the company. With a budget of US$15 million it was lauded as the most expensive musical on Broadway, but the US$6 million spent on advertising ensured *Beauty and the Beast* broke the record for single-day ticket sales, reaching a high point of US$1.2 million, surpassing *The Phantom of the Opera* by more than US$350,000.[13]

On achieving Broadway success Disney created a dedicated theatrical division to plan and execute future endeavours. Thomas Schumacher, president of the sector, stated in 2004:

> Our mission is to produce commercial theatre, not just to fill Broadway theatres. And anyway, Broadway per se has become an artificial definition of commercial work … We have to create productions around the world, because there are not enough venues here, there is not enough audience for all the projects we're currently developing.[14]

In a short period of time, Mackintosh's production strategies began to serve as a reference for the expansion of big-budget musical shows. Urban reform redesigned New York to receive and export Broadway plays, and large American production companies began to see in these strategies a way to expand their shows and optimise their profits.

In Brazil, this new technopolitics found particularly fertile ground to thrive, especially in São Paulo and Rio de Janeiro.

## A law for culture

Brazil has a tradition in musical theatre that dates back to the second half of the nineteenth century, when a frenetic cycle of growth and modernisation connected the city of Rio de Janeiro to the routes of the global theatre market. In that period, the constant presence of touring Portuguese, French and Spanish companies facilitated the development of a large, local, comedic-musical entertainment industry in the city.[15] At the turn of the twentieth century, shows in Rio's Tiradentes Square were attracting crowds[16] to the box office every day, sustaining a chain of artists, technicians and entrepreneurs, and even a cartel of organised investors who defined details like ticket prices and the maximum salaries to be paid to contracted stars.[17]

Entertainment theatre in São Paulo, although on a smaller scale than in Rio, also led to the birth of a mass culture, a process that preceded and accompanied the emergence of radio and records.[18] In this regard, during much of the twentieth century, the revue genre was primarily responsible for creating and maintaining a specialised, professional environment for comedic-musical theatre in Brazil. Gradually, revue aesthetics and artists were absorbed by new mediums, such as radio, television and cinema, until revue finally died out in the 1970s.[19]

Prior to this, Brazilian theatre had been going through a long process of modernisation that involved ambitious artistic programmes and more highbrow audiences. This high-culture theatre, which rejected 'popular' modes of production, was dedicated to staging dramatic plays of literary value. In the 1950s it began a process of professionalisation, particularly in São Paulo where companies imported European texts and directors, and established new standards for Brazilian theatre in terms of production, consumption and aesthetics.[20]

With the growing demand for more 'artistic' theatrical styles and the migration of popular forms of entertainment to new media, music became an intermittent component of the scene in São Paulo and Rio de Janeiro. Throughout the second half of the twentieth century, these cities only saw sporadic, local productions of Broadway plays[21] and, in the 1960s, the emergence of a Brazilian tradition of politically themed musicals influenced by Bertolt Brecht.[22] Despite enduring throughout the military dictatorship of 1964–85, these shows failed to become a regular cultural fixture, or to cultivate an ecosystem of trained professionals, committed audiences or funding that could sustain a market for musicals. However, the role of music in Brazilian theatre underwent a radical change with the approach of the twenty-first century, when local and foreign contexts facilitated the creation of new transnational routes for the commerce of musical theatre. The influencing factors have multiple origins, from London to New York through São Paulo and Rio de Janeiro.

The explosion of musical theatre in Brazil in recent decades is a process that, despite involving the resumption of some national traditions, is mainly based on the import and adaptation of artistic and institutional procedures used abroad. This process did not take place in a premeditated manner, and cannot be understood outside the context that generated a federal law on tax incentives for culture, the *Lei Rouanet*.

Throughout the 1970s, the largest Brazilian cities, Rio de Janeiro and São Paulo, had a stable art-theatre market, made possible by the fame their theatre stars acquired by acting in television soap operas.[23] In the 1980s the box office-based market for naturalistic theatre began to decline because it had to compete with the universalisation of television, which had previously helped sustain it.[24] At the point when the telenovela had captured a large part of the public that previously consumed realistic dramaturgy, the theatre generated alternative, self-referential aesthetics using elements of the Brazilian stage tradition together with new languages of contemporary art, such as dance theatre and performance art.[25]

Looking for new markets independent of the box office, this scene turned to the sponsorship of private companies interested in connecting their brands with an image of innovation. In the last decades of the twentieth century, sponsorship of culture became a reality that grew along with new branches of experimental theatre and a kind of renaissance of musicals.

Initially the Brazilian musicals that emerged in the 1980s did not repeat the Brazilian tradition of large-scale box-office entertainment.[26] Instead the genre was reformatted for the new modes of art-theatre production, transforming into a cultural asset for artistic appreciation, sponsored by companies and promoted by the government. In its search for artistic justification, musical theatre turned to Brazilian cultural memory, addressing themes, songs, singers, authors and texts from the popular traditions of the nineteenth and twentieth centuries.

At the time there were no systematic public policies for cultural promotion in the country. Incentive laws were created both to enable new markets for artistic experience, and to preserve memory and cultural heritage, not only in theatre but in all cultural areas. However, the post-dictatorship period linked the genesis of this cultural legislation to the clash of two opposing forces: the urgency of a systematic policy for culture, and the fear of a possible government dirigisme. In the 1980s the neoliberal ideal of a minimal state was strengthened worldwide, particularly in Brazil, where even sectors of the left feared the cultural intrusion of the state after 21 years of fascist dictatorship strongly marked by censorship.[27] In addition, the economic crisis, hyperinflation, and crippling foreign debt limited the possibilities for state investment in any area.

It is from this paradoxical context – in which urgency in the creation and systematisation of cultural policies clashed with an authoritarian, bankrupt and disreputable state – that the Brazilian cultural legislation, which was simultaneously both specific and ambiguous, arose. The solution the Brazilian government of the 1980s and 1990s found to the dilemma of financing culture was the creation of legislation based on indirect governmental incentives. Inspired by US legislation designed to encourage philanthropic donations, the incentives offered tax deductions to sponsors of arts and culture, aimed at facilitating the investment of civil resources in the cultural market.

The first Brazilian president elected by direct vote following the end of the military dictatorship, Fernando Collor de Mello, reduced cultural investments by around 40 per cent, and extinguished several federal entities that had promoted the performing arts, cinema and other cultural products.[28] Collor bet all his chips on culture as a market and on tax-exemption policies.[29] The *Lei Rouanet* was enacted in 1991 and supported tax deductions as an alternative to direct state investment. From 1991 to 1997, the legislation allowed a partial income-tax deduction for companies that sponsored culture. Initially Brazilian businesses were unenthusiastic about deducting up to 30 per cent of their investment in cultural sponsorships from their taxes, in addition to the abatement for tax purposes of the same amounts as operating expenses.

Two additional types of subsidy provided for by the *Lei Rouanet* – in addition to tax-exempt patronage – would either never get off the ground (as in the case of cultural and artistic investment funds, or FICARTs) or serve mainly to finance government projects (as in the case of the national fund for culture, or FNC). The inadequacy of the subsidy system arising from the legislation was that it failed to provide different ways for the government to engage in different forms of cultural production.[30] The prevalence of the patronage system over others can be explained by distortions that the *Lei Rouanet* suffered in the 1990s as a result of internal political struggles in the Brazilian cultural field.

From 1993 onwards, to offset the disruption the cinema sector had suffered in the Collor era, a movement of Brazilian producers and filmmakers enacted legislation that guaranteed 100 per cent deductions on income tax due, and provided profits of up to 24 per cent for the movie sponsor.[31] In light of this, other artistic sectors demanded equivalent legislation, and in 1997 the *Lei Rouanet* was amended to grant 100 per cent tax deductions on sponsorships in areas such as dance, the visual arts, circuses and theatre. From then on, the *Lei Rouanet* began to really work.

Having lost sight of the original objective of the law, which was to use private capital to promote culture, the Brazilian cultural sphere joined with the government to create a questionable new incentive system in which the sponsoring company defined the work, artist, group or project that would receive incentives (according to the brand's potential returns), and the government contributed by investing all the capital through a full tax-waiver mechanism. When the cost to sponsors was reduced to zero, the *Lei Rouanet* began to encourage a type of marketing that showed little regard for sociocultural issues or the sponsor's image of innovation. In the theatre, the cultural pseudo-market of full tax incentives tended to benefit major musical productions and plays with famous actors or media appeal, reinforcing the star system.

In the case of theatre and other cultural segments, this policy, which could hardly be called public, has survived several economic crises. The *Lei Rouanet* has endured because it is not legally bound by governmental budget constraints, and because it favours a clientelist, elitist cultural policy supported by powerful lobbies.[32] Furthermore, the elitism and anti-liberal bias of these disincentives to private investment in culture are not recognised or understood by a large number of Brazilian cultural agents, let alone by the public.

## When everything intersects: transnational technopolitics in Brazil

In the years following this change to the *Lei Rouanet*, English and American productions designed primarily for export found circumstances in Brazil highly favourable, and in the first decade of the century theatre producers received massive investments to produce musicals in the country. The Brazilian version of *Les Misérables*, created in 2001, managed to raise US$573,841;[33] *A Bela e a Fera* (*Beauty and the Beast*) raised US$463,106 in its first season in 2002 and a further US$1,020,862 in its second season in 2003; the 2004 choreographic play *Chicago* raised US$1,468,489; and *O Fantasma da Ópera* (*The Phantom of the Opera*) raised around US$7,049,272 over two seasons (2005 and 2006) via the *Lei Rouanet*. The Brazilian public received these productions with enthusiasm, with *Les Misérables* attracting 350,000 theatregoers in its 11-month run, *A Bela e a Fera* drawing 600,000 theatregoers in its 19-month season between 2002 and 2003, and *O Fantasma da Ópera* attracting an audience of 880,000 between 2005 and 2007.[34]

The Disney and Mackintosh productions were staged in Brazil by the Mexican company Corporación Interamericana de Entretenimiento (CIE). Founded in 1990, it hosted live events in Mexico City, but in 1991 following an agreement with American ticket sales company Ticketmaster it became responsible for selling tickets for live events throughout Latin America. In 1996 a licensing agreement with Disney's theatre department authorised CIE to stage the conglomerate's productions in Latin America, Spain and Portugal. CIE's first production, in 1997 in Mexico City, was *La Bella y la Bestia* (*Beauty and the Beast*); a huge success, the seats were filled by 650,000 theatregoers over 420 performances.

Capitalisation allowed CIE to expand its operations into Brazil. After acquiring part of a local entertainment company, CIE built new venues and started investing in the musicals market. According to an article in the Brazilian daily newspaper *Folha de S.Paulo*, by the year 2000 the company was the largest live-entertainment conglomerate in Latin America, with revenues of US$400 million that year. The company's CEO in Brazil affirmed: '[CIE] is a partner that can bring a large volume of international shows and that has direct access to the American market … This enables lower prices for international tours in Latin America, better technical conditions, and a larger number of shows.'[35]

For the Brazilian premiere of *Les Misérables* on 24 April 2001, producer Cameron Mackintosh, composer Claude-Michel Schönberg and director Ken Caswell travelled to São Paulo to guarantee the final quality of the production. Schönberg declared that 'when it comes to *Les Misérables*, we are talking about one of the works of greatest cultural importance in the world'.[36] A few years later, for the 2005 production of *O Fantasma da Ópera* (another Mackintosh show), CIE raised around US$2,830,000 through international sponsors including Credicard, Bosch and Ericsson using the *Lei Rouanet*.[37] At the time, the company's then CEO Fernando Alterio said 'I feel comfortable in resorting to the *Lei Rouanet* to produce our shows … During the 18-month season of

*O Fantasma*, around 200 people, including technicians and artists, will be employed.'[38] Alterio ended his reflection by dodging criticisms he had received for using the law, since according to him the malaise came from 'smaller producers, who feel disadvantaged by the great musicals'.

Brazilian artists specialising in Broadway-style musicals since the 1990s, such as Jorge Takla and the duo Claudio Botelho and Charles Möeller, have increased the number of shows staged in the country over the years.[39] Funding acquired through the *Lei Rouanet* has also grown: *My Fair Lady* (2007) raised US$2,999,554, *Cats* (2010) raised US$3,196,948, *Mamma Mia!* (2010) raised US$7,436,667 and *The Lion King* (2013–14) raised US$10,614,124 while attracting 800,000 theatre-goers during its almost 20-month run – a record at the time.[40]

The market expanded with the presence of imported musicals, and specialised producers such as Aniela Jordan, Sandro Chaim and Luiz Calainho, among others. Given the close network of contacts these large producers maintain among sponsors, and their ability to organise lobbies with the government, they have in a way revived the cartel structure active in Brazil in the early twentieth century, mentioned at the beginning of this chapter.[41]

Over the last decade, in parallel with the staging of Brazilian versions of West End and Broadway musicals, Brazilian playwrights, musicians, performers and producers have begun to rely on what they call the Broadway model to mount original projects, assuming aesthetic and administrative conventions inspired by foreign references. If in 1998 Andrew Lloyd Webber denied the existence of a formula, in Brazil, producers, artists, the press and even the public asserted that it existed, at least as a mode of production.[42] Flowing from this, productions centred on stories of Brazilian personalities and events reached the stage, such as *Tim Maia – Vale Tudo, o Musical* (2012), *Rock In Rio – O musical* (2013) and *Elis – A musical* (2014), among others. Meanwhile, Director Gustavo Gasparani attracts audiences of between 3,000 and 4,000 to the national tours of his shows, in which he uses the Broadway model to revive creative expedients of the old revue, with national themes, famous singers from Brazilian pop music and fundraising of up to R$28 million (US$7,837,567) via the *Lei Rouanet*.[43]

## Conclusion

The transformation of Broadway shows into international commodities involved transnational corporate policies and even urban reform.

The consolidation of Broadway shows into the Brazilian theatre market was facilitated by local context (one in which entrepreneurs and inter-mediaries also participated) as well as public policies (British, American and Brazilian) not originally designed for this purpose. Despite this, these policies were decisive for the success of a vast Broadway market in the country.

Broadway does not profit from any kind of tax-deduction system – such donations are reserved exclusively for non-profit organisations. In the land of Uncle Sam, despite the concentrating effect of foundations linked to large corporations – Ford, Rockefeller and Carnegie – there is an ecology of small donors responsible for the bulk of the resources in philanthropy,[44] which ensures some plurality and to a certain extent a democratisation of cultural investment. This is because both individuals and corporations in the US can deduct part of their donations from the income-tax calculation. In Brazil, with the *Lei Rouanet*, only two per cent of the largest and most profitable companies can make use of legal deductions. As a result, the Brazilian version of the tax incentive ensures the state pays for the marketing of very wealthy companies that decide which cultural projects receive sponsorship.[45] In the case of Cameron Mackintosh, the Arts Council offered incentives to a producer who, once he had accrued adequate personal capital, began to promote his English productions in different countries.

In the first half of the twentieth century in the US, the donation system was associated with the decline of entertainment theatre and the rise of high-culture art theatre. The result was the creation of a new mode of production, no longer based on tours and commercial shows to entertain large crowds, but on fundraising through non-profit curatorial entities for non-commercial shows, legitimised as being of high artistic value by urban elites. Thus, theatre, together with opera and dance, entered the restricted domain formerly dominated by museums and the visual arts.[46] The move from commerciality to curatorship laid the foundations for a realistic art theatre that would be professionally maintained for decades, influencing cinema and, ultimately, the entire world.

At the turn of the twenty-first century, the move from the box office to the curatorship and fundraising systems in Brazil involved processes and effects that were completely different from those of the US. Created with the initial intention of promoting non-commercial national projects, the Brazilian tax-incentive policy ended up creating the perfect environment for an internal market for international shows forged in a technopolitics designed to expand profits – as envisioned by Mackintosh in the UK.

By focusing on the sponsor's brand rather than the sociocultural character of the artistic project, the *Lei Rouanet* organised the Brazilian cultural market according to private interests. By covering all the costs of this market with public money, Brazilian law eliminated the need for theatrical sponsors and entrepreneurs to invest in their own projects, thereby eliminating risks, multiplying profits and creating the perfect scenario for the emergence of a typically Brazilian musical experience, forged in the West End or on Broadway.

## Notes

1  The term technopolitics is used in this chapter with its sense extended to cultural realities, as proposed by Christopher Balme in 'Theatrical institutions in motion'. In the specific case of musical theatre in the late twentieth century, technopolitics refers to strategies and power asymmetries in the transferring of cultural expertise to developing nations during neoliberal globalisation. See also the introduction to this volume.
2  Morley and Leon, 1998, 9.
3  Morley and Leon, 1998.
4  Morley and Leon, 1998.
5  Trained as an actor, Field joined the Arts Council in 1957 and expanded the department's resources from GB£1 million to GB£300 million over the 28 years he held office. Information from https://www.ispa.org/news/168252/Remembering-Tony-Field.htm. Accessed 1 July 2022.
6  Morley and Leon, 1998.
7  Morley and Leon, 1998.
8  Gapper, 2016.
9  Davis, 2000.
10  Gramlich, 1976, 416.
11  Leonhardt, 2018.
12  Stempel, 2010, 630.
13  Nelson, 1995.
14  Adler, 2004, 99.
15  Werneck and Reis, 2012.
16  Süssekind, 1986.
17  Mencarelli, 2003.
18  Bessa, 2012.
19  Reis and Marques, 2012, 321.
20  Pontes, 2010.
21  Machado, 2022.
22  Marques, 2014.
23  Unlike most countries, in Brazil the professionalisation of art theatre during the second half of the twentieth century was not brought about by policies on public or private patronage.
24  Guenzburger, 2020, 46.
25  Guenzburger, 2019, 2–3.
26  Machado, 2020.
27  Michalski, 1985.
28  Reis, 2003.
29  Mendes, 2015.
30  Menezes, 2016.
31  Sarkovas, 2005.
32  André Coutinho Augustin (2011) discusses the concentrating character of laws designed to foster culture in Brazil, suggesting that they exemplify the theses of certain critics, such

as David Harvey, Dominique Lévy and Gérard Duménil, according to which neoliberalism stimulates policies to restore the power of a class before it seeks to minimise state involvement in the economy.

33 All values were converted from Brazilian real to US dollars using a tool provided by the Central Bank of Brazil, which adopts the quotation between currencies of the period in question.

34 Cardoso et al., 2016.

35 Medeiros, 2001, B30.

36 Santos, 2001, E1.

37 This market has seen an expansion of sponsors, production companies and funding for almost two decades. Beginning in 2018, political changes in the country started a cycle of sponsorship migration for museum projects and large foundations, which was compounded by the COVID-19 pandemic. It is still too early to assess if the resulting decrease in fundraising for musicals will be seasonal or a trend, and if the so-called Brazilian Broadway will survive it.

38 Folha de S.Paulo, 2005, E3.

39 Machado, 2020.

40 Brasil, 2014, C8.

41 Guenzburger, 2020.

42 Duarte, 2015, 469.

43 Reis, 2020.

44 The American system, initiated in 1913, supports tax deductions for those who make private donations, focusing on various social areas including culture. Inderjeet Parmar describes how the transnational actions of foundations were part of a strategy by US elites to extend their influence over other nations through philanthropic networks (Parmar, 2012).

45 Sarkovas, 2005.

46 DiMaggio, 1992.

# References

Adler, Steven. *On Broadway: Art and commerce on the great white way*. Carbondale: Southern Illinois University Press, 2004.

Augustin, André Coutinho. 'O neoliberalismo e seu impacto na política cultural Brasileira'. 'II Seminário Internacional Políticas Culturais' (online conference proceedings, http://antigo. casaruibarbosa.gov.br/interna.php?ID_S=124&ID_M=2210). Fundação Casa de Rui Barbosa, 2011. http://tinyurl.com/2439sza8.

Balme, Christopher. 'Theatrical institutions in motion: developing theatre in the postcolonial era', *Journal of Dramatic Theory and Criticism* 31 (2) (2017): 125–40. doi:10.1353/dtc.2017.0006.

Bessa, Virgínia de Almeida. 'A Cena Musical Paulistana: Teatro musicado e canção popular na cidade de São Paulo (1914–1934)'. Thesis. University of São Paulo, co-oriented by the Université Paris Ouest Nanterre La Défense, Nanterre, 2012.

Brasil. Lei no 8.313, de 23 de dezembro de 1991. Diário Oficial [da] República Federativa do Brasil, Brasília, DF, 24 dez. 1991. Seção 1, p. 30261.

Brasil, Ubiratan. '"O Rei Leão" encerra temporada no Brasil com recorde de público', *O Estado de São Paulo* (10 December 2014): C8.

Cardoso, Adriana, Fernandes, Angelo José and Cardoso Filho, Cassio. 'Breve história do teatro musical no Brasil: e compilação de seus títulos', *Música Hodie* 16 (1) (2016): 29–44. https://doi.org/10.5216/mh.v16i1.42982.

Davis, Tracy C. *The Economics of the British Stage, 1800–1914*. Cambridge and New York: Cambridge University Press, 2000.

DiMaggio, Paul. 'Cultural boundaries and structural change: the extension of the high culture model to theater, opera, and the dance, 1900–1940'. In *Cultivating Differences: Symbolic boundaries and the making of inequality*, edited by Michèle Lamont and Marcel Fournier, 21–67. Chicago: University of Chicago Press, 1992.

Duarte, Márcia de Freitas. 'Práticas de Organizar na Indústria Criativa: A produção de um espetáculo de teatro musical em São Paulo – SP'. Thesis. São Paulo: Fundação Getúlio Vargas, 2015.

Folha de S.Paulo. '"Produtora se diz 'confortável" em usar lei de incentivo'. *Folha de S.Paulo* (20 April 2005): E3.

Gapper, John. 'Interview: Cameron Mackintosh', *Financial Times* 15 January (2016). https://www.ft.com/content/af6b04f6-ba34-11e5-bf7e-8a339b6f2164.

Gramlich, Edward M. 'The New York City fiscal crisis: what happened and what is to be done?', *American Economic Review* 66 (2) (1976): 415–29.

Guenzburger, Gustavo. 'Transnationality, sponsorship and post-drama: "the flash and crash days" of Brazilian Theatre', *Journal of Global Theatre History* 3 (2019): 38–52. Accessed 4 August 2022. https://gthj.ub.uni-muenchen.de/gthj/article/view/5099.

Guenzburger, Gustavo. *Rio, o Teatro em Movimentos: Estética, política e modos de produção*. Rio de Janeiro: Garamond, 2020.

Leonhardt, Nic. *Theatre Across Oceans: Mediators of transatlantic exchange, 1890–1925*. Cham: Palgrave Macmillan, 2018.

Machado, Bernardo Fonseca. 'Iluminando a Cena: Um estudo sobre o cenário teatral nas décadas de 1990 e 2000 em São Paulo'. Master's dissertation. University of São Paulo, 2012.

Machado, Bernardo Fonseca. 'Social experience and US musical theatre on São Paulo's stages', *Sociologia e Antropologia* 1 (2020): 957–80.

Machado, Bernardo Fonseca. *Discourses on American Musical Theatre Between São Paulo and New York: Theatrical flows at the beginning of the twenty-first century*. Lanham, MD: Lexington, 2022.

Marques, Fernando. *Com os Séculos nos Olhos: Teatro musical e político no Brasil dos anos 1960 e 1970*. São Paulo: Perspectiva, 2014.

Medeiros, Jotabê. 'Grupo Mexicano domina mercado de show biz', *O Estado de São Paulo, Caderno de Economia* 31 March (2001): B30.

Mencarelli, Fernando. 'A Voz e a Partitura: Teatro musical, indústria e diversidade cultural no Rio de Janeiro (1868–1908)'. PhD dissertation. IFCH UNICAMP, 2003.

Mendes, Helen Miranda. *O Palco de Collor: A precarização da política cultural no governo de Fernando Collor*. Rio de Janeiro: Editora Multifoco, 2015.

Menezes, Henilton. *A Lei Rouanet Muito Além Dos (F)atos*. São Paulo: Fons Sapientiae, 2016.

Michalski, Yan. *O Teatro Sob Pressão: Uma frente de resistência*. Rio de Janeiro: Jorge Zahar Editor, 1985.

Morley, Sheridan and Leon, Ruth. *Hey, Mr. Producer! The musical world of Cameron Mackintosh*. New York: Back Stage Books, 1998.

Nelson, Steve. 'Broadway and the beast: Disney comes to Times Square', *Drama Review* 39 (2) (1995): 71–85.

Parmar, Inderjeet. *Foundations of the American Century: The Ford, Carnegie, and Rockefeller foundations in the rise of American power*. New York: Columbia University Press, 2012.

Pontes, Heloisa. *Intérpretes da Metrópole: História social e relações de gênero no teatro e no campo intelectual, 1940–1968*. São Paulo: EDUSP, 2010.

Reis, Ana Carla Fonseca. *'Marketing Cultural e Financiamento da Cultura: Teoria e prática em um estudo internacional comparado'*. São Paulo: Pioneira Thomson Learning, 2003.

Reis, Angela de Castro. 'Aspectos da tradição teatral Brasileira na criação artística contemporânea: apontamentos sobre a obra de Gustavo Gasparani'. In *Cenas Cariocas: Modos, políticas e poéticas teatrais contemporâneas*, edited by Clara de Andrade, Gustavo Guenzburger and Isabel Penoni, 181–94. Rio de Janeiro: Garamond, 2020.

Reis, Angela de Castro and Marques, Daniel. 'A permanência do teatro cômico e musicado'. In *História do Teatro Brasileiro Volume I: Das origens ao teatro profissional da primeira metade do século XX*, edited by João Roberto Faria and Jacó Guinsburg, 321–35. São Paulo: Perspectiva/Edições SESC SP, 2012.

Sagalyn, Lynne B. *Times Square Roulette: Remaking the city icon*. Cambridge, MA: MIT Press, 2001.

Santos, Valmir. 'Miseráveis milionários: "Les Misérables" estreia amanhã em São Paulo', *Folha de São Paulo* 24 April (2001): E1.

Sarkovas, Yacoff. 'Uma herança incômoda', *O Estado de São Paulo* 15 April (2005): D-11.

Stempel, Larry. *Showtime: A history of the Broadway musical theater*. New York: W. W. Norton and Company, 2010.

Süssekind, Flora. *As Revistas do Ano e a Invenção do Rio de Janeiro*. Rio de Janeiro: Nova Fronteira/Casa de Rui Barbosa, 1986.

Werneck, Maria Helena and Reis, Angela de Castro, eds. *Rotas de Teatro: entre Portugal e Brasil*. Rio de Janeiro: 7 Letras, 2012.

# Part III
# Expert networks

# 9

# The Rockefeller roundabout of funding: Severino Montano and the development of theatre in the Philippines in the 1950s[1]

Nic Leonhardt

## Prologue: 're: a person for developing drama in the Philippines'

Dear Professor Montana [sic]:

I was in The Philippines only a few weeks ago and Dr. Gabriel Bernardo of The University of The Philippines and several other scholars mentioned you as one of the people with whom I should talk with regard to the development of drama in The Philippine Islands.

I expect to be in Washington on Thursday and Friday of this week, March 22 and 23, and I should like to take this opportunity for a talk with you if a time convenient for you can be arranged. I expect to be staying at the Hay Adams and wonder whether you would not be good enough to leave word there as to how I can get in touch with you.

Sincerely yours, Charles B. Fahs[2]

This letter leaves the office of Charles B. Fahs, director of the Rockefeller Foundation's Humanities Program, on 19 March 1951. Its addressee is Severino Montano, Philippine playwright, director and, at the time of the correspondence, lecturer at the American University in Washington DC. The letter reveals that Fahs does not know Montano personally, but became aware of him through recommendations – Fahs having apparently returned from a trip to Southeast Asia during which he specifically asked for these recommendations. His request is no small one, and is initially opaque: 'the development of drama in the Philippine Islands'. Whether Montano is a suitable person for his project is something he would like to find out during a meeting in Washington. The letter arouses interest and raises questions. Why does Fahs contact Montano? What interest does he or his client, the Rockefeller Foundation, have in Montano and his work? How is it that Bernardo and 'several other scholars' know Montano and can recommend him? And, above all, who is Montano and why is he regarded as a suitable figure for this not-insignificant task?

The letter is the starting point for this chapter about the promotion of Severino Montano by the Rockefeller Foundation in the 1950s. Despite the letter's brevity it points to essential parameters that were central to Montano's promotion and that are examined here: the initiative of the sponsors, their interest in theatre, their selection and awarding methods and agenda, and the promotion of a candidate – an expert in the field of (Philippine) theatre.

Charles B. Fahs's letter to Severino Montano is in the files of the Rockefeller Archive Center in New York. In the spring of 2018, I undertook a research trip there to obtain an initial overview of the archives, which document the connection between philanthropic enterprise, theatre and its development since the end of the Second World War. Although this connection – theatre, theatre development and philanthropy – may seem unusual at first, closer study shows it to be a fruitful relationship, one that sometimes had a profound effect on the theatre practice and history.

The global political situation after the Second World War resulted in a new awareness of the importance of culture and the arts. Amid the global concern to promote cultural self-understanding, and mutual understanding, theatre received special attention. Alongside the economic and technical rehabilitation of war-damaged countries, theatre was seen as representing potential cultural and humanistic development. At the same time, the development of theatre was often promoted by higher authorities. In 1946, UNESCO – the United Nations Educational, Scientific and Cultural Organisation – was founded, making the promotion of culture, literature, language, education and theatre an international concern. The US played an important role in the postwar structure as a new world power, establishing new foundations and exchange programmes (Fulbright, for example), and giving existing ones, such as the Rockefeller Foundation, a new orientation, away from an intranational to an international promotion of art, the humanities and theatre. However, this philanthropic aid was never free of economic and power-political interests.[3]

It is well known, for example, that the Rockefeller Foundation supported and thus promoted Derek Walcott's Trinidad Theatre Workshop (founded in 1959) for a long period of time with consistent financial resources. The actual extent of the foundation's interest in drama and theatre from the 1930s to the 1960s, however, is revealed by the rich and heterogeneous archival material, which makes it clear that theatre practitioners, academics and authors were supported in order to undertake projects and study trips within the US, outside the US and overseas. The Rockefeller Foundation also supported schools, university departments and colleges between the 1930s and 1950s. In the case of Severino Montano, both individual and institutional sponsorship played a part: he received an 'ad Personam Grant' from the Rockefeller Foundation as well as institutional support for the Philippine Normal College in Manila from which he based his projects from 1952 or 1953 onwards, as will be explained in more detail below. Detailed information on the foundation's subsidy, and Montano's applications and correspondence, can be found in the aforementioned files of the Rockefeller Archive Center in New York. There Montano's work in Manila is also extensively documented, firstly in the reports and letters Montano regularly sent to the foundation to document his work and his need for support, and secondly in the meticulous diaries of the Rockefeller field staff, mainly represented by Charles B. Fahs, Boyd Compton and Compton's assistant, James Brandon. The surviving and never-before evaluated material on Montano's activities financed by the Rockefeller Foundation between 1950 and 1960 piqued my interest, prompting me to follow his career and work in the US, Europe and the Philippines. This chapter gives an insight into the first results and observations on Montano as a case study.

This chapter is divided into three sections. The first provides a general overview of the Rockefeller Foundation's commitment to cultural promotion in Asia, the second examines Severino Montano and his career, and the more detailed third section provides a differentiated insight into his support from the Rockefeller Foundation, and its activities and methods. The following is based on documents from the Rockefeller Archive Center, newspaper notes, Montano's reports and publications, and statements and publications from third parties.

## The Rockefeller Foundation and its promotion of theatre and culture

As mentioned above, after the end of the Second World War the Rockefeller Foundation's support for theatre was no longer limited to the US. Rather, the foundation took international paths in the promotion of the arts and art institutions, especially theatre. The combination of theatre art and academic training, which had proved its worth in the US, was used as a model by the foundation, since it allowed the interweaving of artistic individuality and work with a scholarly environment and expertise. In his 1948 report on the Rockefeller Foundation's Humanities Program, concerning the foundation's reasons for investing in drama from the mid-1930s, David H. Stevens, director of the programme from 1932 to 1949, notes:

> In the sciences and in humanistic studies, the Foundation has depended largely on scientific or academic personnel and institutions, both as a source of judgment on the merit of requests, and for the administration of its grants. That it can sometimes do so in the arts is shown by its grants for university work in drama, and by those approved till now for the encouragement of contemporary work in literature. But in the arts, the term academic is hardly used to characterize work at the forefront of their development; and if the Foundation is to limit its concern with the arts to what can be done through personnel in institutions, it will be neglecting much that might be of most benefit to the arts in general.[4]

In the following years, the Rockefeller Foundation supported numerous individuals and institutions in the US and abroad, at universities and elsewhere, in their theatre work. Asia had already played a major role during Stevens's tenure as director of the Humanities Program, particularly through Asia–US cross-cultural exchange and language training. This axis remained after Charles B. Fahs took over Stevens's position and expanded it to incorporate his own interest in and commitment to Japanese studies and area studies. To quote again from Stevens's report:

> If the humanities have a contribution to make to democratic life and to developing in the minds of men the understanding essential to world peace, then the need for humanities work in Asia is great and urgent. Moreover, the humanities by their very nature require for their growth the absorption of the ideas and values of other

cultures. In cultural isolation they, even more than the natural sciences, are bound to stagnate. Our humanists, like the author of a recent book, can become 'richer by Asia'.[5]

As far as the Philippines – the geographical focus of this chapter – are concerned, it can be noted that after years of occupation, first by the Americans and then by the Japanese, the archipelago became independent in July 1946. Nevertheless, in the 1950s many Americans settled in the Philippines, while locals set off for study, training or political service in America. For this case study of Severino Montano, the permanent exchange between the US and the Philippines – the decades of transatlantic connections and relationships between educational institutions and their graduates – play a crucial role in understanding the dynamics of network relationships in which the Rockefeller Foundation was involved. The foundation's many years of experience in promoting community and university theatres, as well as its personal and institutional network in Asia, formed a strong basis for investing in Asian artists and local Asian institutions. The local and specialist knowledge, and personal networks, of Charles B. Fahs, his colleagues and his successors Boyd Compton and James Brandon, who were responsible for the foundation's Humanities Program between 1950 and 1960, contributed to a consolidation of relations.

The Rockefeller Foundation did not start supporting drama and theatre abroad until the 1950s. As part of the foundation's Humanities Program, theatre had been given higher priority since the 1930s, and funding had been systematically expanded, albeit initially on a solely national level. Why did the Foundation pay so much attention to theatre for over two decades?

From the 1930s, the Foundation broadened its remit to encompass the more specialised field of theatre and drama education. Thus, more and more universities in the US, following the model of the theatre pedagogue George Pierce Baker and his famous 47 Workshop, began to include the study of theatre and drama in their curricula, setting up drama departments, production facilities and playwriting workshops. The Rockefeller Foundation contributed by awarding grants to support these new departments, either in the form of technical equipment or in scholarships for teaching assistants or training. Supporting this theatre work, far from Broadway, gave non-commercial theatre greater value, and university theatre joined community theatre on an equal footing. By 1942, as stated in Stevens's report, 'grants dating from 1934 had given added strength to departments of drama at Yale, Cornell, North Carolina,

Stanford, and Western Reserve'. The largest theatre-related grant went to the National Theatre Conference, founded in 1931 at Northwestern University by, among others, George P. Baker; both the Rockefeller and Carnegie foundations sponsored it, dispensing particularly generous subsidies during the war years.[6]

The foundation's activities in the field of theatre from the late 1940s onwards are inseparable from its methods and principles of promotion, tested in the US in the 1930s. After the war, the foundation attached great importance to the development of literature. Enabling authors to write freely was a priority, and this premise applied to playwriting as well as to radio and film, as Stevens notes:

> The situation in the fields of radio and film is being carefully scrutinized, and also the *international possibilities of drama*. These means of *powerful influence in the cultural life of nations*, as of individuals, have uses beyond their commercial applications that are recognized but not widely realized. How far these forms of expression can be made socially influential toward better appreciation in the arts is an important question today. (Italics mine.)[7]

From its inception, the foundation collaborated with individual and institutional advisers[8] with experience in specific areas of funding, both in terms of potential grants and in terms of subject area. Although the foundation attached great importance to officers' assessments of the Humanities Program and their personal encounters with potential beneficiaries, advisers' opinions were nevertheless important to a network of (often hidden) information. With regard to the promotion of culture – especially literature, education, language and theatre – UNESCO has played an important role since its foundation in November 1946. Its creation coincided with the Rockefeller Foundation's interest in expanding the promotion of the arts internationally. UNESCO was regarded as 'particularly advantageous for such international operation',[9] especially because of its clearly formulated interest in the field of the arts and international relations – the latter having been disrupted by the Second World War and, subsequently, by the political divisiveness of the postwar period.

In his report, Stevens pays particular attention to the International Theatre Institute (ITI), at the time newly founded by UNESCO. In his words: 'One opportunity for the Foundation to give encouragement on a truly international basis may develop shortly in the International Theatre Institute for the organisation of which during 1948 UNESCO has assumed responsibility. UNESCO projects in the other arts may shortly offer similar opportunities.'[10] A private philanthropic foundation networked with an international organisation to expand its international funding policy and its own network – a mésalliance that was not without consequences.

By tracking Montano's activities in the field of theatre, the following sections show how the Rockefeller Foundation's support measures were structured at the level of theatre education and practice. Montano will be the focus here, the theatre author and maker addressed in Charles B. Fah's 1951 letter, quoted at the beginning of this chapter, as 'one of the people with whom I should talk with regard to the development of drama in The Philippine Islands' – addressed or, one might say, identified.

The Rockefeller Foundation was looking for an expert to develop the Philippine theatre landscape, and Montano seemed a suitable candidate. But who was Montano, and what criteria led the Rockefeller Foundation to identify him as an expert in the development of Philippine theatre?

## Severino Montano: playwright, director, manager, pedagogue (1915–1980)

Little is known about Severino Montano outside the context of Philippine theatre history; at best his most successful dramas, including *Sabina*, *The Merry Wives of Manila* and *The Ladies and the Senator*, are well known. In 2001 he was posthumously appointed national artist by the National Commission for Culture and the Arts, the official government agency for culture in the Philippines. The comments on the nomination state that he bridged 'the great cultural divide between the educated and the masses' as 'noted playwright, director, actor and theatre organizer', a 'persevering pioneer in the formation of a Philippine national theatre movement and the professionalization of Filipino dramatic arts'.[11]

Severino Montano was born in Manila in 1915. His interest in theatre was ignited in his teenage years by Marie Leslie Prising, a British actress with Sir Johnston Forbes-Robertson's company who mentored Montano. In 1931 he became president of the dramatic club of the University of the Philippines, and after earning a bachelor's degree in education with a major in English he began teaching there. In 1939 he left his homeland with a scholarship to study acting, directing and economics in the US and the UK. In 1942 he received a Master of Arts degree in dramatics from Yale University, where he also partici- pated in the prestigious 47 Workshop (his teachers included Theodore

Komisarjevsky of the Moscow Art Theatre). He then went to Washington DC to work under President Manuel Quezon and General Carlos Peña Romulo for the Philippine government in exile (1943–6). In 1946 he was sent to London as a technical assistant to the Philippine delegation at the first session of the United Nations General Assembly, and while there he became a follower of the economist and political scientist Harold Laski. In 1948 Montano completed his master's degree in economics at the American University in Washington DC, with a thesis on 'Broadway Theatre Real Estate', and received his doctorate in public administration a year later. This combination of theatre practice, communication, management and political initiative seemed to make Montano suitable for the Rockefeller Foundation's task of promoting the Philippine theatre landscape. Montano brought with him not only expertise and geographical knowledge, but also his own professional, artistic, familial and political network. His artistic and scientific career was characterised by, and founded on, the interdependence of this network. 'It is easy to discover and promote experienced and established older artists', as Stevens put it in his 1948 report, but far more challenging is the 'selection of the brilliant, creative individuals at their time of undeveloped fullness in expression', which does not follow any 'rule of practice or theory of probability'.[12]

Montano's answer to Fahs's request was positive, for he had himself toyed with the idea of returning to his homeland after 12 years abroad, partly for family reasons and partly because of his desire to apply the knowledge he had gained abroad in theatre practice, management and business to cultural work in the Philippines. For his return journey, he planned an extended study trip through cultural centres in Europe and Asia. By experiencing European and Asian theatre he hoped to gain inspiration for his future work in the Philippines, convinced that Philippine theatre could be designed and organised in a similar way to a European national theatre system. The study trip was also intended as preparation for the mission given to him by the Rockefeller Foundation, namely 'the development of drama in The Philippine Islands'. He seemingly considered the mission urgent, for the Philippines had been under Western influence for quite a long time, and this influence had caused the indigenous Philippine theatre traditions to vanish. As James Brandon put it:

> Given the Philippine's long contact with Western culture and the dearth of indigenous theatre in the islands, it is not surprising to find Western spoken drama more widely and more deeply

appreciated here than in any other Southeast Asian country. To the average Filipino 'theatre' means 'Western theatre'. Virtually all drama to which he is exposed is based on Western models. There are no professional theatre troupes.[13]

In a letter to Fahs dated 17 January 1952, Montano identifies three innovations as indispensable for the envisaged development of theatre in the Philippines:

1.  The need for broad technical leadership which can help formulate and guide the fundamental policies in the rounded development of Philippine dramatic art in all its various aspects.
2.  The need for a teacher who can impart the methods of playwriting as practised in the modern theatre and during the golden periods of the theatre history of both East and West.
3.  The need of a leader who can inspire freedom of thought in the theatre, and who can relate this growth to the activities of the free world.[14]

In formulating these needs he simultaneously formulated the programme for his own work while recommending himself as a 'technical' leader, a teacher and an ambassador for 'freedom of thought in the theatre'. After submitting some adjustments to his concepts and travel plans to Fahs, he received an individual grant in 1952 – an 'ad Personam Grant in Aid for a theatre observation route in Europe and South East Asia, including India, en route back to the Philippines', as the title of the grant read.

With the help of this scholarship – mainly covering travel costs of US$3,500 – Montano set off in August 1952 on his roundabout way back to Manila via important theatre centres in Europe and Asia.[15] Immediately after his arrival in Manila in December 1952 he re-established his familial and professional networks there. He had given a workshop in theatre and rhetoric at the Philippine Normal College in 1949, and after his return he continued, and expanded, his work at the college, as outlined below.

The Philippine Normal College opened in September 1901 as the Philippine Normal School, the first college of higher education founded during the American occupation of the Philippines. Under the presidency of Elpidio Quirino (godfather of Montano's sister Jesusa M. Sadam), the school was renamed the Philippine Normal College. The state-funded institution focused primarily on training teachers for Philippine schools (even after the renaming), and saw itself as inculcating democratic ideals and ways of life. Hence, the fact that Montano based his work at the college fitted in well with its general philosophy. He saw the teachers and practitioners he would teach as multipliers of his ideas via their schools in the *barrios*.

Within the various networks involved, it is remarkable that Fahs not only turned to Montano for his expertise, but also that he asked his superiors and former colleagues to comment on Montano's expertise, in addition to the recommendation he received from Gabriel Bernardo. On 23 May 1951 Fahs approached Paul F. Douglass, president of the American University, for a 'confidential comment with regard to [Montano's] ability as a teacher, a writer, and an administrator of drama programmes. Mr. Montano does not know that we are writing to you and what you say will, of course, be kept confidential.'[16] Requests for information about potential scholarship recipients are not uncommon, and can be found in numerous files on both individuals and institutions. In the Rockefeller Foundation's funding measures, the foundation itself maintains at least two main networks that sometimes overlap and sometimes function autonomously: an official network that is open to beneficiaries and an unofficial, quasi-subcutaneous network that is hidden from scholarship recipients. While the former discloses strategies and requirements and communicates them transparently, the latter consists of confidential communication with advisers, individuals and institutions close to the beneficiary, and constitutes a network of advisers as well as internal agreements within the foundation. Within this network, information and recommendations are collected, problem areas discussed and measures that could affect funding considered – measures that elude the knowledge of beneficiaries.

With regard to Montano and his first grant, Boyd Smith, Walter Prichard Eaton (of the University of North Carolina at Chapel Hill) and Anna Cook (of Harvard) are named as referees. In addition, local experts and American delegates in the Philippines were consulted. Gabriel Bernardo, who as noted above had been approached by Fahs in 1951, was contacted by Fahs again in 1954, this time to obtain an assessment of Montano's work and progress. Fahs also contacted Margaret H. Williams, chief cultural affairs officer of the US embassy in Manila, for the same purpose. What did Montano do in Manila, and what did the realisation of Montano's work programme and the Rockefeller Foundation's investment look like?

# Far-flung in the *barrios*, centre-staged in Manila: Montano's theatre development programme in the Philippines

With the help of the grant, Montano employed various measures to promote professional theatre and theatre education during the 1950s in Manila. He was supported in this by his colleagues, some of whom he knew from his studies or from professional contexts. Within a short time, he established a graduate programme to train playwrights, directors, technicians, actors and designers, launched the Arena Theatre playwriting contest,[17] and in November 1955 initiated and organised the first theatre festival in the Philippines in Pangasinan, 110 miles north of Manila. His greatest and most lasting achievement, however, was the Arena Theatre, founded in 1953. Here, pedagogues who taught at schools in surrounding *barrios*, as well as actors, directors, theatre technicians and artists, undertook systematic, professional training in teaching and communication using the means and techniques of theatre. Authors and theatre practitioners, some of whom were later declared national artists of the Philippines, enjoyed their training with Montano and his colleagues at the Philippine Normal College.[18]

The space allocated to the Arena Theatre was initially, and provisionally, the girls' dormitory at the college. Here, workshops took place, and the local theatre group, under Montano's guidance, rehearsed (mainly his) plays. A second branch of the Arena Theatre opened in Bulacan in March 1955, followed by branches in Luzon and the Visayas (another was planned for Laguna). The concept flourished, and was in demand because of its simplicity and economy. The conceptual principles of the Arena Theatre spread to the surrounding educational institutions and theatres. Following the arena style primarily meant staging theatre in a simple setting with little technical effort, a circular arrangement of auditorium and stage, and the production of locally specific, indigenous or foreign (i.e. Western) plays in English and Tagalog. As James Brandon noted in 1967:

> In Manila there are about half a dozen long-established semi-professional community theatre organizations. These groups perform European and American plays for the most part, but they also produce some Philippine plays. One of the most unique is the Arena Theatre of the Philippines. Since its founding twelve years ago it has been attached to Philippine Normal College in Manila. Though university-based, it is organized as a community theatre

project with some sixty branches on the major islands of the Philippines. Each local group produces two or three plays a year. All the plays are written by Philippine authors, among them the best playwrights in the country, and all concern Philippine life. Through the Arena Theatre provincial folk-theatre producing groups are linked with sophisticated, big-city creative artists, to the benefit of both parties.[19]

Montano's nomination for national artist of the Philippines in 2001 states of the Arena Theatre: 'Through the arena style of staging plays, Montano sustained an inspiring vision for Philippine theatre appropriate to local traditions and conditions, thereby integrating his passionate lifelong commitment to, in his own words, "bring drama to the masses".'[20] Montano was convinced that the arena style was 'the original theatre form of all Southeast Asia', one that cultivated 'participation of the audience to its highest degree, and, therefore, is an effective vehicle for the communication of ideas and emotions',[21] as Montano wrote in an Arena Theatre progress report. In the Arena Theatre he saw a renaissance or resumption of a traditional model. Another interpretation of form and concept comes into play here (one that Montano himself does not mention in the source material hitherto explored), an interpretation that sees in the arena style of theatre the adaptation of a model for community theatre that was popular and exported in the 1950s. Naty Crame-Rogers, a long-time associate of Montano and one of his supporters from the very beginning of his career at the Philippine Normal College, remembered him in a biographical tribute in 2001:

> I had returned from Stanford University where my professors, Dr. Norman Philbrick and Dr. Nicholas Vardac were his colleagues at Yale. They had suggested theater-in-the-round as the answer to a developing country's need for theater arts. But since it would be difficult for me to embark on this project alone, I saw in Dr. Montano the leader that the country needed. I went to PNC to volunteer my services as Dr. Montano's first stage manager.[22]

It is relatively clear that Philbrick and Vardac were familiar with Margo Jones's 1951 book *Theatre-in-the-Round*.[23] And even though Montano does not explicitly refer to Jones in his writings, it can be assumed that as an author, director and manager not only interested in theatre but working in it, he would have encountered Jones's book and her ideas when he was in the US.

Margaret Virginia Jones (1913–1955) was a theatre director, producer and advocate of the regional theatre movement. She founded Theatre '47 in Dallas, the first not-for-profit theatre in the US. Throughout her career as a theatre practitioner Jones pursued a vision of decentralised theatres, asserting that the performing arts should be found not only in established cultural centres but also in smaller towns and cities. Community and college theatres, as sponsored by the Rockefeller Foundation, contributed to this decentralisation.[24] Jones herself had benefited from a Rockefeller scholarship, which she applied for in 1944, to study the theatrical landscape of the US, especially in Dallas.[25]

Theatre in the round – also called arena theatre, central staging, arena staging, circus theatre and penthouse style[26] – could be rectangular, circular, diamond-shaped or triangular; it was a theatre without curtains. Jones ascribed manifold benefits – including simplicity, inexpensiveness and the incidental quality of the stage set – to the concept and form of this theatre, and praised its capacity for awakening the audience's imagination despite its simplicity. Theatre in the round renounced opulent production, and the setting promised a high degree of intimacy between performers and the audience. Her pioneering work in Dallas culminated in the book *Theatre-in-the-Round*, which was read by both theatre practitioners and the Rockefeller Foundation, which had supported and co-financed Jones's initiative and recommended it to potential scholarship recipients wanting to pursue similar projects. In the files concerning Montano's promotion there is no mention of Jones's book or ideas, but his mission and vision as a theatre maker and educator were almost congruent with the idea of theatre in the round, both in terms of the design and philosophy of a theatre accessible to a wide audience, and in terms of the initial embedding of arena theatre in an educational context (as noted above, the Philippine Normal College was considered the starting point and hub of the Arena Theatre idea). Yet Montano's insistence on the arena style as a conventional form of Southeast Asian theatre is also justified. It could also be argued that he perceived it as a re-import – the theatre circuit imported and recoded by Western countries (in this case the US and Margo Jones) and then re-imported to Asia.

Conditions at the Philippine Normal College prompted Montano to consider building a modern proscenium theatre, with a capacity of 1,000 seats, just one year after the Arena Theatre began. On 8 April 1954 he mentioned this plan in one of his reports to Fahs, and asked for funding from the Rockefeller Foundation. Fahs hesitantly gave a negative response in a letter dated 19 April 1954, pointing to the possibility of local subsidies, as the Foundation was generally unable to provide funds for buildings. But Montano's idea did not fade away. His interest in theatre management and design, and above all his vision and mission for the development of theatre in the Philippines and the promotion of national culture, led him to consolidate the idea, at the end of the 1950s, of turning the Arena Theatre into a national theatre for the Philippines. The theatres in the countries and cities he had visited in 1952, including England, Germany, Japan, France and Italy, served as models; these 'modern governments', as he noted in his progress report, 'long recognized the value of the theatre as a necessary component in the life of the individual, and have established government theatres'.[27]

The proposed national theatre had to be 'inexpensive enough to meet all sorts of marginal conditions', but also designed in such a way that it would reach 'every nook and corner of the land'. Only in this way could 'enlightenment and cultural advantages … be brought to the grass-roots. Through the economical nature of arena staging, we can achieve our purpose.'[28]

The concept and a first architectural design for the national theatre can be found in Montano's report on the proceedings of the Arena Theatre. The young architect C. J. Abgayani produced a detailed plan for the stage, classrooms, offices and workshops.[29] A note by Boyd R. Compton reveals that these plans were presented to Rockefeller Foundation representatives during a visit to the Philippines. Compton noted:

> With some fanfare, the new plan for an Arena Theatre building on the Philippine Normal College campus was presented. Architect C.J. Agbayani has designed a building which would contain an arena theatre auditorium and enough class and rehearsal rooms for a full dramatic course. The cost would be P. 300,000, of which some P. 28,000 have already been promised by senatorial pork-barrel funds … CBF [Charles B. Fahs] made it quite clear that the RF would not be able to contribute to the costs of construction, then sidetracked the discussion to the subject of theatre equipment. He spoke of the possibility of getting an RF promise of a certain sum for equipment, providing the funds for building are raised locally and the Philippine Normal College provides salaries for an adequate staff. The idea seemed to interest the group, but discussion did not proceed much further.[30]

Reports like this one by Compton, called officers' diaries (reports by Rockefeller representatives and programme managers on their travels to sponsored institutions and scholarship holders), are, in their detail, valuable sources for understanding the activities of sponsors and scholarship recipients (see also chapter 13 in this volume). In addition to general description, they contain critical comments and explicit recommendations for follow-up grants or adjustments to the allocation of grants. The records reveal that the officers spent weeks travelling to visit and interview the recipients of scholarships and grants, as well as visiting other cultural and educational institutions, and US embassies. In addition, the Rockefeller Foundation maintained contact with local representatives to keep abreast of sponsored individuals' activities. This monitoring was not specific to Southeast Asia, but was rather part of the usual funding procedure. The foundation's funding strategies included the continuous monitoring of beneficiaries, which encompassed in-person visits from officers of the Humanities Program.

The idea of turning the Arena Theatre into a national theatre with its own dedicated building was never realised, probably because of the exorbitant cost, for which there was simply no sponsor to be found. In the early 1960s, James Brandon wrote to Boyd Compton about Montano, who in his eyes was a 'remarkable fellow – artist to his fingertips but also quite obviously a skilful organizer'. In Brandon's view Montano had achieved much, and yet so little of what he hoped to achieve. Montano's school had not provided him with enough funds to continue his grass-roots programme, and he was therefore tempted, as Brandon noted:

> … to switch schools and push for this new theatre-complex as a National Theatre. This can't be an easy choice for him, because if he suceeds [sic] in getting his new plant, the direction of his work will inevitably be toward greater professionalism in production, higher costs, and less-grass-roots work … (This may be a heretical thing to say, but I'm convinced that much of the remarkable success of his program is due to the lack of facilities not in spite of it).[31]

The Rockefeller Foundation had identified Montano as a potential candidate for the development of the theatre in the Philippines, his extensive knowledge of dramaturgy, theatre construction, communication and management making him apparently ideal for the task. At the Philippine Normal College he used all these skills and abilities to realise his vision, supported by a collegial network of theatre directors, theatre educators and technicians. The college seemed to him an ideal hub for his agenda and vision. Montano focused on plays by Filipino authors on Filipino themes – in English as well as in Tagalog – and this, together with the economic arena style of the productions, made his theatre programme highly suitable for imitation in schools and decentralised locations. The idea of a decentralised theatre scene, as described by Margo Jones in *Theatre-in-the-Round*, seemed to have been realised. Jones had argued that the performing arts should not only be present in theatre capitals, but also in small towns and provinces, and viewed community and college theatres as suitable forms for this.[32]

## Conclusion

In his 1948 report on the Rockefeller Foundation's Humanities Program, David H. Stevens noted that the promotion of young nations was a particular concern of the foundation, requiring special initiatives and programme adaptations:

> Conditions in Asia will require Foundation programs different from those current in the United States. In countries, which are decades behind the United States in educational development, the Foundation's help may be appropriate in fields in which the Foundation is no longer active in its program at home. Much of the current humanities program can, however, be applied to Asia with advantage. In many fields the progress made in the United States becomes the basis for effective assistance abroad.[33]

Charles B. Fahs's 1951 letter, with which this chapter opened, had an impact on the career of a theatre maker and educator, and on the theatre landscape of a country that had only achieved independence a few years before it received Rockefeller Foundation funding. Based on the foundation's experience of promoting college, university and community theatres in the US, it developed a funding model that it applied to developing nations, with necessary adaptations for each country or region. Over a period of almost 10 years, the foundation repeatedly granted Severino Montano small endowments with which to procure literature, media and technical equipment for the Arena Theatre, and with which to supplement his wages and offset his travel expenses as part of his Arena Theatre programme. All in all, between 1952 and 1959, the Rockefeller Foundation supported the Arena Theatre project with US$32,000, the largest portion of which was apportioned to Montano's salary. The foundation did not see itself as the main financier of the 'development of drama in The Philippine Islands', but only as a co-sponsor, with the expectation that the Philippine Normal College or the Philippine government would ensure continuity and sustainability. However, this was difficult due to the school's limited resources. Boyd R. Compton noted this in his officer's diary on 8 September 1958:

> Philippine Normal College President Emiliano Ramirez took BRC and CBF to breakfast and then to school. He apparently wanted to show his good will and interest in the Arena Theatre program, but nothing much more … He has high hopes that more 'pork barrel' money will be found for the theatre building. In his view, the AT movement is already an integral and important part of the PNC curriculum. With the present Board of Directors and Department of Education policy, the AT has strong support and can be considered permanent. It will be difficult, however, to get Severino Montano a full faculty position for next year. ER assured us that he will get the funds for SM's 'item' soon.[34]

In the 1950s, personal and institutional networks went hand in hand with Rockefeller's support of Montano and his Arena Theatre. The support Montano received from the foundation encompassed both individual *ad personam* scholarships for his study trips and education, and scholarships for the development of his Arena Theatre and theatrical management and educational programme at the Philippine Normal College and in the surrounding provinces. But by the end of the decade, Montano's support from the foundation had been largely phased out, except for a few minor travel grants.

Sociologists Helmut K. Anheier and Siobhan Daly note that philanthropic foundations are 'one of the main sources of support for global civil society organizations' – organisations that are in turn building a more open global order and trying to 'humanize globalization'.[35] The political scientist Inderjeet Parmar clearly views this reading with suspicion, arguing that even if philanthropic foundations theoretically contributed to the spread of democratic ideas and the reduction of social grievances, especially in developing countries, such foundations were 'intensely political and ideological and are steeped in market, corporate, and state institutions … they are a part of the power elite of the United States'.[36] The networks extending from such foundations were also networks of power, of the economic and intellectual elite; the foundations' influence was not limited to promoting 'the well-being of mankind throughout the world', as John D. Rockefeller put it in the nineteenth century. It is precisely such interdependencies and areas of interest that will have to be further investigated in future studies.

The initiatives advanced by Severino Montano in the Philippines, and the measures taken by the Rockefeller Foundation in developing drama in the Philippines, represent only preliminary findings. Further research is needed to get closer to the interdependencies and networks that led to Montano's theatrical achievements in the US and the Philippines, and the promotion and administration of his work by the Rockefeller roundabout of funding.

## Notes

1 Research for the paper on which this chapter was based was funded by the European Research Council under the European Union's Horizon 2020 research and innovation programme (grant agreement no. 694559 – DevelopingTheatre). An earlier and slightly different version of the paper was published in the *Journal of Global Theatre History*.

2 Charles B. Fahs to Severino Montano, American University, Washington DC, 19 March 1951. Rockefeller Archive Center, Montano, Severino (drama) 242R, Box 19, Series 1.2, Projects 242, Philippines.

3 See Parmar, 2012.

4 Stevens, 1948, 27. David Harrison Stevens (1884–1980) initiated important programmes in drama, film, radio, literature, linguistics and international cultural exchange. He began his work in the field of theatre by funding regional and community theatres and university drama departments.

5 Stevens, 1948, 17.

6 Minutes of the Rockefeller Foundation regarding the National Theatre Conference, 4 June, 1938. Rockefeller Archive Center, Rockefeller Foundation records, projects, RG 1.1, series 200.R, box 255, folder 3042. Regarding the founding purpose of the National Theatre Conference, the Rockefeller Foundation's minutes read: 'The National Theatre Conference is a co-operative organization of directors of community and university theatres. Its purposes are to improve the quality of non-commercial drama and to increase its social significance in all sections of the country ... The Conference was established in 1932 with different purposes than those now in force. Its first president was the late George P. Baker of Yale University. He and his colleagues in the original group desired to bring the members of the Conference into relationship with the professional theatre. They were concerned with methods of finding professional opportunities for their own students and with the general status of the profession outside of metropolitan centers.' The National Theatre Conference website reads: 'In 1925 a group of leaders of such university programs including George Pierce Baker at Yale, Thomas Wood Stevens at Carnegie Tech, Frederick Koch at the University of North Carolina, Chapel Hill, E. C. Mabie, at the University of Iowa, and Garrett Leverston, at Northwestern University called a series of conferences that led to the founding of the National Theatre Conference. The NTC was initially organised and adopted its name in 1931 at a conference at Northwestern University. In 1932, at a second conference at the University of Iowa, a constitution was adopted and officers were first elected.' Accessed 1 August 2019. https://www.nationaltheatreconference.org/about.html.

7 Stevens, 1948, preface.

8 In his review of the Rockefeller Foundation's Humanities Program, Stevens stresses the importance of these representatives, whom he calls advisers: 'Advisers are a great resource, as in awarding of fellowships, wherever the sources of information are highly critical or unusually close to the contact equally. There the officer has an alternative for his own primary evidence of considerable value. On his own, however, he will talk with the individual repeatedly, if possible, and will care less about secondary sources of opinion, which may be friendly or unfriendly, casual or judicious.' Stevens, 1948, 39.

9   Stevens, 1948, 21.
10  Stevens, 1948, 31.
11  National artist folio for 2001, published by the Order of National Artists (ONA), National Commission for Culture and the Arts, Manila. I would like to thank Sabrina Tan from the ONA for kindly making the folio available.
12  Stevens, 1948, 38.
13  Brandon, 1967, 78f.
14  Severino Montano to Charles B. Fahs, 17 January 1952. Rockefeller Archive Center, Montano, Severino (drama), 242R, Box 19, Series 1.2, Projects 242, Philippines.
15  Montano provided detailed reports on his journey through the theatre centres of Europe and Asia, an evaluation of which will be the subject of a separate paper.
16  Rockefeller Archive Center, Montano, Severino (drama), 242R, Box 19, Series 1.2, Projects 242, Philippines.
17  The Arena Theatre playwriting contest led to the discovery of Wilfrido D. Nolledo, Jesus T. Peralta and Estrella Alfon.
18  Crame-Rogers, 2001, 101–8.
19  Brandon, 1967, 79.
20  National artist folio for 2001, published by the Order of National Artists (ONA), National Commission for Culture and the Arts, Manila. I would like to thank Sabrina Tan from the ONA for kindly making the folio available.
21  Montano, 'Progress Report', 1948, n.p.
22  Crame-Rogers, 2001, 103.
23  Jones, 1951.
24  See Jones, 1951, 17. 'What our country needs today, theatrically speaking, is a resident professional theatre in every city with a population of over one hundred thousand … I assure you that the best way to assure quality is to give birth to a movement which will establish permanent resident professional theatres throughout the country.'
25  In Jones's application for the Rockefeller scholarship she described her intention to get 'a concrete picture of the present American theatrical scene', to 'spend enough time in Dallas to begin to know the city, its people, schools, libraries, museums, etc.' and to 'talk to young creative theatre people in the country', from among whom she planned to recruit 20 'for the creation of a resident theatre in Dallas'. Jones, 1951, 53.
26  The first theatre of this kind is considered to be the Glenn Hughes Penthouse Theatre in Seattle, founded in 1940.
27  Montano, 'Progress Report', 1948, n.p.
28  Montano, 'Progress Report', 1948, n.p.
29  The design formed part of Abgayani's qualification thesis, supervised by Severino Montano. Born in 1925, Abgayani graduated in civil engineering from the University of Santo Tomas in 1949, and completed his architectural studies at the same university in 1953 with a graduation thesis on 'A Study of the Arena Theatre for Philippine Normal College'; Severino Montano was his principal assessor. From 1949 Abgayani worked in various construction jobs, practising as an architect from 1953 onwards. See Montano, 'Progress Report', 1948, n.p.
30  Compton, 1958a.
31  James Brandon to Boyd Compton, 18 November 1963.
32  'There has been notable progress in the educational theatre. Every year more colleges and universities are establishing drama departments, and those which already have them are adding new courses to their curriculums and enriching their staffs with professional theatre people. This is of vast importance because most of our young theatre people will emerge from this kind of theatre. Since its main duty is the preparation and training of actors, technicians, playwrights and directors, the university theatre must approach professional standards as much as possible, both by having instructors with professional experience and by assuming a sound theatre attitude in its productions.' Jones, 1951, 11f.
33  Stevens, 1948b, 18.
34  Compton, 1958a; Compton, 1959.
35  Anheier and Daly, 2005, 159.
36  Parmar, 2012, 1–2.

# References

Anheier, Helmut and Daly, Siobhan. 'Philanthropic foundations: a new global force?'. In *Global Civil Society,* edited by Helmut Anheier, Marlies Glasius and Mary Kaldor, 158–77. London: Sage, 2005.

Brandon, James R. *Theatre in Southeast Asia*. Cambridge, MA: Harvard University Press, 1967.

Compton, Boyd R. 'Officer's Diary', 1958–1959. Rockefeller Archive Center, South-East Asia, 905 Com, 1958a.

Compton, Boyd R. 'Officer's Diary', 8 September 1958b. Rockefeller Archive Center.

Compton, Boyd R. 'Officer's Diary', 23 May–6 July 1959. Rockefeller Archive Center.

Crame-Rogers, Naty. 'Severino Montano: titan of the Philippine theatre'. In *National Artist of the Philippines*, Vol. 2: *1999–2003*, edited by the Cultural Center of the Philippines, 101–7. Pasig City: Anvil, 2003.

Jones, Margo. *Theatre-in-the-Round*. Westport, CT: Greenwood Press, 1951.

Leonhardt, Nic. 'The Rockefeller roundabout of funding: Severino Montano and the development of theatre in the Philippines in the 1950s', *Journal of Global Theatre History* 3 (2) (2019): 19–33.

Parmar, Inderjeet. *Foundations of the American Century: The Ford, Carnegie, and Rockefeller foundations in the rise of American power*. New York: Columbia University Press, 2012.

Stevens, David H. 'Preface'. *Rockefeller Foundation Humanities Program Reviews, 1939–1949* (15 April 1948).

Stevens, David H. *Humanities Program Reviews, 1939–1949* IV 2A34, Box 4, Folder 13, David H. Stevens.

# 10
# Metin And: creating a theatrical epistemic community in Turkey
Hasibe Kalkan

The changing political situation after the Second World War brought the US and Turkey closer than before, ultimately resulting in Turkey's accession to NATO in 1951. The US, as a rising world power, aware that military and financial support would not be enough to build an ideological wall against the Warsaw Pact, expanded its radius to a wide variety of fields, including the humanities. A large number of American organisations were either founded specifically for this reason, such as the Fulbright Program, or reoriented, such as the Rockefeller and Ford foundations. The Rockefeller Foundation was convinced that the dissemination of its values was best achieved through the arts. Therefore, the foundation started to support the training of young artists in Turkey, donating over US$792,000 to purchase new equipment and develop human resources in the field of the arts.[1]

Using the example of the Rockefeller-funded scholar Metin And, the aim of this chapter is to describe the role that individual representatives played in the founding of theatrical epistemic communities in Turkey, and the kind of knowledge that was created and disseminated. Metin And, the adopted son of a wealthy winegrowing family from Ankara, Turkey, created a foundation of knowledge including over 1,500 articles and more than 50 books in Turkish, German and English, among other languages. As a scholar, university professor and critic of dance, theatre and opera, And had a profound influence on Turkish cultural life, especially in the field of theatre education.

The term 'epistemic communities' was introduced by the political scientist Peter M. Haas. According to him:

> ... an epistemic community is a network of professionals with recognized expertise and competence in a particular domain

or issue-area. Although an epistemic community may consist of professionals from a variety of disciplines and backgrounds, they have (1) a shared set of normative and principled beliefs, which provide a value-based rationale for the social action of community members; (2) shared causal beliefs, which are derived from their analysis of practices leading or contributing to a central set of problems in their domain and which then serve as the basis for elucidating the multiple linkages between possible policy actions and desired outcomes; (3) shared notions of validity – that is, inter-subjective, internally defined criteria for weighing and validating knowledge in the domain of their expertise; and (4) a common policy enterprise – that is, a set of common practices associated with a set of problems to which their professional competence is directed, presumably out of the conviction that human welfare will be enhanced as a consequence.[2]

Christopher Balme extends the term epistemic communities to encompass cultural and artistic phenomena. He proposes 'that the idea of an epistemic community can be adapted to describe how theatre artists, scholars, critics, and pedagogues organised themselves using the same elements of professionalisation, organisational structures, and trans-national connectivity that distinguish scientific and technical epistemic communities'.[3]

I would argue that such a community was constituted after the founding of the Republic of Turkey in 1923. The republic was established by breaking away from the political and social traditions of the Ottoman Empire in a much more radical way than the Westernisation movement that started in the nineteenth century. This break was mainly realised, especially in military and bureaucratic spheres, through reforms implemented by knowledge-based experts trained in Western values. In the 1920s and 1930s, theatre became an art form of increasing importance. It was accepted as an important tool for disseminating a shared set of normative beliefs and principles that provided a value-based rationale for the social actions of community members, forming what Haas describes as an epistemic community. During this period, theatre in the Western tradition was considered an important tool for the establishment and dissemination of Western values as an alternative to Ottoman religious values. The most important representative and practitioner of this idea in Turkey was the actor and director Muhsin Ertuğrul. He aimed to establish a national theatre tradition based entirely on Western values capable of making a radical break from Ottoman heritage. Before the late

Ottoman Empire, traditional theatre forms – such as the shadow theatre, middle play,[4] and storytellers – existed alongside classical European theatre, and especially the many adaptations that were popular at the time. Yet from 1927, when Ertuğrul became the artistic director of the Ottoman imperial theatre Darülbedayi, to 1949, when he was appointed general director of the State Theatre, he gave the institution the identity of a city theatre. In both the subsidised theatres Ertuğrul directed, only plays based on Western models were consistently performed. Like a lot of intellectuals who closely followed developments in France, Germany and Russia during these years, Ertuğrul tried to learn more about Western art forms, and to this end he studied acting in Paris. On returning home he worked as an actor and instructor at the City Theatre in Istanbul, which was established in 1914 under the name Darülbedayı. In the following years he travelled to Berlin and Moscow to follow developments in Western theatre, also gaining experience with cinema as an art form. In 1927 he assumed the position of general artistic director of the Istanbul City Theatre. In the years that followed, Ertuğrul contributed to the establishment of a conservatory providing acting training in accordance with Western standards. As a manager, actor, director, educator and publisher he also helped spread knowledge of Turkish theatre culture, in the Western sense, in many fields.

The Rockefeller Foundation increased its activities in Turkey during the Cold War. In addition to its long-standing areas of support, such as public health and medicine, the foundation became active in education, in the humanities and in the social sciences, helping policymakers better understand the forces shaping economic, social and political relations.[5] An English literature scholar named John Marshall was hired by the foundation to accomplish its goals in the Middle East. He made regular and extensive trips to Turkey to develop an international knowledge network. Inderjeet Parmar defines this type of network as follows:

> By an international knowledge network is meant a system of coordinated research, results' dissemination and publication, study and often graduate-level teaching, intellectual exchange and financing, across national boundaries. The international networks may also include official policymakers and international aid and other agencies.[6]

In order to establish such a network in Turkey, Marshall sought out people and institutions that could help him find suitable people to realise the foundation's goals. In the field of theatre, which had greatly increased in importance for the foundation during the Cold War, Muhsin Ertuğrul became an important advisor to Marshall. It was important for them to find talented individuals who had the ambition and language skills to continue their education in the US. But the aim of the Rockefeller Foundation was not only to familiarise their scholarship recipients with Western developments, but also to encourage them to build an artistic tradition that considered its own cultural sources. This had been a critical point in the cultural life of Turkey for many years. The turn of educational and administrative institutions toward the West, and their renunciation of Ottoman traditions, was addressed and criticised by many political and cultural figures, and by ambassadors from various countries. Only the field of music seemed to cope with this challenge. In 1948 Marshall noted during one of his first visits to Turkey that 'there is a good deal of activity in Turkey in the field of music: most Turkish composers have had a good deal of activity but are using Turkish Themes in their compositions'.[7] The theatre, on the other hand, was consistently Westernised in those years without considering the Ottoman tradition in any way. Although criticism of the absolute rejection of traditional forms in theatre was voiced in the founding years of the republic, it took another political change before anything happened.

After the death in 1938 of Mustafa Kemal Atatürk, the founding father of the Republic of Turkey, the country continued to be ruled by a single party that still pursued Atatürk's goals of a Western-oriented, secularistic society. According to Feroz Ahmad:

> … despite the radical reforms that transformed Turkey's legal and institutional structure, the public only marginally benefited, while expectations rose dramatically. They were dissatisfied with a state that constantly imposed its will without regard for their feelings; the politics of secularism was never explained to them and they never understood how they benefited from it. Everything that was supposedly done 'for the people' had to be done in spite of the people in many places. (Translation mine.)[8]

The situation changed in 1950 with the electoral victory of the Democrat Party (founded in 1946), which ended the 27-year, one-party reign of Atatürk's Republican People's Party (CHP) and started a new era. The Democrat Party had a more right-wing stance than the CHP, and in a way it would not be wrong to place the party in a traditional or conservative perspective in terms of the importance it attached to religion, tradition and Ottoman history, as Elif Nagihan Türköz explains in her thesis

'Türkiye'de muhafazakar kimliğin inşası' ('The construction of conservative identity in Turkey').[9] These political changes were reflected in all areas of public life, including the theatre. Many plays dealt with the effects of the more liberal economic policies and the religious influence of the time, and in some cases the locations of the plays shifted from the city to countryside villages. But the playwrights of the 1950s were not yet ready to formally detach themselves from Western influences. As mentioned above, there was criticism in the founding years of the republic about the theatre's absolute rejection of traditional forms. In the 1950s this criticism was voiced even more loudly, and the Rockefeller Foundation became aware of the problem. John Marshall, the foundation's officer in Turkey, described the problem in his reports as follows:

> But Turkey has clearly now come to a stage of national development where its faculties are needed in national thinking. To take an example from the humanities, Turks sadly need clarification as to their past, and particularly, their recent past. They have emerged now from the Dogmas … of the regimes of Ataturk and the one party system; in a sense, the advantages of the break with the past that those dogmas allowed have been realized. Increasingly evident now is a psychological hunger to come to terms with all that went before. How good and how bad, to put it bluntly, was the Ottoman Empire after all? … What is there in the literature of Turkey before romanisation, from which Turks educated since are literally cut off, because of their inability to read Turkish written in Arabic characters and in an older vocabulary? A people without a history may be theoretically happy; but a complete break with history … leaves elements of at least psychological unhappiness.[10]

Metin And criticised this break with traditional theatre particularly loudly and openly in his reviews; John Marshall became aware of And through the pieces he wrote on literature, ballet and culture for the magazine *Forum*. In 1956 some of Metin And's texts were translated by the Rockefeller Foundation, after which it decided to grant him a fellowship for one year in New York.

## Metin And: a new beginning for Turkish theatre

While Muhsin Ertuğrul reflected the ideology of the founding of the republic, and strived for the recognition and dissemination of Western theatre in Turkey, Metin And, while adopting the values of the republic, searched for a different Turkish theatre under the influence of the changing political climate. In his book *Atatürk and Theatre*,[11] And wrote that the Westernisation movement was misunderstood by theatre makers such as Ertuğrul, and that Atatürk had suggested a different path in his speeches about the arts. According to And, Atatürk's specific talent was to balance incompatible opposites; according to Atatürk's vision, the main aim for the arts should be to produce something original by blending the old and the new. In And's assessment, Muhsin Ertuğrul caused great damage to Turkish theatre because his concept of the form was not a living theatre, a theatre that established an interactive relationship with the audience. Instead it was a theatre obsessed with formal features, a theatre that was far from original, rather than being a place where the audience had fun.[12]

Metin And wrote and lectured on a wide range of fields, from the history of Turkish theatre to Ottoman mythology and daily life, dance, and opera. Based on different sources, he tried to replace the theatre knowledge laid down by Muhsin Ertuğrul, which was mostly based on Western sources. In this context, And disseminated his knowledge both in Turkey and abroad, acting as a kind of cultural ambassador. Due to his multifaceted work, Talat Sait Halman characterises And as a contemporary Renaissance person.[13]

Born on 17 June 1927 in Istanbul, And was the son of Reşit Çavdar, the general manager of a bank, and Seniha Çavdar, a housewife. And was a typical child of the republic, his childhood years moulded by the republic's founding ideals. This might explain his idealistic attitude in the following years. And attended Galatasaray High School, founded during the Tanzimat period (1839–76), a period of Westernisation, to train bureaucrats for the Ottoman Empire. The school offered a secular education to people of all religions, in French as well as Turkish. In 1946 And graduated from high school and entered the faculty of Law at Istanbul University. After graduating in 1950 he went to London to pursue a master's degree in international economic law at King's College London. Although one third of England was in ruins at the time, there were many cultural and artistic events, and Metin tried to follow them as much as possible. He also travelled to France and Scandinavian countries to watch theatre, opera and ballet performances. One day, while conducting research for his thesis on a special condition in bilateral trade agreements, he realised the work was not for him, and decided to leave the thesis unwritten. He was now sure he wanted to work in the performing arts. However, before returning home he spent four months working for a large champagne company in Germany, having accepted an offer from his uncle and aunt, Sevda and Cenap And, who owned the Kavaklıdere winery in Turkey. The childless couple had chosen Metin as their heir, and ultimately Metin was adopted by the Ands, returning to Ankara in 1953 as Metin And to manage the Kavaklıdere winery.

The Anatolian city of Ankara had replaced Istanbul as the Turkish capital after the establishment of the republic. It was turned into a showcase for the new state, which had turned its face towards the West: in addition to official buildings, theatres and museums designed by famous German architects such as Bruno Taut, the new capital boasted wide roads and parks. Balls, theatre performances and concerts were held in abundance, and there was an active cultural and artistic life. While working as the manager of the Kavaklıdere winery, And wrote articles on various subjects for *Forum*. In 1957 And became the owner of *Forum*, for which he continued to write, mostly about literature. As noted above, it was his writing in *Forum* that led to his scholarship from the Rockefeller Foundation in 1956. In an interview with the writer Füruzan, Metin And described the moment he learnt about the scholarship:

> One day I got a call from the American Embassy. They said, 'The cultural director of the Rockefeller Foundation wants to meet with you'. I went and looked, Bülent Ecevit[14] was also there. I said, 'What's up?' He said, 'John Marshall called me, he wants to talk to me about something.' When it was my turn, I went in, and there was a very polite and extremely cultured man. He knows Turkey like the back of his hand. 'We have translated your ballet articles in the Forum and elsewhere. After reading them, we have decided to give you a scholarship from the Rockefeller Foundation.'[15]

As part of the scholarship, And was sent to New York to watch ballet performances, theatre and opera, attending performances by world-renowned companies such as the Martha Graham Dance Company and the New York City Ballet. In the year and a half he spent there, he also took classes at theatre schools. The Rockefeller Foundation introduced And to three critics, with whom he attended performances, and who taught him how to write newspaper criticism: Brooks Atkinson, theatre critic for the *New York Times*; John Martin, contemporary dance critic for the same paper; and Walter Terry, dance critic for the *New York Herald Tribune*. According to And, writing reviews in the US was a commercial practice, and very important for the success of a play. However, he believed such reviews were not approached aesthetically, and that they therefore lacked in-depth analysis and did not say much to the enthusiast.[16]

And not only wrote criticism after his return to Turkey, drawing on his training as a critic in the US, but also thought about the practice of writing criticism in detail, and tried to define it. He determined there were nine types of critics, including critics who focus on the news value of a performance like a journalist, critics who write academic articles about the plays they watch, and critics who consider the theatre a political arena. If we evaluate And according to his own criteria, it can be said that he was a critic who guided, warned and advised his readers, and partly approached performances like an essayist. It should be noted that his reviews also have academic aspects.

After And's return to Ankara, at the invitation of Bülent Ecevit he began writing dance and theatre criticism for the *Ulus* newspaper in a weekly column titled 'Sahne'. Thanks to these columns, which he wrote for fifteen years, And became more widely known as a critic, and his sphere of influence expanded. Ballerina Meriç Sümen Kanan, who served as the general director of the State Opera and Ballet for many years, appreciated And for his contributions to the field as an expert in the establishment and development of Turkish ballet. She stated that not only did he write articles describing and evaluating what he observed, but also informative and educational pieces.[17] In his newspaper and magazine articles, And traced the origin and importance of Turkish traditional dances and of dance in Islam in addition to classical ballet. Together with Kemal Baytaş, undersecretary of the Ministry of Culture, And also persuaded the Ministry of Culture to establish a state folk dance ensemble, and on 7 May 1976 the ensemble performed its first show in Ankara.[18]

From 1954, when he started writing regularly, until his death in 2006, And published a total of 1,346 articles. These articles show the kind of knowledge that was created and disseminated by him. In his article comparing Byzantine and Turkish theatre, he takes the reader on a journey through time, nations and cultures. In his series of articles on the representation of Turks in European arts and shadow play, he charts a course that eliminates the boundaries between nations and cultures. In addition to music, ballet, opera and theatre, he researched and published on miniatures, mythology, puppetry and daily life in the Ottoman period. In his magazine and newspaper articles, he shared his experiences of developments abroad at a time when television was not yet widespread and people in Turkey had limited opportunities to travel. The transfer of information provided by these articles was a source of inspiration for various artists and institutions. And's assessments and demands regarding cultural policies had a direct impact on the cultural and artistic life of the period.

When John Marshall returned to Turkey in 1958 he met And again, after which he reported to the Rockefeller Foundation:

> And is to play a more and more constructive role in the arts in Ankara. On this visit, it became clear that he is more and more respected by everyone for his impartiality, lack of any personal ambition, and desire to make himself and his Money as useful as possible. At home and abroad he has certainly been taken with the idea of a philanthropic role and is beginning to play it.[19]

As a knowledge-based expert partly trained in Western values, And conducted research on foundations in the US during his fellowship in 1956, and dreamed of establishing a music foundation in Turkey. Ultimately he decided to give up his inheritance right to the Kavaklıdere winery to establish this foundation, but because of problems within the family the foundation was not established until years later. Furthermore, And was excluded from the foundation, and therefore resigned from his position at the winery.

From then on, And continued his life as an educator in addition to his writing. In 1958, at the instigation of Prof. Dr İrfan Şahinbaş, also a fellow of the Rockefeller Foundation and head of the American literature department at Ankara University (a department founded by Şahinbaş in 1957), a theatre institute was established that treated theatre as an academic discipline, conducted research and provided education on the subject. Such a branch of education was needed to produce qualified playwrights and critics, and a conscious audience. Influential people such as Muhsin Ertuğrul believed that Turkish theatre could reach the level of Western theatre, to which it looked up, through such education. In the newly established department, Metin And attended playwriting classes financed by the Rockefeller Foundation and delivered by theatre producer, critic and academic Kenneth MacGowan. The department of theatre, which started with a two-year programme in 1958, was reopened as a four-year diploma programme in 1964–5. And worked there as a lecturer until 2006, and as an administrator for a few years.

During this time And focused on researching and teaching areas that had been neglected for years in Turkey's Westernisation adventure. He dealt with the subject of Turkish theatre in four stages, each stage representing an important political turning point. This resulted in four books:

*Traditional Turkish Theatre: Shadow theatre, middle play, meddah and
    puppet theatre;*
*Turkish Theatre in the Tanzimat Period and the Istibdat Period (1839–1908);*
*Turkish Theatre in the Constitutional Monarchy Period (1908–1923);* and
*Republican Period Turkish Theatre (1923–1983).*

With these books, And created a corpus that is still the most important
reference source in the field of Turkish theatre history.

And included mythology in his syllabus, but he preferred to teach his
students Sumerian, Hittite, Hebrew, Phrygian and Assyrian mythology
rather than the familiar Greek mythology. By tracing Anatolian history
and traditions, And created a foundation for a Turkish identity, and thus
for Turkish theatre, that was specific to the republican period and not
confined to Islamic identity, as it was during the Ottoman Empire. And
encouraged his students to familiarise themselves with the culture in
which they lived, and to produce artistic works that were nourished by
it. In an interview with Füruzan, he explained that his students wrote
and staged plays based on the study of local and traditional subjects
including folklore, Anatolian conversation traditions and Hacı Bektaş
Veli ceremonies.[20] These plays were performed at the annual Istanbul
Music and Art Festival as well as at the university, bringing them to a
wider audience. Among the students trained by And, three individuals
in particular should be mentioned: Nurhan Karadağ, who specialised in
plays based on Anatolian myths and traditions, and combined elements
of traditional Turkish theatre with contemporary practices, also teaching
courses in this area; Ayşe Selen, who combined the meddah tradition
(traditional oral storytelling) with contemporary storytelling; and poet
and novelist Murathan Mungan, author of the *Mesopotamia Trilogy.*
Mungan, who grew up in the south-eastern Anatolian region of Turkey
with the myths of the region, has attempted to adapt traditional narratives
in the form of tragedy, and has successfully done so in the plays *Mahmud
and Yezida, Taziye* and *Deer and Curses.* In these plays, Mungan uses local
dialect and, at the same time, poetic language to talk about the blood
feuds between tribes, impossible loves, oppressed women who can only
survive in the traditional patriarchal order by giving birth to children,
and curses passed down from generation to generation. In this way, the
author draws the Western audience of the country into a world with
which they are completely unfamiliar using a theatrical format they
know.

An exploration of cultural and theatrical traditions meets the
reader in And's first book on traditional Turkish theatre, *Geleneksel*

*Türk Tiyatrosu*, which was published in 1969. In 1985 the book was reissued in a slightly revised version. In the preface to the second edition, And pointed out that although interest in traditional theatre had not increased as much as he had hoped in the 16 years since the first edition, there had been some changes in the theatre world. For example, in the 1980s a graduate of Ankara University's theatre department conducted regular shadow and puppet theatre performances at the State Theatre; a competition organised by the Ministry of Tourism selected 12 shadow-theatre performances to continue this traditional art throughout Turkey; and the first festival of traditional theatre was held in three different Turkish cities. In the 1960s, a relatively liberal political climate prevailed in Turkey, allowing texts by left-wing authors to be translated and published; now Bertolt Brecht's texts could also be translated and published, leading to lively discussion about the similarity between the alienation effect and traditional Turkish theatre. A number of Turkish authors, including Haldun Taner, Turgut Özakman and Oktay Arayıcı, processed traditional Turkish elements, which had become more topical, in their texts.[21] Although the developments in playwriting that started in the 1960s and continued into the 1970s led to the emergence of a new consciousness in Turkish theatre, the creative works that emerged from this consciousness, which were remarkable in terms of developing their own original language, remained in a limited number in Turkish theatre literature. According to theatre researcher Yavuz Pekman, Turkish theatre continued to struggle with finding its own language and identity at this time.[22]

The question of the identity of Turkish theatre was consistently an important topic for authors and scholars in Turkey, prompting And to talk about it abroad. With his travels, And sought not only to spread knowledge of Turkish culture and art beyond national borders, but also to follow across cultural boundaries the historical traces of the Turks that have influenced theatre since time immemorial. He gave lectures at New York University for two semesters, at Tokyo University for one semester and at the Justus Liebig University Giessen in Germany for one semester. In addition to the numerous international symposia and conferences And attended during his career, he also undertook a number of research and conference trips, including one in 1962 to the Soviet Union, where he attended ballet and theatre performances and gave lectures. In 1964 he undertook a lecture tour with stops in Beirut, Baghdad, Tehran, Kabul, Karachi, Lahore, New Delhi and Bombay; in 1965 he travelled through 13 German cities giving lectures on Turkish theatre and its transnational influences; in 1966 he made a similar lecture tour through 11 US cities; and in 1978 he gave 30 lectures at 14 US universities, including Princeton, Columbia, Yale and the universities of Chicago and Michigan. In the 1980s his travels led him to China, where he gave a lecture on the influence of Turkish theatre on Chinese theatre (1983), and to Japan where he again gave lectures on Turkish theatre (1985). These many lecture tours illustrate the wide international network And established with other specialists in both the West and the East. According to the American sociologist Mark Granovetter, these were largely hetero-philic networks with weak ties that allowed knowledge flow in both directions.[23]

Some of And's books reveal his concern with the transnational transfer of knowledge. For example, in the book *La Scena Italiana in Turchia – La Turchia sulla Scena Italiana*, published in Italian and also available in a Turkish translation, he deals with the work of Italian artists in the Ottoman Empire and their influence on Italian art, as well as the representation of Turks in Italian stage art; the book is also a well-researched source on the historical relations between the two countries, and their exchanges in the field of art. A similar approach is taken in his book *Gönlü Yüce Türk: Yüzyıllar Boyunca Bale Eserlerinde Türkler* (The Turk with the Great Soul: The Turk in the ballet works of the centuries). Another book that deals with cross-border influences in the arts, examining the role of Turkish stage art, is *Drama at the Crossroads: Turkish performing arts link past and present, East and West*.[24] And summarised the aim of the book as follows:

> This study has certain objectives. Firstly, to define the basic patterns of the rituals and predramatics of the ancient cultures of the Near East. Secondly, to elucidate the forms of the earlier rituals and predramatic performances in the Turkic and Islamic countries. And thirdly, to clarify the relationship between the first and the second through extant materials and survivals. Though the expansion of Turkic and Islamic cultures spread these out centrifugally in different areas away from one another, here the focus is especially on the eastern Mediterranean regions and on Central Asia, because the repeated patterns seem so clear and so explicit. When they are considered as a whole, it seems unreasonable to think that all these similar observances are unrelated.[25]

And walks a labyrinthine and at times risky path in the book, as the time span he examines is gigantic, knowledge about the way people lived in the distant past is insufficient, and Islamic culture has developed from a complex mix of cultures. And defines the Turkish dramatic art of Asia Minor as based on five areas of influence: place, ancestry, empire, Islam and Westernisation.[26] The impact of place goes back to the Turks encountering pre-existing cultures in the regions where they settled, the traces of which can be found mainly in village plays and rituals. The impact of ancestry relates to the fact that the Turks brought traditional cultural and religious characteristics with them from Central Asia. The impact of the Ottoman Empire on dramatic art came from ruling over a multitude of peoples on three continents, where a degree of cultural exchange took place. In And's assessment, Islam was a hindrance to the development of dramatic art, but the influences of Arab and Iranian culture must also be taken into account in understanding Turkish dramatic art. However, the greatest influence on today's Turkish theatre is attributed by And to Westernisation. For this reason, he placed a special emphasis on the Tanzimat period, because in his opinion it had not received the recognition it deserved with regard to the development of Western theatre in Turkey.

The steps taken during the Tanzimat period reflect a contradictory tendency: emulating the theatre of a world that is incompatible with the structure of one's own society, as opposed to taking efforts to ensure the writing of original works, and the formation of a local sensibility in the establishment of a national theatre. Innovative Ottoman sultans such as Selim III, Mahmud II and Abdülmecid, who decided to open up to the West in response to political and economic pressures, and the literati that shared this view, played a significant role in the introduction of Western theatre to Turkey. Through the mediation of foreign embassies in Istanbul and the initiative of minorities who could approach the West more easily, Western forms were tried out in various branches of art, and theatre as an institution began to attract great interest from the palace and the public. The support of the palace was not limited to foreign troupes coming to Istanbul, and theatre halls were built in the Çırağan, Dolmabahçe and Yıldız palaces. The first Turkish play written in the Western dramatic form was *Şair Evlenmesi* (1860) by İbrahim Şinasi, which was written to be performed at the Dolmabahçe Palace theatre. Meanwhile Italian, French, German and Austrian theatre, opera and ballet companies, and world-famous artists such as Adelaide Ristori and Sarah Bernhardt, gave performances in Istanbul and Izmir, making these cities important art centres.[27]

For Metin And, this period of Turkish theatre history is the most interesting. In his opinion, nowhere else, and at no other time, was there such a creative and stimulating engagement with a foreign culture as during the Tanzimat period. He describes in the preface of his book about the Tanzimat theatre, *Tanzimat ve İstibdat Döneminde Türk Tiyatro (1839–1908)*, how much he empathised with the artists of the time, how he laughed and cried with them while researching the period. But he also points out that, based on documents, he was neutral when he wrote about this period.[28] This information is important because it reveals how And dealt with historical material and put it down on paper. After he had empathised with the historical context of his subject and determined he therefore understood it, he put his feelings aside and tried to write about the material in as neutral and source-based a way as possible. In his estimation he is as neutral as a Vaka'nüs (a chronicler in the Ottoman Empire who recorded data about important personalities without offering an interpretation).[29] In his books, And refrains from talking about people, works or productions in an interpretative and evaluative way. For example, he describes the period from 1908 to 1923, relatively neutrally, as a period in which the atmosphere of freedom that came with the restoration of constitutional monarchy in 1908 brought a great vitality to theatrical life in Istanbul. Many writers and artists who wanted to exercise their right to participate in and influence the government, granted to citizens by the constitution, considered the theatre a convenient tool to reflect their views. Plays took as their subjects victories from Ottoman history, heroic epics, polygamy, extramarital affairs, women's rights, exploitation and corruption in the villages. The art of theatre, which was mostly supported by Armenian actors during the Tanzimat period, became stronger and more widespread with the participation of Turkish actors during the Second Constitutional Period. Thus, the foundations of the republican theatre after 1923 were laid with the training opportunities the period provided to new writers and theatre artists. Efforts were also made to explain theatre to the public and to educate people on audience etiquette: theatregoers were instructed through programmes and flyers to come to the theatre in clean, dark clothes, not to speak loudly during the play and not to eat nuts or peanuts.[30]

However, in the following volume on the theatre of the republic from 1923 to 1973 (on the occasion of the fiftieth anniversary of the founding of the republic), And takes a clear stand, explaining in detail the mistakes made in the founding of modern theatre, especially by Muhsin Ertuğrul. As explained above, Atatürk's idea of an innovative theatre was to balance incompatible opposites; in other words, the main aim for the arts should be to produce something original by blending the old and the new. And emphasised that Atatürk desired to establish a kind of people's theatre, a theatre intended for the people that would raise their cultural understanding. But in And's opinion, the founders of theatre in the early republic did not succeed in implementing Turkish theatre with traditional elements because they did not think traditional theatre forms were actually art. Ertuğrul wanted to raise the audience's aesthetic understanding mainly with productions of the classics, and thus, according to And, turned the theatre into a kind of intellectual museum. Despite his criticisms of Ertuğrul, however, And cannot avoid writing about him in almost every chapter of the book because he was active as an actor, director, trainer and theoretician in almost all areas of the theatre, and had a decisive influence on its development. And accuses Ertuğrul of having created a one-man theatre culture, closed to criticism. Under Ertuğrul's direction, Western theatre was copied (through translation), and new Turkish texts were created according to the same patterns, staged at subsidised theatres under his directorship. And, on the other hand, explicitly advocated for the creation of a new memory in theatre. But he also made it clear there was no point in simply adopting formal elements from traditional Turkish theatre forms, such as Ortaoyunu (middle play) or Karagöz (shadow theatre figure), in order to create '[one's] own, national theatre'. According to And, all that was needed to call a play Turkish was a Turkish author bringing their own personal world of experience into the play. In dealing with traditional forms, he gives the example of Carlo Gozzi and Carlo Goldoni, who not only copied forms of the commedia dell'arte but also examined their essence and transferred them to their time.[31]

In a figurative sense one can speak of a third space for Turkish theatre, one that neither adheres to Ertuğrul's strict Western standards nor restricts itself to traditional forms, but that occupies an in-between position according to Stuart Hall's idea of an identity that 'knows where it comes from, where it's at home, but which also lives in a symbolic way, being aware that they are creators in a third space which must continuously be repositioned and defined'.[32] And's research was not only about reconstructing theatre history; he also loved Ottoman history and art in general. He created a memory of the Turks' cultural roots with his work, moving from Islamic culture and pre-Islamic rituals to Turkish Ottoman miniatures and public life in the Ottoman Empire. Remembering these roots was, in his opinion, important for the foundation not only of a 'true national theatre' but also of a 'true Turkish identity'. He also tried to offer a corrective to the Western influence introduced to Turkish theatre by Ertuğrul. In And's opinion, a multitude of achievements attributed to Ertuğrul actually predated him, but had not been recognised previously. In this respect, And's main concern was to make the Western theatre of the minorities of the Ottoman Empire (Armenians, Greeks and Jews) and its influence on Turkish theatre visible, because this knowledge was largely forgotten after the foundation of the Turkish republic.

The following diagram represents how And created networks and transmitted his knowledge.

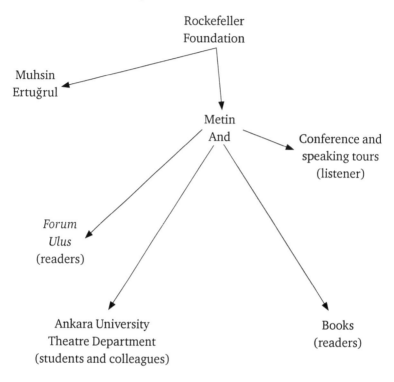

The diagram not only shows the areas in which And developed networks and imparted knowledge, but also, interestingly, that he has nothing in common with Ertuğrul, the most influential figure of twentieth-century Turkish theatre. Both were highly regarded and both were supported by the Rockefeller Foundation, but their ideas about what modern Turkish theatre should look like differed greatly.

## Conclusion

Talat Sait Halman compared Metin And's work to an imposing tree of life with deep roots in the earth, its fruitful branches representing the many different fields in which he worked[33] – a tree that has endured, bearing fruit that has been picked and consumed by many people over the years. There are three main ways in which And spread his branches, passing the fruit to others: as a critic, with numerous texts on dance, theatre and cultural life abroad and at home, which appeared in *Forum*, the *Ulus* newspaper and, from time to time, in other publications; as a scholar, his extensive research published in a total of 54 books and other texts, and passed directly to students through his teaching; and as a speaker, at the many conferences and lectures he gave around the world.

As a theatre historian, And is distinguished by his detailed research and reconstruction of Turkish theatre history. But above all he stands for a theatre history that overcame the political caesura of 1923, the founding of the Republic of Turkey. The reform movements of the nineteenth century led to a rapprochement with European art and culture, but this was often met with mistrust by the general public. Engaging with Western art was reserved for a courtly elite and the military and bureaucratic ruling classes, while the general population continued to entertain itself with traditional forms. With the founding of the republic, theatre based on the Western model was ascribed an important social function: to communicate the values and ideals of the newly founded republic to broad sections of the population. And stands for a different Western-oriented theatre. He criticised the strict copying of Western models in art, especially in theatre, and advocated a return to the cultural roots of the Turks. This was not, however, a nostalgic, wistful yearning for times past, but rather an effort to create a basis for a creative and confident confrontation with tradition leading to a contemporary theatre of its own. In conclusion, it can be said that And not only filled gaps in knowledge that arose during the Westernisation process, but also had a clear vision for the identity of Turkish theatre. As a critic, teacher and author he disseminated this knowledge across national borders, and thus, in the spirit of the Rockefeller Foundation, established a network of specialists who have had a lasting influence on Turkish theatre.

## Notes

1  Rose, 2008, 22.
2  Haas, 1992, 3.
3  Balme, 2019, 4.
4  'Middle play' is one of many different names given to a form of folk theatre; the basis of Turkish folk theatre comes from the middle play. Middle play is a theatre without a fixed text, and has a system that is passed from master to apprentice. It is considered a revival of Hacivat and Karagöz, the traditional Turkish shadow play. Middle play is rooted in the people, and critiques societal problems through comedy. The middle play is improvised in the open and among the people.
5  Rose, 2008, 4.
6  Parmar, 2002, 13.

7   Marshall, 1948, 12.
8   Ahmad, 1995, 151.
9   Türköz, 2011, 71.
10  Marshall, 1955, 11.
11  And, 1983, 9.
12  And, 1983, 2.
13  Halman, 2007, 12.
14  Bülent Ecevit, journalist and fellow of the Rockefeller Foundation, worked with And at *Forum* magazine and served as prime minister of Turkey in the 1970s and 1990s.
15  And, 1999, 56.
16  And, 1999, 58.
17  Sümen Kanan, 2007, 188.
18  Halman, 2007, 15–16.
19  Marshall, 1958.
20  And, 1999.
21  And, 1985, 5–6.
22  Pekman, 2002, 209.
23  Granovetter, 1983, 44.
24  And, 1991, 4.
25  And, 1991, 5.
26  And, 2004, 9.
27  General Directorate of State Theatres, 2017.
28  And, 1972, 118.
29  And, 1973, 12.
30  General Directorate of State Theatres, 2017.
31  And, 1963, 17.
32  Hall, 1994, 25.
33  Halman, 2007, 12.

# References

Ada, Serhan. 'Sınırsız bir merakla oyuna adanmış: Metin And ile Ankara'da söyleşi'. In *Metin And'a Armağan*, edited by M. Sabri Koz, 97–116. Istanbul: Yapı Kredi Kültür ve Sanat Yayınları, 2007.

Ahmad, Feroz. *Modern Türkiye'nin oluşumu*. Istanbul: Sarmal Yayınevi, 1995.

And, Metin. 'Yazarlarımızın yerli kaynaklar'ı', *Forum* 232 Aralık (1963): 23–5.

And, Metin. *Tanzimat ve İstibdat Döneminde Türk Tiyatrosu (1839–1908)*. Ankara: Türkiye İş Bankası Kültür Yayınları, 1972.

And, Metin. *50 Yılın Türk Tiyatrosu*. İstanbul: Türkiye İş Bankası Yayınları, 1973.

And, Metin. *Ataç Tiyatroda*. Ankara: Kültür ve Turizm Bakanlığı Yayınları, 1982.

And, Metin. *Atatürk ve Tiyatro*. Ankara: Devlet Tiyatroları Yayınları, 1983.

And, Metin. *Geleneksel Türk Tiyatrosu: Köylü ve halk tiyatrosu gelenekleri*. Istanbul: Inkilap Yayınları, 1985.

And, Metin. *Drama at the Crossroads: Turkish performing arts link past and present, East and West*. Istanbul: Isis Verlag, 1991.

And, Metin. 'Interview with Füruzan', *Sanat Dünyamız* 72 (1999): 12–28.

And, Metin. *Başlangıcından 1983'e Türk Tiyatro Tarihi*. Istanbul: İletişim Yayınları, 2004.

Balme, Christopher. 'Building theatrical epistemic communities in the Global South: expert networks, philanthropy and theatre studies in Nigeria 1959–1969', *Journal of Global Theatre History* 3 (2) (2019): 3–18.

General Directorate of State Theatres. 'Bati Tiyatrosu'. Accessed 12 July 2017. https://www.kultur portali.gov.tr/portal/bati-tiyatrosu.

Granovetter, Mark. 'The strength of weak ties: a network theory revisited', *Sociological Theory* 1 (1983): 201–33.

Haas, Peter M. 'Epistemic communities and international policy coordination', *International Organization* 46 (1) (1992): 1–35.

Hall, Stuart. *Rassismus und Kulturelle Identität*. Hamburg: Argument Verlag, 1994.

Halman, Talat Sait. 'And'ımız anıtımız'. In *Metin And'a Armağan*, edited by M. Sabri Koz, 12–18. Istanbul: Yapı Kredi Kültür ve Sanat Yayınları, 2007.

Marshall, John. 'Art in humanities', diary entry 10 December (1948): 11–12. Rockefeller Archive Center. Accessed 12 July 2020. https://raccess.rockarch.org/aeon.dll?Action=10&Form=10.

Marshall, John. 'Art in humanities', diary entry 5 March (1955): 3–5. Rockefeller Archive Center. Accessed 12 July 2017. https://dimes.rockarch.org/xtf/search?keyword=john%20marshall%20;f1- geogname=Turkey.

Parmar, Inderjeet. 'American foundations and the development of international knowledge networks', *Global Networks* 2 (1) (2002): 13–30.

Pekman, Yavuz. *Çağdaş Tiyatromuzda Geleneksellik*. Istanbul: Mitos Boyut Yayınları, 2002.

Rose, W. Kenneth. 'The Rockefeller Foundation's fellowship program in Turkey, 1925–1983', Rockefeller Archive Center, 2008. Accessed 19 August 2021. https://rockarch.issuelab.org/resource/the-rockefeller-foundation-s-fellowship-program-in-turkey-1925-1983.html.

Sümen Kanan, Meriç. 'Metin And'. In *Metin And'a Armağan*, edited by M. Sabri Koz, 188. Istanbul: Yapı Kredi Kültür ve Sanat Yayınları, 2007.

Türköz, Elif Nagihan. 'Türkiye'de muhafazakar kimliğin inşası'. Afyonkarahisar: Afyon Kocatepe Üniversitesi, 2011.

## 11

# Augusto Boal's transnational networks of the Theatre of the Oppressed

## Clara de Andrade and Christopher B. Balme

## Introduction

The Brazilian director and activist Augusto Boal is one of the defining figures of international postwar theatre. His method, known as the Theatre of the Oppressed, is employed around the world, and his influence can only really be compared to that of Stanislavsky and Brecht. Although methods such as forum theatre, invisible theatre and legislative theatre are well known, and are today part and parcel of the applied theatre toolbox, what is less well understood is how the remarkable diffusion and dissemination of these modalities took place. How did the techniques of a radical, transgressive theatre – developed in exile under extremely difficult, sometimes dangerous circumstances – coalesce into the institutional form known as Theatre of the Oppressed?

This chapter traces Boal's journey and that of his method as an example of theatrical institutionalisation, developing from a loose network to a much more fixed institutional form.[1] The chapter is divided into five sections: the first outlines key concepts, such as networks and institutionalisation, and situates Boal's career within the context of institutional theory; the second and third traces Boal's journey as an example of a circulating method that gained in institutional strength as it moved through different national and cultural contexts, from Brazil to Argentina to Peru to France, where it gained a much more secure financial foundation and organisational form; the fourth section explores how the method spread to other countries, such as India, before Boal returned to Brazil from exile in 1986, becoming a city councillor in Rio and implementing the concept of legislative theatre. The final section traces how in the late 1990s and 2000s Boal's method became part of transnational flows that achieved dissemination throughout the world.

## From networks to institutionalisation

The concept of institution is notoriously difficult to pin down, even in disciplines such as sociology, economics and political science, for which it is a major field of research. Theatre studies has tended to avoid the term altogether, or to regard it, in the spirit of the avant-garde, as something to be overcome and transcended; institutionalised theatre with its associations of rigidity and tradition is something to which the avant-garde, experimental theatre practitioner is opposed on principle.

The last three decades have seen a revolution in institutional theory usually subsumed under the label of neo-institutionalism. This reconceptualisation of the relationship between institutions and organisations has provided a much more flexible framework for understanding how institutions affect our daily lives, and revealed that there are few domains, including theatre, that are not in some way influenced by institutional structures. Neo-institutional approaches tend to draw a clear distinction between institution and organisation, with the former referring to abstract rules and frameworks that are manifested in individual organisations, the two levels linked by reciprocal relationships.[2]

According to neo-institutional theory, the relationship between institutions and the societies in which they are located is determined by a desire and need for legitimacy. As noted by Jeannette Colyvas and Walter Powell, 'Legitimacy is perhaps the most central concept in institutional research',[3] and can be defined as a set of beliefs by which collectives not only accept rules and constraints, but bring their practices in line with these rules and ideas. This institutional 'cognitive pillar'[4] means that such cognitive frameworks are often more important than normative ones, such as laws, which makes them very conducive to change. A key indicator of institutionalisation is the status of taken-for-granted-ness – a central cognitive pillar for any institution. A key factor in any kind of institutionalisation is the co-optation of prevailing ideas that provide the ideological basis for legitimisation.

Theatre scholars tend to concern themselves with the organisational level – individual artists, theatres and theatre companies – because it is here that theatre is made and becomes visible. Less visible is the institutional level, which in most cases involves some form of exogenous support such as a ministry of culture, a state-funded university or private funding, be it institutional aid or private, usually tax-deductible, financial support. All these forms of exogenous support create rules and constraints, which are nevertheless highly mutable. It is in the interaction between the institutional and the organisational level that structures amenable to theatre historiographical analysis emerge.

There are three discrete areas that need to be disambiguated in the example of Boal's Theatre of the Oppressed: individual actions, connections through networks and institutionalisation in the sense of semi-permanent structures independent of specific individuals or groups. Augusto Boal's role as charismatic founder provides the chronological beginning of the process. There exists a tradition in twentieth-century theatre – indeed it may even be a feature of theatrical modernism – of charismatic artists establishing institutionalised organisations with a claim to permanence. Stanislavsky's Moscow Art Theatre, Brecht's Berliner Ensemble and Giorgio Strehler's Piccolo Teatro are all examples of largely private initiatives acquiring permanence through state support.[5] The concept of charisma refers to Max Weber's essay[6] on forms of legitimate authority or rule, of which charisma is institutionally the most unstable because it is so closely tied to the biological body of a special individual.[7] As we shall see, Boal's Theatre of the Oppressed has survived the passing of its progenitor, and has already established relatively firm institutional structures, albeit in the form of networks.

Networks are by definition a set of relations or edges between nodes. From this basic understanding, network theory has developed a much more nuanced understanding of the types and functions of networks. Networks are probably at their most efficacious when sustained by heterophilic or weak ties as opposed to homophilic or strong ones.[8] While this may sound counterintuitive, network theory has demonstrated empirically that heterophilic networks are more conducive to innovation than homophilic ones. As sociologist Mark Granovetter argues, homophilic networks such as families or clans are strong in terms of internal cohesion but often resistant to change: 'New ideas will spread slowly, scientific endeavors will be handicapped, and subgroups separated by race, ethnicity, geography, or other characteristics will have difficulty reaching a modus vivendi.'[9] As we shall see, Boal's Theatre of the Oppressed begins as an ego network – that is, one centred on an individual – but quickly transforms into a heterophilic one by forming ties and connections in many different countries and cultures, especially with state and philanthropic funding bodies. This latter phase, in which the network takes on visible organisational form, is the result of institutionalisation processes in the stricter sense.

When we speak of institutionalisation, even in the heuristic sense employed here, we mean the gradual recognition of a network or organisational field as important and therefore in some way worthy of permanence. The means by which individuals and organisations coalesce into a field and thereby attain institutional legitimacy is one of the main concerns of organisational studies.[10] The path to legitimacy is invariably a historical process that can be reconstructed. In an early study, sociologist Paul DiMaggio traced how the largely amateur little theatre movement in the US gained professional legitimacy by adopting the organisational and legal form of the trustee-governed, non-profit enterprise already established for the visual arts and classical music.[11] A more recent investigation into early educational cinema in the US defines institutionalisation in terms of 'a stabilization of sorts – the coalescing of various one-off experiments or isolated initiatives into a field characterised by regularised modes of production, distribution, and exhibition', as well as the establishment of 'norms and conventions'.[12] In both these examples one can observe a transition from loosely organised networks – meaning in this case usually informal groups of like-minded individuals and associations – to more permanent organisational forms, potentially leading to political recognition in the form of charters, incorporation or regular subsidy.[13] These processes are often accompanied by trends towards professionalisation, which allows employees to shift easily between organisations, a clear sign of the isomorphism required of any organisational field.[14]

In the following examination of Boal's Theatre of the Oppressed we will reconstruct the institutionalisation process through which a charismatic founder built an informal network that, when it moved to France in the 1980s, found political legitimacy within the framework of the new cultural policies, which privileged social development, advanced by the socialist government. From a small group connected by loose associations the network grew into an established organisational field, expanding again after Boal returned to Brazil and entered politics, and gained further legitimacy in the context of the cultural policies promoted by the first Lula government (2003–10). From there the method grew transnationally, establishing itself in numerous countries.

## Theatre of the Oppressed: a circulating method

Before the creation of the Theatre of the Oppressed, during the 1950s and 1960s, Augusto Boal had already established an international network of contacts in the theatre world. After an internship at Columbia University and a period as a visiting student at the Actors Studio in New York in the 1950s, he returned to Brazil with experience of playwriting, gained in John Gassner's seminars, and Stanislavsky's 'method'. By the 1960s, as director of the Teatro de Arena in São Paulo, Boal was well known in international theatre circles, having toured with his group to the US (thanks to Joanne Pottlitzer and Richard Schechner), and taken part several times in the Nancy International Festival in France at the invitation of the then festival director, Jack Lang. This early network, as well as Boal's subsequent life in exile, certainly contributed in the following decades to the transnational expansion and growing legitimisation of the Theatre of the Oppressed worldwide.

In his early career, Boal gained extensive experience as an author, director and introducer of new theatrical techniques at the Teatro de Arena, where he created workshops on naturalistic acting, taught seminars on dramaturgy, and wrote and staged acclaimed plays such as *Opinião* and *Arena Conta Zumbi* that offered powerful denunciations of Brazil's military dictatorship. In his search for a theatre that was liberating (for both practitioners and the audience) and politically engaged, and that could survive under dictatorial regimes, he started researching techniques that would later give rise to the Theatre of the Oppressed. By transferring the means of art production to the audience, he became an investigator of the artistic processes through which ordinary people became the authors of their own aesthetic experience – something he first explored through his newspaper theatre technique. In one of the most repressive periods of Brazil's military dictatorship, during the government of General Médici, the creation of scenes produced overnight using the morning newspapers was a way to escape harsh censorship, which after 1968 increasingly targeted plays and theatre groups.

In 1971 Boal was kidnapped and arrested by the military dictatorship. He underwent torture and systematic interrogation, and was kept in solitary confinement for a month in the Department of Political and Social Order. He was then held as a political prisoner at the Tiradentes penitentiary in São Paulo for two more months. That same year he went into involuntary exile, living outside Brazil for the next 15 years and experiencing another form of censorship, as he was prevented from working in his own country.[15] The Theatre of the Oppressed was shaped while Boal was on the move during his exile – from 1971 to 1986 – crossing borders and experiencing different political regimes.

Like the newspaper theatre technique, created as a reaction to the intensification of censorship in Brazil, Boal's proposals for the radical transformation of the actor–spectator relationship emerged as a political and aesthetic response to the authoritarianism that plagued the South American continent. The method's development initially followed the trajectory of Boal's travels in Latin America. Setting off for Argentina in 1971, which at the time enjoyed the cover of being a 'democratic dictatorship',[16] Boal experimented with invisible theatre with a group of actors from Buenos Aires. After that, in Peru, while taking part in a literacy programme inspired by the Brazilian educator and philosopher Paulo Freire, and working with people from different indigenous groups who spoke multiple dialects, Boal investigated non-verbal communication, which led to the development of the image theatre technique. While in Peru, Boal said he 'discovered'[17] forum theatre, a modality of the Theatre of the Oppressed in which the spectator joins the scene, becoming an actor or 'spect-actor'. Confronted with a scenario of oppression, the spectator is invited to directly intervene, suggesting and re-enacting a dramatic action that might resolve the conflict. By first performing the action on stage, the 'spect-actor' can rehearse the transformation of reality itself. In forum theatre, the most internationally widespread technique of the Theatre of the Oppressed, the performance is in Boal's words 'a preparation for action'.[18]

After a period in Portugal Boal lived principally in France, where he developed techniques designed to uncover a subject's internalised oppression, known as the cop in the head and the rainbow of desire. During this period a greater systematisation and dissemination of his techniques began. From France, the Theatre of the Oppressed spread to countries in Africa and Asia. Only then did the method travel to a re-democratised Brazil. An understanding of the development of the Theatre of the Oppressed in France is key to comprehending its subsequent transnational expansion and institutionalisation.

## Theatre of the Oppressed in France: the starting point

Augusto Boal arrived in France at a moment of cultural effervescence. His presence, and the publication of his book *Theatre of the Oppressed* in French in 1979, provoked an intense debate on the applicability and adaptation of the Theatre of the Oppressed method in new countries. During Boal's exile in Paris, an entire generation of theatre artists, intellectuals and pedagogues gathered around him and founded the first group devoted to researching and practising the Theatre of the Oppressed, the Groupe Boal. Following the rapid spread of Theatre of the Oppressed techniques, the group saw an urgent need to found a reference centre for the method.

The institutionalisation of the Boal method began with the establishment of the first centre for the Theatre of the Oppressed, a non-governmental organisation. The centre d'étude et de diffusion des techniques actives d'expression (Méthodes Boal), or Le CEDITADE, founded in Paris in 1979, acted as a studio for the development and adaptation of the method, and for research and reflection, while at the same time providing a centre for the diffusion of Theatre of the Oppressed techniques. This ongoing transformation of the Boal method was documented in newsletters – *Bulletins du Théâtre de l'Opprimé* – published by the Groupe Boal. These newsletters drew attention to previously unknown articles by Boal and his collaborators, as well as publishing reports of new practitioners in Germany, Belgium, Canada and Brazil. By facilitating the exchange of information among Theatre of the Oppressed practitioners from different countries, the Parisian journal acted as a tool for circulating the method[19] and contributed to the formation of an international network of practitioners.[20] During this period, author and critic Émile Copfermann, editor of Boal's books in France, played a central role in introducing the Theatre of the Oppressed to the French public. Besides being initially responsible for editing the *Bulletins du Théâtre de l'Opprimé*, the writer presented Boal's work to the artistic-intellectual world and re-established connections with influential individuals such as Jack Lang, who would soon become minister of culture in the government of François Mitterrand.

Until that point, the members of Groupe Boal had aligned their experiments in different types of social and political intervention in France with a search for distinct forms of economic support. The group also experimented with forum theatre in corporate contexts, such as by creating workshops for employees of Air France. However, this intervention method was not considered Theatre of the Oppressed by Boal or his followers. Another form of support explored by the Paris group was to integrate the Theatre of the Oppressed into the institutional framework of French art theatre by performing in theatres – and charging accordingly – rather than performing in social centres or on the street.[21]

Between these attempts, social changes in 1980s France favoured the group's adaptation to modes of production connected to the funding of the social-development field. In 1981 François Mitterrand was elected France's first socialist president, and the subsequent financial support provided by Mitterrand's government was paramount to the institutionalisation and spread of the Theatre of the Oppressed.

The Boal method arrived in France at precisely the moment when public policy regarding theatre shifted from a notion of cultural democratisation to one of cultural democracy, grounded in the concept of culture as a social development and an expression of local culture.[22] Thus, the Theatre of the Oppressed was applied as a mediation methodology within local communities and in social centres across France. The method gained cachet in the new and increasingly important context of cultural democracy, and of culture as a form of social development. The centre for the Theatre of the Oppressed in Paris was primed to co-opt these new French policies, thus accelerating both the institutionalisation of the method and the professionalisation of its practitioners.

By moving into the field of local political action, the Theatre of the Oppressed reached a point of institutional no return. New practitioners, adapting the method to local cultural realities, started to perform forum theatre independently with social groups from their own cities. Such dynamics of appropriation, and the simultaneous diffusion of techniques, contributed to experiments with the method in other European countries, thereby multiplying significantly the number of practitioners. Additionally, the multicultural experience with excluded groups in France prepared the Theatre of the Oppressed for a dialogue with the diverse cultures it encountered on its path towards internationalisation.[23]

The projects and pioneering expeditions of the Groupe Boal paved the way for an even larger-scale diffusion of the Theatre of the Oppressed method, which was disseminated through workshops given by Boal and by the members of the CEDITADE. Between 1979 and 1984 these workshops took place in several European countries and further afield in Réunion, Canada and Brazil.

In the 1990s, following the dissolution of the CEDITADE, several independent groups sprang up, contributing to an increasingly autonomous diffusion of the method. In addition, the publication of Augusto Boal's books in French and English, and subsequently several other languages, from the late 1970s, allowed the Theatre of the Oppressed to spread all over Europe and to countries in Africa and Asia that Boal and the French had not yet visited.[24]

## Exchanges and institutionalisation

In adapting to cultural policies in France, the Theatre of the Oppressed acquired methodological and institutional characteristics that served as parameters for its subsequent globalisation. The growing institutionalisation of the method demanded by the French state subsidies – its localised methods and ideological convergence with the prevailing cultural policies, the NGO status of the CEDITADE and the professionalisation of its practitioners – established a way of working that could be adopted in other countries and territories.

The foundation of the first centre for the Theatre of the Oppressed instituted a set of techniques that served as a model for new centres in the same NGO format, some examples of which follow.

1.  The Jana Sanskriti Centre for the Theatre of the Oppressed in Badu, West Bengal, India, founded by Sanjoy Ganguly in 1985. It serves to practise and disseminate the Theatre of the Oppressed with 30 local satellite teams through the Federation of Theatre of the Oppressed, India, which consists of around 25,000 people in the region of Kolkata. Jana Sanskriti hosts the *Muktadhara* International Forum Theatre Festival, which has been organised bi-annually since 2004.
2.  Centre for the Theatre of the Oppressed in Rio de Janeiro, Brazil, founded by Augusto Boal in 1986. Managed by a collective, it acts alongside social movements such as the Landless Workers' Movement and is part of the network of Pontos de Cultura (cultural hubs), which consists of more than 3,000 small centres for the promotion and dissemination of culture.
3.  Centre for the Theatre of the Oppressed of Maputo in Mozambique, founded by Alvim Cossa in 2012. It acts alongside the Mozambique Network of Community Theatre, which consists of about 120 groups and works with the support of UNICEF.

Nowadays, such centres act as diffusion hubs for the Theatre of the Oppressed method, thereby strengthening the method's institutional profile around the world. In the case of the Brazilian centre, it is possible to study how transnational flows contributed to the method's institutionalisation. In 1986, inspired by the success of the French centre in employing the Theatre of the Oppressed within education, Boal developed a similar project for the public-school network in Rio de Janeiro named Fábrica de Teatro Popular (popular theatre factory). At the invitation of anthropologist Darcy Ribeiro, then a member of Rio de Janeiro's left-wing government, Boal was able to return from his 15-year exile and finally bring the Theatre of the Oppressed to his native Brazil. This project was integrated into the broader movement of Brazilian re-democratisation, and helped Boal introduce the aforementioned

French notion of cultural democracy to Brazil,[25] establish the country's first Theatre of the Oppressed practitioners and found the Centre for the Theatre of the Oppressed in Rio de Janeiro (CTO Rio).

In the 1990s, during Boal's tenure as city councillor, he and his new collaborators in Rio developed an innovative way of using the Theatre of the Oppressed that became known as legislative theatre.[26] In this new modality, forum theatre was used as a tool for the radical democratisation of institutional politics through the direct participation of citizens in the drafting of legislature. Thirteen of the proposals that arose from the forum theatre performances, which took place inside or in front of the Municipal Chamber, were approved as laws as a result of legislative theatre.[27]

In 1996, with Boal no longer serving as city councillor, the CTO Rio began searching for new forms of institutional and financial support to continue this pioneering experiment in legislative theatre. From 1998 to 2000, the CTO Rio was sponsored by the Ford Foundation to further develop legislative theatre work.[28] The project included a training branch alongside community groups.[29] Legislative theatre spread quickly across Brazil and the rest of the world, with various forms of institutional support contributing to its diffusion. Today legislative theatre is practised and researched worldwide, from Brazil to Taiwan.[30]

Amid the growth of the legislative theatre, a shift in cultural policies in Brazil after 2004 contributed significantly to the institutionalisation and transnational expansion of the Theatre of the Oppressed. Inspired by the concept of cultural democracy, the Programa Cultura Viva (living culture programme) was implemented during the first Lula government and promoted a national network of cultural hubs.[31] This network helped spread the Theatre of the Oppressed across Brazil through a project called Teatro do Oprimido de Ponto a Ponto (Theatre of the Oppressed hub to hub).

In 2008, an international branch of the programme facilitated the expansion of the method to provinces in four African countries: Angola, Guinea-Bissau, Mozambique and Senegal. The aim of this project was the formation of international cultural hubs dedicated to the dissemination of the Theatre of the Oppressed throughout the African continent, combined with an affirmation of Brazil's historical and cultural bonds with Africa.[32]

In this cultural exchange, Brazil exported a social technology in the form of a set of techniques – the Theatre of the Oppressed – as well as a new form of cultural policy that was conducive to the dissemination of the Theatre of the Oppressed. In this way, both the Theatre of the Oppressed and the idea of democracy activated via hubs in an autonomous cultural network circulated transnationally, taking the same route from Brazil to Africa and then to other countries in Latin America. The confluence of these projects resulted in the largest training program for multipliers of the Theatre of the Oppressed ever run by the CTO Rio.[33]

Beyond cultural policies, social funding has been mainly responsible for the survival of the CTO Rio and the continuity of its work in Brazil, mostly through projects in areas of high poverty and violence, such as the communities and slums of Rio. The ability of the Theatre of the Oppressed to integrate with social development, especially following the election of Jair Bolsonaro in 2019, has enabled it to escape recent cuts in arts sponsorship carried out by Bolsonaro's far-right government.

In the case of Brazil, where the CTO Rio can look back on more than 30 years of continuous work, the spread of the Theatre of the Oppressed method resembles the initial stages of its dissemination in France. In both countries, the activities of the centres for the Theatre of the Oppressed were made viable by integrating the method into social-development policies.

## Transnational networks of the Theatre of the Oppressed

The integration of the Theatre of the Oppressed within community networks through socially oriented endeavours reflects an epistemic shift, starting in the 1970s, in the field of culture. At the time there was a broad move in theatre that questioned the model of high culture, and that led to projects where theatre was redefined as a tool for social development. This led ultimately to the field of applied theatre and its many subfields, of which theatre for development is probably the best known, and to which the seminal contribution of the Theatre of the Oppressed is undisputed.[34] By adapting his techniques to policies of cultural democracy and social development, Augusto Boal found ways to systematise and disseminate his method on a transnational scale.

As a sign of recognition of his global importance, it is worth mentioning that, in addition to being a candidate for the Nobel Peace Prize, Boal was appointed world theatre ambassador by the International Theatre Institute (ITI) in March 2009, a few months before his passing. On the same occasion, he was chosen by the ITI to make a statement on World Theatre Day in his last public appearance, in Paris.

After Boal's death, the Theatre of the Oppressed continued to circulate transnationally through the diverse networks created to disseminate the method. Several additional international networks, some of them connected to the previously mentioned Theatre of the Oppressed centres, have formed since then: the Francophone countries' network, Réseau Théâtre de l'Opprimé; the Federation of the Theatre of the Oppressed, India, managed by Jana Sanskriti; the Asian network, started by the Afghanistan Human Rights and Democracy Organization (AHRDO); the Ma(g)dalena International Network, composed of theatre groups that are practitioners of the Feminist Theatre of the Oppressed; the Mozambique Network of Community Theatre in Africa; and the Latin American Theatre of the Oppressed Network (ReLATO), which brings together several Central and South American countries. These networks connect practitioners and groups from different countries, who meet frequently to carry out an exchange of practices at international conferences and festivals of the Theatre of the Oppressed in Africa, Asia, Europe and the Americas.

Through these networks, the Theatre of the Oppressed crosses borders, circulating as a political tool for activists, often through social projects and with the support of international and non-governmental human-rights organisations. In a dialectical process that conjoins local transformation and network expansion, the method engages with Arjun Appadurai's concept of 'imagination as a social practice', and connects to the growing number of 'diasporic public spheres' to which most of the activist movements in the post-national world are now connected in a 'post-national network of diasporas'.[35]

## Conclusion

The Theatre of the Oppressed, begun and developed during its founder's exile, acquired both mobility and an open methodological approach that enabled its dissemination through transnational networks. The method's capacity for adaptation is directly connected to its modularity. These characteristics of the Theatre of the Oppressed made it amenable to change and adaptation, and allowed it to absorb the influence of the local cultures, policies and aesthetic traditions of the places where it was applied, which enabled its survival in culturally and geographically diverse contexts.[36]

In an expansion comparable only to that of the methods of Stanislavsky and Brecht, Augusto Boal's method spread throughout the world, and today it is practised on all five continents. The director that helped bring Stanislavsky's method and the ideas of Brecht to Brazil is the same one who brought a theatrical method to the rest of the world: the Theatre of the Oppressed.

In the case of the Theatre of the Oppressed, network structure and institutionalisation are not antithetical entities, but rather mutually conditioning processes that enabled the ideas and practices of one charismatic theatre artist to form resilient structures – structures that have not only been sustained over a 50-year period, but have mutated and attained, at least for the present, the signs of permanence typically associated with institutions. Boal, as a product of the theatre-modernist avant-garde, would probably be appalled at the thought of his method being labelled as 'institutionalised', but the fact that his method has survived his passing and now enjoys numerous offshoots and centres of practice suggests that it is indeed an institution in its own right.

## Notes

1   This chapter is the result of a collaboration conducted during Clara de Andrade's term as a visiting fellow at the Centre for Global Theatre History and the European Research Council's Developing Theatre project at the Ludwig Maximilian University of Munich in 2020.
2   Following Douglass North's definition, it can be said that institutions define 'the rules of the game' and constitute 'the humanly devised constraints that shape human interaction', whereas organisations are the individual players, 'groups of individuals bound by some common purpose to achieve objectives'. North, 1990, Chapters 3 and 5.
3   Colyvas and Powell, 2006, 308.
4   Scott, 1995, 35.
5   Balme, 2019, 170.
6   Weber, 1968.
7   The other two forms of authority are legal-bureaucratic and traditional. The former regulates succession through legal means such as a constitution, while the latter privileges practices such as primogeniture to formalise structures of authority.
8   Ferguson, 2018, Chapter 6.
9   Granovetter, 1983, 202.
10  See DiMaggio and Powell, 1983, and Scott, 1995.
11  DiMaggio, 1992.
12  Dahlquist and Frykholm, 2019, 3.
13  Definitions of the term 'network' are highly contextual. For more on the concept in theatre history see Balme, 2020.
14  DiMaggio and Powell, 1983.
15  Andrade, 2014.
16  Boal, 2000, 291.
17  Boal, 2000, 197.
18  Boal, 1985, 141.
19  Andrade, 2017.
20  For more on the *Bulletins du Théâtre de l'Opprimé* and the transnational development of the Theatre of the Oppressed in France see Andrade, 2017.
21  CEDITADE, 1982.
22  Urrutiaguer, 2014, 155.
23  Andrade, 2017, 181.
24  See Andrade, 2017 and Ganguly, 2010.

25 Much like the Theatre of the Oppressed in France, the Brazilian project Fábrica de Teatro Popular (popular theatre factory) was grounded in a vision of *animation socioculturelle* (community-based cultural activities) influenced by French cultural policies.
26 Schechner et al., 1998.
27 Boal, 1998.
28 The authors acknowledge the generosity and contribution of Professor Victor Hugo Adler Pereira, who provided access to his research entitled 'Teatro e Movimentos Sociais' conducted in 2000–2 and funded by the Brazilian National Council for Scientific and Technological Development under his coordination and the Ler-UERJ project at the Rio de Janeiro State University (UERJ).
29 Bendelak, 2000.
30 See Bendelak, 2016, 25 and Centro de Teatro do Oprimido, 2016, 32.
31 Based on the principle of shared management between public power and sociocultural agents, the Brazilian Programa Cultura Viva (living culture programme) was created to foster and connect diverse cultural manifestations that were already being autonomously carried out all over the country.
32 See the website of CTO Rio. https://www.ctorio.org.br/home/.
33 Santos, 2016, 28.
34 Prentki, 2015, 15–16.
35 Appadurai, 1996, 48, 38, 228 respectively.
36 Andrade, 2017, 217–18.

# References

Andrade, Clara de. *O Exílio de Augusto Boal: Reflexões sobre um teatro sem fronteiras*. Rio de Janeiro: 7Letras, 2014.
Andrade, Clara de. 'Teatro do Oprimido de Augusto Boal na França: transformações locais e expansão transnacional'. PhD thesis. Federal University of the State of Rio de Janeiro: 2017.
Appadurai, Arjun. *Modernity at Large: Cultural dimensions of globalization*. Minneapolis: University of Minnesota Press, 1996.
Balme, Christopher. 'Theatrical institutions in motion: developing theatre in the postcolonial era', *Journal of Dramatic Theory and Criticism* 31 (2) (2017): 125–40. https://doi.org/10.1353/dtc.2017.0006.
Balme, Christopher. 'Institutional aesthetics and the crisis of leadership'. In *The Routledge Companion to Theatre and Politics*, edited by Peter Eckersall and Helena Grehan, 169–72. Abingdon: Routledge, 2019.
Balme, Christopher. *The Globalization of Theatre 1870–1930: The theatrical networks of Maurice E. Bandmann*. Cambridge: Cambridge University Press, 2020.
Bendelak, Olivar. Interview given to the research team of Teatro e Movimentos Sociais. Rio de Janeiro: Rio de Janeiro State University (UERJ), 2000.
Bendelak, Olivar. 'Teatro legislativo', *Metaxis* 8 (2016): 22–5.
Boal, Augusto. *Theatre of the Oppressed*. New York: Theatre Communications Group, 1985.
Boal, Augusto. *Legislative Theatre: Using performance to make politics*. New York: Routledge, 1998.
Boal, Augusto. *Hamlet e o Filho do Padeiro: Memórias imaginadas*. Rio de Janeiro: Record, 2000.
Boal, Augusto. *Hamlet and the Baker's Son: My life in theatre and politics*. New York: Routledge, 2001.
Britto, Geo. 'Na terra Brasilis', *Metaxis* 8 (2016): 20–1.
CEDITADE. 'Théâtre de l'opprimé direction Augusto Boal: enjeux la vie – spectacles forum'. Spécial encarte – programme. Théâtre de l'opprimé, 8 December 1982.
Centro de Teatro do Oprimido. Special issue, 'Teatro do Oprimido de ponto a ponto', *Metaxis* 6 (2010).
Centro de Teatro do Oprimido. Special issue, 'CTO 30 anos', *Metaxis* 8 (2016).
Cohen-Cruz, Jan and Schutzman, Mady, eds. *A Boal Companion: Dialogues on theatre and cultural politics*. London and New York: Routledge, 2006.
Colyvas, Jeannette A. and Powell, Walter W. 'Roads to institutionalization: the remaking of boundaries between public and private science'. In *Research in Organizational Behavior:*

*An annual series of analytical essays and critical reviews*, edited by Barry Staw, 27, 305–53, 2006.

Dahlquist, Marina and Frykholm, Joel, eds. *The Institutionalization of Educational Cinema: North America and Europe in the 1910s and 1920s*. Bloomington: Indiana University Press, 2019.

DiMaggio, Paul. 'Cultural boundaries and structural change: the extension of the high culture model to theater, opera, and the dance, 1900–1940'. In *Cultivating Differences: Symbolic boundaries and the making of inequality*, edited by Michèle Lamont and Marcel Fournier, 21–67. Chicago: University of Chicago Press, 1992.

DiMaggio, Paul J. and Powell, Walter W. 'The iron cage revisited: institutional isomorphism and collective rationality in organizational fields', *American Sociological Review* 48 (2) (1983): 147–60. https://doi.org/10.2307/2095101.

DiMaggio, Paul and Powell, Walter W. 'Introduction'. In *The New Institutionalism in Organizational Analysis*, edited by Paul DiMaggio and Walter W. Powell, 1–38. Chicago: University of Chicago Press, 1991.

Ferguson, Niall. *The Square and the Tower: Networks and power, from the Freemasons to Facebook*. New York: Penguin, 2018.

Ganguly, Sanjoy. *Jana Sanskriti: Forum theatre and democracy in India*. London: Routledge, 2010.

Granovetter, Mark. 'The strength of weak ties: A network theory revisited', *Sociological Theory* 1 (1983): 201–33.

Jackson, Adrian. 'Augusto Boal: A theatre in life', *New Theatre Quarterly* 25 (2009): 306–9.

North, Douglass C. *Institutions, Institutional Change and Economic Performance: The political economy of institutions and decisions*. Cambridge: Cambridge University Press, 1990.

Prentki, Tim. *Applied Theatre: Development*. London and New York: Bloomsbury Methuen Drama, 2015.

Santos, Bárbara. 'Identidade estético-política', *Metaxis* 8 (2016): 26–9.

Schechner, Richard, Chatterjee, Sudipto and Boal, Augusto. 'Augusto Boal, city councillor: legislative theatre and the chamber in the streets: an interview', *TDR* 42 (4) (1998): 75–90.

Schutzman, Mady and Cohen-Cruz, Jan, eds. *Playing Boal: Theatre, therapy, activism*. New York: Routledge, 1994.

Scott, Richard. *Institutions and Organizations*. Thousand Oaks, CA: Sage, 1995.

Urrutiaguer, Daniel. *Les Mondes du Théâtre: Désenchantement politique et economie des conventions*. Paris: Harmattan, 2014.

Weber, Max. *Max Weber on Charisma and Institution Building: Selected papers*. Chicago: University of Chicago Press, 1968.

# 12
# Cecile Guidote, PETA and the ITI
Rebecca Sturm[1]

Cecile Guidote founded the Philippine Educational Theatre Association (PETA) in 1967 to support not only the development of Philippine theatre, but also of society. With these goals, PETA was part of a trend of using theatre as a tool of nation building within the decolonising world. This chapter examines how this trend allowed Guidote to quickly establish PETA as part of an international network of like-minded theatre artists. The support she drew from various sources, including UNESCO, the International Theatre Institute (ITI), the Rockefeller Foundation and La MaMa Experimental Theatre Club, resulted in the first Third World Theater Festival, hosted by PETA in Manila in 1971. When martial law forced Guidote into political exile in 1972, she worked with other exiles and theatre artists from minority ethnic groups in New York while PETA continued creating and performing plays in Filipino, both endeavours supported by the international contacts Guidote had established.

Because of PETA's widely influential model of grassroots theatre, its plays and methods have already been the subject of considerable research. Previous studies have considered PETA in the context of the movement that Eugène Van Erven called the theatre of liberation,[2] its role in the history of Asian and Philippine theatre,[3] its methods, and the themes of its plays.[4] PETA itself has also published an account of its history.[5] This chapter aims to add to this research by focusing on its founder, Cecile Reyes Guidote, and situating her in an international network of theatre experts that supported and informed the establishment of PETA. Nic Leonhardt's research on Severino Montano has explored the attention that US organisations such as the Rockefeller Foundation paid to the development of theatre in the Philippines in the 1950s. The 'permanent exchange between the United States and the

Philippines, the decades of transatlantic connections and relationships between educational institutions and their graduates'[6] that was central to Rockefeller's interest is also crucial to understanding the support Guidote received.

## A theatre for the nation: the inception of PETA

Cecile Guidote discovered and developed her interest in theatre in an educational context that also provided her with connections to Catholic and US cultural organisations important to PETA's initial success; she was exposed to Western drama in high school and later became involved with college theatre groups. A scholarship from James B. Reuter, an American Jesuit priest who taught at Ateneo de Manila University and was himself a director and producer of theatre, allowed her to join the Ateneo Graduate School summer drama workshop in 1960, after which she worked as an assistant to Reuter. In 1964 she received a Fulbright-Hays scholarship, sponsored by the Bureau of Educational and Cultural Affairs of the US Department of State, to study at the State University of New York at Albany (SUNY Albany). There, Guidote, concerned with the absence of professional theatre training in the Philippines, drafted a short outline for the development of Philippine theatre. The proposal received the attention and approval of Edward Mattos, cultural affairs officer at the US embassy in the Philippines, who recommended Guidote for a JDR III Fund grant to train under Paul Baker at the Dallas Theater Center (DTC). At the DTC Guidote wrote as her master's thesis a comprehensive proposal for the development of a national theatre for the Philippines. With this topic, Guidote touched upon contemporary developmental discourses, as evidenced by the broad support she received in the US; through additional grants she attended conferences and festivals, and experienced the work of US repertory theatre companies. During this period she met US theatre artists and producers, and cultural officials from various private and public organisations such as the Rockefeller Foundation, the US Office of Education, the American Educational Theatre Association, the American National Theatre and Academy (ANTA) and the US centre of the ITI, which offered advice on the future of Philippine theatre. Among them were US experts concerned with the development of theatre in the Global South, including Paul Bruce Pettit, chairman of the drama department at SUNY Albany, who had recently been a consultant and guest director at the new National Theatre of Cyprus. Herbert L. Shore, a member of the Afro-Asian Theatre

Project, spoke to Guidote about his preparation for the establishment of a national theatre in Tanzania.[7] She also came into contact with theatre artists from the Global South similarly supported by US organisations, such as fellow DTC student Yu Deok-hyeong, with whom she discussed the operation of the Seoul Drama Center and the approach and theories of its founder Yu Chi-jin.[8] While writing her thesis, Guidote kept in touch with her Philippine contacts, who helped secure local support for the realisation of her project.

Guidote's proposal provided a survey of the condition of theatre in the Philippines at the time before mapping out her ambitious plans for the development of theatre. She intended her thesis to serve a similar function to the proposal from English actor and dramatist Harley Granville-Barker for a national theatre,[9] which enabled the establishment of such an organisation in the UK.[10] Her proposal referred to many Western forms of theatre from different time periods, political systems and societies, and subsumed dramatists such as Chekov, Brecht, Gorki, Hauptmann, Ibsen, Jonson, Molière and Shakespeare in the category of European subsidised repertory theatre without acknowledging their differences.[11]

Guidote's understanding of national theatre illustrated her alignment with the idea, shared by the theatrical epistemic community, of theatre as a 'discrete artistic and cultural form'.[12] She argued for theatre as a medium of cultural reform by highlighting its potential capacity to preserve and enhance the cultural identity of the Philippines in changing times,[13] its ability to instil moral values in an audience,[14] and its educational value 'as a principal method of disseminating ideas' on various subjects.[15] Through the staging of foreign plays, the audience was to gain 'a deeper understanding of the countries from which the dramatic works originate'.[16] To prove theatre's importance as a tool of social development she provided historical examples including Periclean Athens and Elizabethan England, implying a causal link between human progress and the vibrant, innovative theatre of these periods.[17] Defined as an instrument of social change, theatre is not valued for its commercial opportunities, and Guidote's proposal barely addresses the financing of the project, presupposing considerable state subsidies justified by the idea of theatre as a social good. Since the proposed national theatre aspired to reach all Filipinos, it was intended to feature traditional and modern forms of both Philippine and European performance, and encompass a wide range of genres. To appeal to a broader audience including workers and peasants, Guidote suggested that plays be translated into Tagalog.

Owing to the geographical and societal realities of the Philippines, Guidote imagined the national theatre not as a single repertory theatre house or company, but as a decentralised network of interrelated groups promoting different genres of theatre for different audiences. Concerning the national theatre's organisational structure, her proposal was strongly and explicitly influenced by the ANTA: a trust fund or foundation, supported by a congressional bill, would provide funding for the theatre's operation.[18] To meet professional standards and deliver professional-level training to theatre artists, Guidote argued for the necessity of a central agency to coordinate new theatre groups and artists, and proposed the establishment of a Central Institute of Theatre Arts in the Philippines (CITAP). The CITAP would be based in the dramatic arts centre that Guidote envisioned as its headquarters and communications centre as well as versatile performance venue for different theatre groups. CITAP would also coordinate federations of theatre groups and artists.[19] One of these hypothetical associations she called the Philippines Educational Theater Association, imagining it to be composed of children's, school, community and workers' theatre.[20]

Guidote's views on possible international contacts and exchange can also be attributed to ANTA's example. The academy's cooperation with the US federal government, and its successful international tours and exchange programmes, had become an important pillar and raison d'être for ANTA, which linked it to the ITI.[21] Guidote suggested the same for the Philippines (with a national ITI centre hosted by CITAP), allowing foreign guest artists to visit the Philippines and Filipino theatre artists to travel to and experience theatre in other countries.[22]

Guidote's suggestion was timely, as in the 1960s the ITI was struggling to live up to its claim to internationality. Throughout this period, the ITI increased its efforts to expand its network to support the theatre of the Global South. With the launch of the University of the Theatre of Nations, fellows of the university from Global South countries were able to attend courses delivered by the university programme.[23] However, membership fees for local ITI centres were often too high for prospective member nations, even when adjusted to reflect the wealth of the respective country (in accordance with UNESCO practices).[24] As Christopher Balme writes, the funding of 'imported institutional forms of dubious legitimacy' was not a high priority for governments in the decolonising world.[25] Associate centres were introduced, allowing theatre artists from countries unable to pay the membership fees to contribute to the ITI, but high travel costs made attending and partici-pating in ITI events impossible for many. At the ninth ITI world congress in Vienna in 1961, ITI Secretary General Jean Darcante informed the general assembly that theatre artists from various African countries were interested in joining the ITI, but were prevented from doing so by financial reasons.[26] To mitigate the problem of insufficient funding, theatre artists from Global South countries interested in connecting with the ITI began to establish regional networks. This idea was pioneered by Latin American countries who from the 1950s were represented in the ITI to a more substantial degree than other regions of the Global South. They founded the Institute of Latin American Theatre (ILAT) to represent the countries of South and Central America in the ITI, and to facilitate the exchange of theatre arts and knowledge on a regional level. A similar development happened in the Arab states: Arab theatre experts met in 1965 to discuss the problems facing theatre in the Arab world, and resolved to collaborate on the development of Arab theatre.[27] When they met again in 1966 to establish an Arab theatre committee, they were already expanding their reach beyond the Arab world: one of those in attendance, the journalist and poet Som Benegal of the Indian ITI centre, shared with the Arab theatre artists the resolutions of his East–West theatre seminar, hosted only months prior in New Delhi, which addressed the differences between Western and traditional Asian theatre.[28] Via regional networks, the connection of theatre artists from the Global South with the ITI network began to take shape.

Likely informed about the ITI's ongoing trend towards regionalisation, and maybe encouraged by her contacts in ANTA and the ITI's US centre, Guidote proposed that the Philippines could serve as a central office for an Afro-Asian federation of ITI centres. She argued that the Philippines' colonial history and ethnic diversity made the country ideal for such a position, and that its Spanish heritage provided a connection with the ILAT.[29] The Philippines would thus play a deciding role in the organisation of the epistemic theatre community in the Global South.

## PETA, the international theatre community and the first Third World Theater Festival

After finishing her master's degree in 1967, Guidote returned to the Philippines and secured the support of religious and educational organisations, and of leading figures in Philippine theatre and education, for the founding of PETA.[30] PETA was established that same year, with its most prominent bodies being the Kalinangan Ensemble (PETA's professional performing arm),[31] and CITAP (the first performing arts academy in the Philippines).[32] She encouraged Tagalog translations of foreign drama and the creation of new plays in Tagalog,[33] and gathered a prolific group of theatre, television and music artists, along with officials and cultural workers, to organise theatre productions, seminars and workshops throughout the Philippines.[34] She collaborated with Teodoro Valencia, influential journalist and member of the National Parks Development Committee, who allowed the Kalinangan Ensemble to transform a portion of the ruins of the historic Fort Santiago in Manila into the open-air, in-the-round Rajah Sulayman Theater. Alejandro Roces, writer and former secretary of education, became PETA's first president.[35]

In accordance with her proposal, Guidote immediately began to use her existing connections in the US to expand her international contacts in service of PETA by moving it into the ITI's orbit. From 1968 to 1971, PETA devoted its national conventions to celebrations of World Theatre Day.[36] The Philippines joined the ITI as an associate centre in 1967,[37] the fourth Asian country to join after India (1950), Japan (1951) and South Korea (1956), and in 1971 Guidote established PETA as the host of the Philippine ITI centre.[38] Another JDR III Fund grant allowed her to attend the 1967 ITI world congress in New York, where she established relationships with ITI delegates from around the world that she hoped would be beneficial to Philippine theatre artists. In her attempts to secure foreign support for PETA she disregarded the cultural frontiers of the Cold War, successfully initiating relations with theatre artists from socialist countries despite the fact that the Philippines was considered a key US ally. When she learned that the ITI centre of the German Democratic Republic (GDR) had agreed to an artistic exchange with the Venezuelan centre, allowing Venezuelan theatre artists to study in the GDR and sending an East German guest director to Venezuela, she surprised one of the East German delegates by inquiring about similar possibilities for the Philippines. Although the German delegates were initially hesitant,[39] they began to invite PETA artists to the East Berlin theatre festival, and to events organised by the German ITI centre.[40] In 1970 PETA invited Czechoslovakian theatre director Ladislav Smoček to stage Brecht's *The Good Person of Szechwan* in English, and in 1971 American director Brooks Jones came to stage the same play in a Tagalog translation.[41]

In order to promote its work internationally and stimulate artistic exchange, PETA decided to organise an international theatre festival; 1971 marked the 400th anniversary of the founding of Manila and as such would provide a suitable occasion for the event. To secure financial support for the festival, a PETA delegation attended the round-table talk on Arab theatre in Beirut in 1969 sponsored by UNESCO and the

Lebanese ITI centre. There, Alejandro Roces proposed the idea of a 'Third World' theatre festival, to take place in November 1971. The festival would be linked with an international conference on 'the development of theatre in developing countries', with a focus on indigenous theatre and contemporary performance. The proposal was accepted and granted funding by UNESCO, with theatre director Ellen Stewart 'designated as a UNESCO Expert to assist in the organisation, implementation and coordination of the project with the PETA Secretariat in Manila'.[42] As founder and artistic director of La MaMa Experimental Theatre Club in New York, Stewart was an internationally connected and successful theatre manager. La MaMa had completed several European tours and was in the process of establishing several satellite theatres abroad, mostly but not solely in Western countries. This had allowed Stewart to establish transnational connections, and to bring famous theatre artists such as Polish director Jerzy Grotowski to New York. Stewart had a huge impact on the trajectory of Guidote's career, and the 1971 festival in Manila was only the start of their long collaboration.

With its proposal for a festival, PETA had approached the international theatre community at a crucial moment. The first United Nations development decade had fallen far short of expectations, prompting the UN and UNESCO at the end of the 1960s to reaffirm their commitment by declaring a second development decade.[43] UNESCO-affiliated organisations such as the ITI were encouraged to focus their efforts on supporting the cultural development of the Global South. Theatre artists from the Global South were to be given an official space within the ITI in the form of a specialised committee: the Committee for Third World Theatre (CTWT). There were, however, many questions about the committee's scope and responsibilities that needed discussion. Thus, at the 1971 ITI world congress in London, a working committee met to discuss possible approaches. Of the different proposals discussed for how the ITI could support theatre in developing nations, most were vague on funding and implementation. The most tangible was PETA's Third World Theater Festival, since it was already fully funded and had secured UNESCO's support. At the time of the ITI congress, the festival was to take place in six months and was already well into the planning phase, and its success was not dependent on the ITI's financial or administrative support; the ITI needed to simply offer access to its network and provide an international platform by declaring the festival its first official event. Guidote became the first secretary of the nascent CTWT, Stewart its official consultant.[44] The ITI's endorsement was pivotal as it allowed PETA to reach a much broader international audience, but the ITI had little influence on the festival programme, which was largely determined by PETA's and Guidote's connections and philosophy.

With the promotion of Filipino theatre being one of PETA's main goals, the festival featured Tagalog productions of *Cyrano* and Eugène Ionesco's *The Bald Soprano*. Other Southeast Asian performances included a Philippine production of Verdi's *Aida*, traditional Khmer dance drama, Indonesian wayang kulit shadow-puppet play and an excerpt from the Malaysian play *Hang Jebat*.[45] Korean theatre director and Guidote's fellow DTC graduate Yu Deok-hyeong was supported by the Rockefeller Foundation to travel to Manila and stage a Tagalog version of his radio play *Dhyana* with PETA's Kalinangan Ensemble.[46] In PETA's own account of its history, the performance is described as 'the festival's greatest achievement' – one that concretised Guidote's vision of a 'multidisciplinary fusion and cross-pollination of traditions interlaced with contemporary theatrical expression to produce fresh insights on life and culture'.[47] The accompanying conference was attended by 37 delegates from 16 countries.[48] Most Global South participants came from Southeast and East Asia (Indonesia, the Khmer Republic, Korea, Malaysia, the Philippines), some from sub-Saharan Africa (Ghana, Nigeria, Uganda, Sudan) and one from Egypt. In addition, there were observers from various Western and socialist countries.

The press coverage in Manila was celebratory. The festival and conference were portrayed as a contribution to a united community of theatre professionals that could transcend political boundaries. The evidence presented was that the Khmer Republic had sent a 30-person theatre troupe despite the ongoing Cambodian Civil War, that the East and West German delegates embraced at the inaugural reception and that the delegates from Egypt and Israel, Ahmed Zaki and Jesaja Weinberg, worked together 'hand in hand' during the conference.[49] Many of the participants were similarly positive about the festival's theatrical accomplishments: Jean Darcante declared the successful realisation of the festival and conference a significant step for the development of theatre in the developing world:

> For the theatre of the Third-World they represent an exalting possibility of knowledge and progress. This will be more important and better than any other festival throughout the world. It will be an act of faith of the theatre people of Africa, Asia and Latin America whose presence is absolutely necessary for the world, as much for the future of our theatre as for indispensable peace.[50]

During the conference great emphasis was placed on celebrating indigenous theatre and affirming the independence of Global South theatre artists from European theatre. At the centre of this was Ellen Stewart, who counselled the delegates 'to have faith in their own theatrical systems':[51]

> Why do you accept these self-impositions of Western standards? You are the ones who created theater in the world! There is need of a revamping of attitudes: search for and establish your own individual identities; give of yourselves! It does not matter whether theatre consists of sound and image more than dialogue, or of dance and song more than acting. Perhaps it is more important to MAKE theatre than to WRITE theatre. Believe in yourselves and in your heritage, in what you have; do not pay lip-service to the Western world![52]

Several of the challenges facing theatre in developing nations were discussed: limited audiences, the lack of funding and the dependence on European theatre tradition. In line with PETA's aims, the resolutions arising from these discussions stressed the importance of bringing 'performances to popular audiences in both urban and rural communities' in support of community development, and emphasised the significance 'of local playwrights who [would] reflect in their creations the problems and endeavours of their respective communities and countries'. PETA was thus able to introduce its approach to theatre both to fellow theatre practitioners and to a larger community of international theatre experts interested in the development of theatre in the Global South.

The Third World Theater Festival served as the beginning of a loose series of ITI 'Third World' festivals, followed by events in Shiraz in 1973, Venezuela in 1976 and South Korea in 1981. These festivals represent the most significant output of the CTWT, which otherwise struggled with internal political quarrels and inactivity, the latter a result of members being prevented from contributing by either a lack of funding or by political unrest in their home countries.

## The Committee for Third World Theatre during the Cold War

Guidote's successful career in the Philippines was brought to an abrupt stop when Ferdinand Marcos declared martial law in 1972. She came into conflict with Imelda Marcos when she refused the first lady's offer to become the first artistic director of the new Cultural Center of the Philippines, a prestigious project that nevertheless did not align with Guidote's vision for cultural development in the Philippines. Guidote fled the country in March 1973, joining her activist husband Heherson Alvarez in New York.[53] During her exile, which lasted 13 years until the end of the Marcos regime, of which she remained an outspoken critic,[54] Guidote continued her work in the US within her established network. She founded the Philippine Educational Theatre Arts League (PETAL), hosted at La MaMa, as an extension of PETA to provide emigrated Filipinos with theatre training and the opportunity to join an ensemble. Together with Stewart she established the Third World Institute of Theatre Arts Studies (TWITAS) to facilitate cross-cultural exchange between artists from the Global South and minority artists from the US through workshops and collaborative productions, several of them directed by Guidote herself.[55] She also became funding chair of the International League of Folk Arts for Communication and Education (FACE), in which capacity she initiated and directed UN cultural programmes for human-rights education.

Now that the field of 'Third World theatre' had been consolidated within the ITI, with the first Third World Theater Festival its inaugural event, the development of the CTWT became contested. 'Third World theatre' was a much more difficult concept to define than those of the ITI's other specialised committees, which dealt with topics such as music theatre, dance and theatre education. The term 'Third World' was a demarcation based on political and geographical considerations with no clear or universally agreed-upon definition. While it was meant to describe countries not aligned with either NATO or the Warsaw Pact, in practice it was often conflated with 'developing countries' and associated with the decolonising world including socialist countries in the Global South with strong Eastern bloc ties, such as Cuba. It became necessary to determine what defined 'Third World theatre', what common material or artistic problems and considerations existed, and how the ITI could provide support. No understanding of the terms 'Third World' or 'Third World theatre' was shared by the different ITI centres, with perspectives influenced by different schools of thought including the older develop-mentalist model, dependency theory and the principle of proletarian internationalism of socialist countries.[56]

The conflict festering within and around the CTWT mostly centred on Ellen Stewart and the prominent role she occupied as the committee's official consultant. Darcante took issue with the fact that Stewart often acted on her own authority, and considered the way La MaMa dominated

CTWT proceedings potentially neo-colonial.[57] Stewart was also viewed sceptically by ITI delegates from socialist countries, who suspected her to be an agent of US interests in the Global South. At the Third World Theater Festival conference, the German delegates expressed concern about the direction of 'Third World' theatre in the ITI and Western influences:

> In any case, it should be noted – which was not news to us – that the La MaMa Theatre troupes, which exist in a large number of Western countries, are obviously in the business of getting certain national aspirations under their wing. Thus, Ellen Stewart candidly stated that she was willing and able to send staff to any country in the world free of charge to build up La MaMa troupes. Knowing that this company receives a substantial part of its funding from the Ford and Rockefeller Foundations, it is easy to see who is behind this 'magnanimous' funding policy.[58] (Translation mine.)

This American influence was also a factor among 'Third World' conference participants, such as Guidote and Yu Deok-hyeong, who had studied in the US and whose work had been, and still was, supported by US philanthropic foundations. When the CTWT was officially established and its statutes finalised at the next ITI congress, in Moscow in 1973, the socialist countries of the ITI tried to use their 'home advantage' to redirect the trajectory of the committee.[59] While Guidote was reaffirmed as secretary of the CTWT, her collaboration with Stewart situated her on the opposing side in the eyes of theatre artists from other Global South countries who wanted to reduce the influence of either the West or the Global North in general. The second Third World Theater Festival took place in Shiraz in 1973 as part of the seventh Festival of Arts, and as with the first festival the ITI's name was attached to an already planned and funded project. At this second conference of the CTWT the opposition against Stewart became much more pronounced. According to a report from an observer from the West German ITI centre, the 'comparatively strong Arab "front" dominated with its own ideas about organisation and activity', and tried to 'fend off an allegedly existing US-American and European-Western sphere of influence in favour of a future emphasis on cultural independence' (translation mine).[60] Guidote and Stewart's proposal for a La MaMa workshop with theatre artists from minority ethnic groups was rejected. In addition, since Guidote was no longer operating in the Philippines, it was decided to transfer the CTWT secretariat from the Philippines to Iran.[61] The push to eliminate Western influence from the CTWT continued at the committee's next meeting, in Beirut in March 1974: Guidote and Stewart learned about the meeting second hand, and some participants, such as Yu, did not receive an invitation.[62]

This attempt to curtail either Western or general outside influence revealed the limitations of the CTWT. Like other ITI committees, the CTWT was financially dependent on the initiatives of CTWT member countries, as the ITI did not have the budget to support it. In the Global South in particular, the organisation of events and meetings was severely limited by the lack of financial resources. Such events and meetings could only take place with external funding, such as from UNESCO, or with the support of ITI centres from the Global North. At the next ITI world congress, in West Berlin in 1975, Darcante deemed the CTWT's inactivity a failure and questioned the ITI's approach to the theatre of the Global South.[63] In addition to the third Third World Theater Festival, in Venezuela, CTWT's programme for the next two years primarily featured initiatives by ITI centres from the Global North, which needed the ITI's approval for legitimisation only. Among the initiatives were six different PETAL-TWITAS proposals.[64] Despite being portrayed by ITI theatre artists from socialist countries as opponents when it came to their influence on the CTWT, Guidote and Stewart managed to maintain their contacts and involve ITI theatre artists from socialist countries in theatrical exchange. After Guidote's unsuccessful attempt to bring East German theatre director and CTWT consultant Fritz Bennewitz to the Philippines in 1972,[65] she and Stewart brought him to work on La MaMa and TWITAS projects with actors from minority ethnic groups three times between 1977 and 1979. Even after she was removed from the position of committee secretary, Guidote continued to participate in the CTWT, and in 1985 became its co-president when it was renamed the Committee for Cultural Identity and Development.[66]

## Conclusion

PETA changed when no longer under Guidote's leadership. After she left the Philippines, a group of CITAP graduates took over PETA's organisation. They implemented collective leadership, and 'developed a progressive orientation that manifested itself in a less top-down attitude, a new concept of a socially committed artist-teacher, a method of collective creation, and a genuine concern to build counter-culture for liberation'.[67] But despite PETA's later artistic and structural reorientation, away from the focus shaped by Guidote's ties to Catholic and US cultural networks, her vision and network were decisive to PETA's success. Her background in and focus on education crucially influenced PETA's approach. As Christopher Balme notes, and as was evident during Guidote's run as head of PETA, the idea of theatre as a tool for social change and development aligned PETA with the funding agendas of various non-governmental organisations. This approach was so successful it spread to several other countries, mainly in South and Southeast Asia.[68]

In its early days PETA built on Guidote's transnational connections with theatre experts, cultural officials, philanthropic foundations and NGOs, which included contacts in the Eastern bloc. Fritz Bennewitz's 1974 trip to the Philippines to speak about his experience adapting Brecht's *The Caucasian Chalk Circle* to Marathi theatre marked the beginning of a long collaboration between Bennewitz and PETA. He returned to Manila in 1977 to direct an adaptation of *The Caucasian Chalk Circle*,[69] adapted and translated into Tagalog by Franklin Osorio and Lito Tiongson under the title *Ang Hatol Ng Guhit Na Bilog*, and in total worked on 13 performances in the Philippines.[70] In 1976 composer and PETA member Lutgardo Labad was invited to an ITI seminar in East Germany for theatre artists from the Global South, where he presented PETA projects intended to contribute to the development of a national theatre culture.[71] This allowed PETA to benefit from East German Brechtian expertise, and to introduce a different circle of theatre practitioners to its approach. In an act that Michael Bodden describes as 'cross-cultural appropriation', PETA's socially critical productions engaged in 'a reinterpreting and retooling of Brecht's ideas or techniques rather than a stuff imitation'.[72] While adapted to the Philippine situation, these productions were not necessarily aligned with the Cold War agendas that facilitated this exchange of theatrical knowledge.[73]

## Notes

1   Rebecca Sturm's research for this chapter received funding from the European Research Council under the European Union's Horizon 2020 research and innovation programme (grant agreement no. 694559 – developing theatre).
2   Van Erven, 1987; Van Erven, 1992.
3   Fernandez, 1980.
4   Bodden, 1996, 24–50.
5   Samson, 2008.
6   Leonhardt, 2019, 22.
7   Guidote-Alvarez, 2003, xviii–xix.
8   For more on Yu Chi-jin, the Seoul Drama Center and its support by the Rockefeller Foundation, see Creutzenberg, 2019.

9   Granville-Barker and Archer, 1970.
10  Guidote-Alvarez, 2003, xv.
11  Guidote-Alvarez, 2003, 27.
12  Balme, 2022, 272.
13  Guidote-Alvarez, 2003, 35.
14  Guidote-Alvarez, 2003, 42.
15  Guidote-Alvarez, 2003, 36.
16  Guidote-Alvarez, 2003, 72.
17  Guidote-Alvarez, 2003, 39.
18  Guidote-Alvarez, 2003, 70.
19  Guidote-Alvarez, 2003, 111.
20  Guidote-Alvarez, 2003, 106.
21  Canning, 2015.
22  Guidote-Alvarez, 2003, 103.
23  See Iacob, 2022.
24  For a more detailed account of the ITI's financial struggles, see Iacob, 2024.
25  Balme, 2022, 272.
26  '9. kongress des ITI: bericht des generalkomitees'.
27  Darcante, 1965, 89–90.
28  'Arab theatre seminar Casablanca'.
29  Guidote-Alvarez, 2003, 104.
30  Samson, 2008, 18.
31  Samson, 2008, 29–46.
32  Samson, 2008, 47–60.
33  Cruz, 1998, 213–15.
34  Cruz, 2003, 216–17.
35  For a more detailed account of PETA's founding see Samson, 2008, 17–28.
36  Samson, 2008, 62–3.
37  '25 jahre mitgliedschaft des zentrums DDR des Internationalen Theaterinstituts'.
38  Samson, 2008, 64.
39  Letter from Hans Michael Richter, 1967.
40  'Erfüllungsbericht', 1970.
41  Torres, 1989, 139.
42  'Report of the Third World committee'.
43  United Nations, 'Resolutions adopted on the reports of the second committee', 39–49.
44  'Report of the Third World committee', 3.
45  Goquingco, 1971.
46  Carunungan, 1971.
47  Samson, 2008, 66.
48  Partido, 1971.
49  Goquingco, 1971.
50  'Third-world festival', 1971.
51  Sanchez, 1971.
52  Goquingco, 1971.
53  Galvez, 2003, 181–8.
54  Butterfield, 1982.
55  Horn, 1992.
56  'Bericht über die mitarbeit auf dem 14. kongreß des Internationalen Theaterinstituts', 1971.
57  Letter from Jean Darcante to the attendees of the Shiraz conference, 1973.
58  'Bericht über die teilnahme an der 1. theaterkonferenz und einem theaterfestival der "Dritten Welt" vom 18.11.–2.12.1971 in Manila sowie über aufenthalt in Tokio vom 3.–5.12.1971'.
59  'Bericht über den XV. weltkongreß des Internationalen Theaterinstituts in Moskau vom 27. Mai bis 1. Juni 1973'.
60  'Kurzbericht des BRD ITI über die Shiraz konferenz'.
61  'Bericht'.
62  Copy of letter from Cecile Guidote to Jalal Khoury, 1973.
63  'Secretary general's report: XVIth Congress'.
64  'Proposed projects and program of activities noted and approved 1975–1977'.

65   Letter from Cecile Guidote to Fritz Bennewitz, 1972.
66   '21st Congress', 48.
67   Van Erven, 1992, 133.
68   Balme, 2022, 284.
69   'Bericht über aufenthalt in der Republik der Philippinen', 1970.
70   John, 2012, 284.
71   Fiebach, 1977.
72   Bodden, 1997, 380.
73   Bodden, 1997, 386.

# References

## Archival sources

'21st congress: theatre/new world visions: Toronto: 1–8 June'. BArch DR107/75.
'9. kongress des ITI: bericht des generalkomitees'. BArch DR1/20438.
'Arab theatre seminar Casablanca: 17 to 20 November 1966: resolutions'. BArch DR107/74.
'Bericht über aufenthalt in der Republik der Philippinen', 10 December 1970. BArch DR1/10653a.
'Bericht über den XV. weltkongreß des Internationalen Theaterinstituts in Moskau vom 27. Mai bis 1. Juni 1973', 31 July 1973. In 'ITI weltkongresse'. Archive of ITI Germany.
'Bericht über die mitarbeit auf dem 14. kongreß des Internationalen Theaterinstituts'. In 'ITI weltkongresse'. Archive of ITI Germany.
'Bericht über die teilnahme an der 1. theaterkonferenz und einem theaterfestival der "Dritten Welt" vom 18.11.–2.12.1971 in Manila sowie über aAfenthalt in Tokio vom 3.–5.12.1971'. BArch DR107/51.
'Bericht: 2. festival/konferenz des theaters der Dritten Welt in Shiraz (Iran) 1973'. BArch DR107/4.
'Erfüllungsbericht: arbeitsplan 1970', 31 December 1970. BArch DR1/12950.
'Kurzbericht des BRD ITI über die Shiraz konferenz'. In 'Dritte Welt von 1971 bis 1973'. Archive of ITI Germany.
'Proposed projects and program of activities noted and approved 1975–1977' (excerpt). In 'Dritte Welt von 1971 bis 1973'. Archive of ITI Germany.
'Report of the Third World committee'. BArch DR107/51.
'Secretary general's report, XVIth congress'. In 'ITI weltkongresse'. Archive of ITI Germany.
Copy of letter from Cecile Guidote to Jalal Khoury, 24 February 1973. In 'Dritte Welt von 1971 bis 1973'. Archive of ITI Germany.
Letter from Cecile Guidote to Fritz Bennewitz, 17 June 1972. BArch DR107/51.
Letter from Hans Michael Richter, 30 August 1967 (excerpt). BArch DR107/51.
Letter from Jean Darcante to the attendees of the Shiraz conference, 2 October 1973. In 'Dritte Welt von 1971 bis 1973'. Archive of ITI Germany.
United Nations. 'Resolutions adopted on the reports of the second committee'. United Nations General Assembly, twenty-fifth session, 39–49. Accessed 6 September 2022. https://undocs.org/A/RES/2626%20(XXV).

## Published sources

Balme, Christopher. 'Theatre-historiographical patterns in the Global South 1950–1990: transnational and institutional perspectives'. In *The Routledge Companion to Theatre and Performance Historiography*, edited by Tracy C. Davis and Peter W. Marx, 269–89. London: Routledge, 2022.
Bodden, Michael H. 'Class, gender, and the contours of nationalism in the culture of Philippine radical theater', *Frontiers: A Journal of Women Studies* 16 (2–3) (1996): 24–50.
Bodden, Michael H. 'Brecht in Asia: new agendas, national traditions, and critical consciousness'. In *A Bertolt Brecht Reference Companion*, edited by Siegfried Mews, 379–98. London: Greenwood Press, 1997.
Butterfield, Fox. 'Opera group in pact with Philippines', *New York Times* 16 October (1982): A3.

Canning, Charlotte. *On the Performance Front: US theatre and internationalism*. Basingstoke: Palgrave Macmillan, 2015.

Carunungan. 'Alamang: dream come true', *Manila Times*, 30 November (1971).

Creutzenberg, Jan. 'Dreaming of a new theatre in Cold War South Korea: Yu Chi-jin, the Rockefeller Foundation and the Seoul Drama Center', *Journal of Global Theatre History* 3 (2) (2019): 34–53. https://doi.org/10.5282/gthj/5118.

Cruz, Isagani R. 'Cecile Guidote-Alvarez', *Philippine Star*, 12 November (1998).

Cruz, Isagani R. 'Cecile Guidote Days', *Philippine Star*, 18 June (2003).

Darcante, Jean. 'Colloquium on the modern Arab theatre', *World Theatre* 14 (1) (1965): 89–90.

Fernandez, Doreen G. 'From ritual to realism: a brief historical survey of Philippine theater', *Philippine Studies* 28 (4) (1980): 389–419.

Fiebach, Joachim. *Theatre and Social Reality: International colloquy for theatre people from countries of the Third World*. Berlin: Tastomat, 1977.

Galvez, Virgilio. 'Epilogue'. In *Theatre for the Nation: A prospectus for the national theater of the Philippines*, by Cecile Guidote-Alzvarez, 181–8. Quezon City: De La Salle University Press, 2003.

Goquingco, Leonor Orosa. 'Babel overcome: one world through theater', *Manila Bulletin*, 28 November (1971). From the archive of ITI Germany.

Granville-Barker, Harvey and Archer, William. *A National Theatre: Scheme and estimates*. Port Washington: Kennikat Press, 1970.

Guidote-Alvarez, Cecile. *Theater for the Nation: A prospectus for the national theater of the Philippines*. Quezon City: De La Salle University Press, 2003.

Horn, Barbara L. *Ellen Stewart and La MaMa: A bio-bibliography*. Westport, CT: Greenwood Press, 1992.

Iacob, Viviana. 'The University of the Theatre of Nations: explorations into Cold War exchanges', *Journal of Global Theatre History* 4 (2) (2022): 68–80.

Iacob, Viviana. 'Cold War mobilities: Eastern European theatre going global'. In *Performing the Cold War in the Postcolonial World: Theatre, film, literature and things*, edited by Christopher Balme, 43–67. London: Routledge, 2024.

John, David Gethin. *Bennewitz, Goethe, Faust: German and intercultural stagings*. Toronto: University of Toronto Press, 2012.

Kollektiv des Zentrums DDR des ITI. '25 Jahre mitgliedschaft des zentrums DDR des Internationalen Theaterinstituts', 1984.

Leonhardt, Nic. 'The Rockefeller roundabout of funding: Severino Montano and the development of theatre in the Philippines in the 1950s', *Journal of Global Theatre History* 3 (2) (2019): 19–33.

Partido, Corazon R. 'Without much ceremony, Third World theater participants convene', *Manila Times*, 24 November (1971).

Samson, Laura L. *A Continuing Narrative on Philippine Theater: The story of PETA*. Quezon City: Philippine Education Theatre Association, 2008.

Sanchez, Ephraim. 'A critical resume: Third-World theatre conference: questions and issues raised', *Manila Chronicle*, 28 November (1971).

'Third-world festival: renaissance theater director lauds Philippine initiative', *Manila Times*, 7 October (1971).

Torres, Maria Luisa F. 'Anticipating freedom in theatre'. In *Brecht in Asia and Africa: The Brecht yearbook XIV*, edited by John Fuegi and Marc Silberman, 134–51. Hong Kong: International Brecht Society, 1989.

Van Erven, Eugène. 'Theatre of liberation in action: the people's theatre network of the Philippines', *New Theatre Quarterly* 3 (10) (1987): 131–49.

Van Erven, Eugène. *The Playful Revolution: Theatre and liberation in Asia*. Bloomington: Indiana University Press, 1992.

# 13
# Robert W. July and the 'future' of theatre in Africa
Christopher B. Balme

> Most of the time I could swear I was in, say, the Carolina Piedmont.
> – Robert W. July, diary, 1958

On 27 January 1958 Robert William July, the Rockefeller Foundation's new director of humanities and officer for Africa, set foot on the continent for the first time in Dakar, Senegal:

> First day in Africa and lots of impressions – vivid, various, powerful, and probably not to be trusted at all … The local Africans – Senegalese – seem to comprise all shades of skin color although most are very black and, indeed, the lighter ones may be from other parts of the country (there seems to be little evidence of intermarriage) … In this vast area live about 20,000,000 people of many different tribes and languages and cultures. This variousness of culture, along with difficulty of transportation and communication, and the comparatively unwesternized characteristic of the population presents one of the basic problems in developing and governing a country which will be, for all practical purposes, independent within three or four years.[1]

When July first touched African soil he brought with him values and expectations acquired through years working at the Rockefeller Foundation. He was both overwhelmed by and sceptical of such sensory excess. He registered skin colour, the 'blackness' of the population – a recurrent motif in his early diary entries – and grasped the enormity of the task that lay ahead: development amid a lack of Westernisation. A week later, having arrived in Accra, he was astounded by the modernity of the African cities he had seen, and admitted he could be in 'Carolina Piedmont' – a reference to the deindustralised eastern Appalachians with its considerable African-American population.

July had arrived a Rockefeller Foundation expert. His expertise was in higher education, particularly history but also including the arts more generally. As an officer of the Rockefeller Foundation he fulfilled a double function: first as an intermediary tasked with identifying people of potential who could be sent to the US or the UK for further education; and second as an academic expert, an historian dedicated to building expertise in the field of African history, a discipline he actively promoted as an agent of the foundation, and contributed to with his later publications. His job was also to envisage the future of the African states that had or were about to gain independence – their needs and aspirations – and harness his professional know-how to the considerable financial resources of the Rockefeller Foundation.

July's arrival coincided with a momentous phase in the Rockefeller Foundation's involvement in the developing world. In the areas of the humanities and social sciences the foundation was recalibrating and internationalising its activities. 'Development' had been primarily a concern in the American South, where the foundation had a long-standing involvement in combating poverty and raising educational standards as a path to improving overall living standards. Advocating for development, both inside and outside the US, related explicitly to President Harry S. Truman's Point Four Program and his call to combat 'underdevelopment'. It also meant imagining or projecting the future – a realm of possibilities and potential projects that could be actively shaped with the resources of a major philanthropic foundation.

Rockefeller's involvement in multiple geopolitical locales poses the question of if the Foundation thought in terms of a single future – although it seemed to be the assumption in the 1950s that it was singular concept – or of multiple futures that stood in a relationship of asymmetry with one another. The intellectual framework behind such thinking was a new conceptualisation of the future as a horizon of expectation that could be actively shaped. This was a secular future that could be planned for with the help of experts – scientific, administrative and cultural. Marking a shift from prophecy to prognosis, it was a future that could be both 'desired' and planned for, as historian Elke Seefried puts it:

> … the concept and understanding of the future now acquired a double meaning. On the one hand, they included a prophetic component, which was teleologically conceived from an end of

history and saw things coming towards the present. On the other hand, the prognostic component now came to the fore, which envisaged the future from the past and present and assumed that what could be expected could to a certain extent be derived from the past and present. This expectation could be derived and desired in a normative mode or extrapolated in a more empirical-positivist sense.[2] (Translation mine.)

The figure of the expert is crucial to understanding futurity in terms of agency as well as just normative expectation. The social figure of the expert emerged as a key player in 'political planning processes – i.e. application-based and procedure-based anticipations of the future'.[3]

## The future according to Rockefeller

In 1958 Warren Weaver, director of the Rockefeller Foundation's natural sciences division and vice president of its natural and medical sciences division, published a report entitled 'A quarter century in the natural sciences'. In it he expressed satisfaction 'because we have the intellectual tools for predicting the future as well as understanding the past'.[4] While referring specifically to the motion of planets, his claim was implicitly framed in wider terms because, under the heading 'men', he emphasised the centrality of the human factor:

> The way to advance work in any field whatsoever is to seek out the well-trained men of capacity and character, men who are imaginative and energetic – and then back them. If one is giving broad and sustained support to an area, he must also be concerned to help create a future flow of such persons – that is, he must help create attractive circumstances for the recruitment and training of younger personnel.[5]

Shaping the future was predicated on finding the right men – those 'of capacity and character' – to do the job. They were, in today's jargon, high potentials, and necessary to effect change. As we will see, the overwhelming focus of July's work was to identify such men and, occasionally, women.

The Rockefeller Foundation's annual report for 1958 identified the two principal purposes of the foundation's work in the developing world: 'One is the support of humanistic scholarship and of work in the arts in the countries of the region; the other, the encouragement of understanding and appreciation of the area in the West.'[6] Two years later the foundation defined its mission 'to lie, broadly, in the field of social dynamics', and warned that 'those countries that look to the future from a position of national underdevelopment must realise that grave problems lie ahead and that choices must be made which will determine the course of their history for many years to come'.[7] Following this, the foundation adjusted its support policies and began focusing on university education, particularly in Africa, to aid developing nations in 'their continuing forward progress'.[8] Universities needed to acknowledge their 'main responsibility for educating future leaders in developing areas of the world', and provide 'research-oriented advanced training'.[9] The university, because of its commitment to research, was where the future was shaped.

In 1962 the Rockefeller Foundation celebrated its first 50 years with an explicit commitment to shaping the future, and not just alleviating the problems of the present: 'The fact that we live in a world of change is constantly recognised by the Foundation, as is the necessity of continuous adjustment to change, and, accordingly, of planning for the future.'[10] In concrete terms this meant apportioning funds 'to be devoted to institution building', which meant 'both direct and indirect support of this overseas university development program'.[11] The foundation also identified an urgent need to focus on food production and land economics 'in preparation for the hungry hordes of the future'.[12]

If we think of Cold War development projects we might think of the Aswan Dam or the Green Revolution in agriculture – technological megaprojects that harnessed both scientific research and engineering expertise. However, the civil and mechanical engineer had an interest in the cultural field as well. The Rockefeller Foundation recognised that the arts were an integral part of the development agenda. While the lion's share of the foundation's theatre-related funding went into transforming the US theatrical scene into an artistically ambitious non-profit model with a network of regional theatres, the foundation also attempted – with much more modest means – to do something similar in the postcolonial world.

The cultural work of the Rockefeller Foundation was suspended between various scenarios of uncertainty and framed by nuclear warfare, hungry hordes and faith in institution building in the form of research-oriented universities. This led, as I have written about elsewhere, to substantial support for the establishment of a school of drama at the University of Ibadan, and many smaller grants for university theatre departments and experimental laboratories in the developing world.[13]

In the 1960s cultural development was formulated as a funding stream of the Rockefeller Foundation, which went hand in hand with US-centric university development. The foundation's support of higher education needs to be viewed against the background of human capital theory. In the words of Gary Hess: 'Development thinking assumed the importance of education, embodied in "human-capital" theory. Investment in education brought a high rate of return, human-capital theory assumed, because it increased labor productivity, promoted technological innovation, and enhanced equality.'[14] However, by the end of the decade the tone had changed significantly. The foundation's annual report for 1969 concluded: 'The university of the future is being shaped today in an atmosphere of crisis; too often reforms are introduced to meet the exigencies of the hour.'[15] Nigeria had descended into civil war, and, against the background of the Vietnam War, universities had become sites of dissent, and in many cases of outright opposition to US foreign policy.

The foundation's reports of the 1960s are suffused with futurity, which is inherent in the development paradigm, whose teleological assumptions are built into the word itself. Both the language and perspective of the reports reflect a broader shift in both Western capitalist and Eastern socialist thinking, which, despite ideological antagonisms, shared several assumptions about modernisation and its application in countries in the postcolonial world.[16] Both systems were predicated on future thinking, be it the US futures market or the Soviet five-year plan.

## Robert W. July: Rockefeller's man in Africa

Born in New York in 1918, Robert William July (figure 13.1) studied history at Columbia University, graduating with an MA in 1939. He served in the US Navy Reserve during the Second World War and returned to Columbia in 1945. There, in 1951, he obtained his PhD with a dissertation on the New York politician Gulian C. Verplanck. He joined the Rockefeller Foundation in 1948, becoming assistant director for humanities in 1955, and for the humanities and social sciences in 1962, holding the latter post until 1968 when he left the foundation to take up a professorship in history at Hunter College and the Graduate School of the City University of New York. He held visiting professorships at the University of Ibadan's institute of African studies from 1963–6, and at University College in Nairobi (now the University of Nairobi) from 1966–8. During his tenure as an academic he produced several notable works on African

**Figure 13.1**    Portrait of Robert W. July, circa 1958. Source: Courtesy of Rockefeller Archive Center.

history: *The Origins of Modern African Thought*, 1967; *A History of the African People*, 1970; *Precolonial Africa: An economic and social history*, 1975; and *An African Voice: The role of the humanities in African independence*, 1987. The subtitle of *An African Voice* (which drew heavily on a Rockefeller Foundation-funded conference at Bellagio organised by July)[17] illuminates the thread running through July's activities as assistant director for the humanities and later as an academic. For July, humanists encompassed 'artists, writers, musicians, educators, as well as political figures of a philosophic or reflective bent of mind'.[18]

July's work at the Rockefeller Foundation focused initially on the General Education Board, which was devoted to improving higher education in the American South, and involved supervising the board's fellowship and scholarship programmes. Promotion to assistant director of humanities meant continuation of this work, but for developing nations in Asia, Africa and Latin America. The fellowship programme for the humanities was 'designed to provide advanced study to individuals in a number of fields in the arts, letters, and related areas, the purpose ... being to prepare the most promising intellectual leadership in a number of countries for enlarged professional responsibilities'.[19] From 1958 July concentrated his activities on sub-Saharan Africa, visiting virtually all countries in the region in annual visits until 1968. From 1963 he lived permanently on the continent, holding the aforementioned posts at the University of Ibadan and subsequently at University College, Nairobi.

July's voluminous diaries (each year comprises over 100 pages of single-spaced typescript) reflect a double perspective. On the one hand they are a form of institutional communication directed at an organisation – the Rockefeller Foundation – intended to provide a basis for funding decisions. On the other they have the character of field notes, and contain remarkably frank assessments of individuals and organisations. While not libellous, they are clearly written with the expectation of confidentiality. The entries contain both implicit and explicit formulations of Rockefeller Foundation funding policies, and hence provide a perspective on the foundation's overarching strategy during this period of involvement in Africa. Although nowhere laid out systematically, July articulates these policies on numerous occasions, meaning that a systematisation can be attempted:

1. On the eve of Anglophone and Francophone Africa's political independence, the Rockefeller Foundation saw an opportunity to promote higher education as an essential component of nation building. This had already been recognised by the colonial powers (for example by the UK in the 1945 Elliot report), but the provisions of the departing colonial powers were, in July's assessment, woefully inadequate for the populations of the relevant emerging nations.[20] In addition, the UK's colonial administration seemed bent on replicating the elitist British Oxbridge model, buttressed by an array of technical colleges, in selected African countries.

2. The overriding motivation for July's recommendations was predicated on an acceleration of African involvement in the humanities on both a staffing level and on a curricular level. He frequently expressed frustration with British expatriate academics who seemed wedded to the standards and expectations of their home countries. An emphasis on Africanisation – even if July didn't use the term – finds institutional expression in various institutes for African studies, to which the Rockefeller Foundation devoted considerable resources, especially in terms of staff development. To July's mind, such institutes provided a space to engage in serious research into a 'culturally matrixed' African culture, whose lineaments had already been formulated by the advocates of negritude in the 1930s.[21]

3. Wherever appropriate, July emphasised the need for more research and qualified staff to engage with Islamic culture. The obvious, even dominant, presence of Islamic culture in West and East Africa was

reflected little, if at all, in the teaching and research of African higher education institutions.

4. A search for a new function for the arts in Africa under postcolonial conditions is a recurrent motif. July became convinced over the course of his visits that dance and theatre were the most central, integrative art forms, and would provide a kind of fulcrum for the other arts – visual, oral and musical.

July's territory included both Francophone and Anglophone Africa. His remit was broad: apart from identifying potential academics in humanities departments (mainly history and literature), he focused on improving library holdings, and occasionally supporting museums and performing-arts groups.

July's 1958 diary reveals a curious intellectual overwhelmed by the sensory experiences of a new continent but also galvanised to effect change for the better. His confessions reveal an ethnocentric bias. His frequent references to 'negroes' can be put down to the accepted usage of the time, and he is highly critical of the 'color bar' whenever he encounters it (for example in the Belgian Congo). His characterisations of interlocutors sometimes contain humorous vignettes: 'JB is a very pleasant attractive Englishman of the lion hunting type who has spent a good deal of time in Africa ... can't wait to get back ... probably feels a bit rusty on strangling rhinos or whatnot.'[22]

July's first trip to Africa established a pattern that would be repeated in the years to come, with minor variations. His seven-week itinerary for 1958 is shown in table 13.1.[23]

In subsequent years, the trips, and the list of interlocutors, became longer. In 1958 July visited 13 cities; in 1963 he made it to 23, including most of the sub-Saharan African countries.

July always began his annual tours in Paris. The first entry in his 1961 diary reads:

> I went over to the office of the Congress for Cultural Freedom for a long talk with John Hunt about some of the Congress's recent activities in Africa ... Evidently the Congress has plans for the development of public library services in Africa with particular reference to the French territories where, under the French system, very little has been developed ... And Hunt also spoke of the establishment of a cultural centre in Ibadan which has been sponsored by Wole Soyinka, Ulli Beier, and others interested in the arts and letters. Presumably funds are being supplied by the western region government.[24]

**Table 13.1** Robert W. July's tour itinerary, 1958

| Date | Location | Institutions | Persons (selection) |
|---|---|---|---|
| Jan 23–26 | Paris | UNESCO, Commission for Technical Cooperation in Africa (CCTA) | Georges Balandier, J.-P. LeBoeuf, John Bowers |
| Jan 26–31 | Dakar | Institut Français de l'Afrique Noire (IFAN), University of Dakar, Department of Education | Louis Massé, Théodore Monod, C. Arnavon, Diallo Thely, R. Mauny, Joseph Ki Zerbo, N'daw Alassane, Sonar Senghor, Pierre Verger |
| Jan 31–Feb 2 | Abidjan | IFAN, Museum of African Art and Culture | J.-L. Tournier, B. Holas |
| Feb 2–8 | Accra | USIS, Ghana Information Service, University College Ghana, Afro-American Institute, Accra Museum | J. H. Nketia, R. H. Stoughton, D. Kimble, Kofi Antuban, J. D. Fage |
| Feb 9–12 | Lagos | USIS Library, Lagos Museum, Nigerian Broadcasting Service | Chinua Achebe, Kenneth Murray |
| Feb 12–14 | Ibadan | University College | G. L. Axworthy, Kenneth Dike, C. L. Geary |
| Feb 15–16 | Oyo, Ife | Museum in Ife | |
| Feb 16–19 | Ibadan | University College, USIS, Nigerian College of Technology | K. O. Dike, S. Adebo, Bernard Fagg, S. O. Biabaku |
| Feb 20–24 | Jos | Jos Museum | A. J. Spicer, B. Fagg |
| Feb 25–26 | Zaria | Northern Region Literary Agency, Nigerian College of Arts, Science and Technology | A. J. Carpenter, A. A. Shillingford |
| Feb 26–28 | Kano | British Council, School of Arabic Studies | M. Eltenton, M. Hiskett |
| March 1–5 | Leopoldville, Brazzaville | Lovanium University, Poto Poto Art School, École des Arts et de l'Artisanat, Institut d'Études Centreafricaines, l'École Saint Luc | M. Gillon, Pierre Lods, M. D. Biebuyck |
| March 7–12 | Entebbe, Kampala | Makerere University College, USIS, School of Art, East African Institute of Social Research, Uganda Museum | B. de Bunsen, Kenneth Ingham, Prince A. K. Nyabongo, Roland Oliver, P. Gutkind, R. W. Beachey |
| March 14 | Paris | [blank in source] | Alfred Métraux, Michel Leiris |

Source: July, 1958.

July's visit to the Congress for Cultural Freedom (CCF), famously (but at the time covertly) funded by the CIA, illustrates the high degree of interconnectedness between American philanthropic organisations, both legitimate and fake. The CCF was the largest of the many CIA front organisations and conduits used to divert US taxpayers' money to cultural projects across the globe.[25] July's remarks underline the CCF's interest in the postcolonial world: the Mbari Club, founded by Ulli Beier, received most of its funds from the CCF – that is, from the CIA.

On 8 February 1961 July flew to Uganda where he visited Makerere University College, one of three campuses of a projected University of East Africa also encompassing the universities of Nairobi and Dar es Salaam. At that time the UK Colonial Office was still planning a federation of Uganda, Kenya and Tanganyika – one of many failed projects for federations of former colonies. Most of July's interlocutors were expatriate Brits, and in his diary he reveals his frustration with their lack of energy and imagination in encouraging African writing, music and theatre productions. Of Gerald Moore, a name familiar to students of postcolonial literature, at the time in charge of extramural studies at Makerere, he noted:

> … old colleague of Ulli Beier, Moore wants to encourage writing in East Africa but has found little to work on. I'm not certain whether his energy matches his enthusiasm for he has done nothing to solicit work from Makarere students.[26]

It becomes clear from July's numerous value judgements and occasional recommendations for funding that he is primarily interested in effecting as rapid a transition as possible to universities staffed by and providing courses and research of relevance to Africans.

More encouraging was a meeting with Maxwell Jackson, director of the newly opened Uganda National Theatre. Jackson had been in post for a year and July was impressed by his activities, especially in encouraging the production of African drama and music. July noted approvingly that the Ugandan government had underwritten the theatre and its activities for five years, and that Jackson was intent on forming a resident company of African performers. Discussions on Rockefeller Foundation support, while ultimately inconclusive, revolved around 'help toward equipment, costumes, musical instruments etc., and assistance toward touring in the rural areas'.[27] While noting Jackson's energy and professionalism, July remained sceptical that he would stay in his post for long, and he was especially frustrated that there seemed to be no cooperation between Makerere University College and the university's English department.[28] From Uganda July continued to Nairobi, Salisbury in Southern Rhodesia, the Republic of the Congo, the Ivory Coast, Senegal and Nigeria.

## Soyinka and the school of drama at Ibadan

An extended stay at the University of Ibadan led to renewed connections with Ulli Beier, Ezekiel Mphahlele, Martin Banham, Geoffrey Axworthy and Wole Soyinka. The latter had received a two-year Rockefeller Foundation grant, which July had brokered in 1959, to research traditional 'Nigerian drama', and had been travelling across the country in a foundation-funded Land Rover 'recording traditional ceremonies and religious rites which have already had an influence on his writing', July notes.[29] July had first met Soyinka in London in April 1959 after being alerted to him by the staff of the English department at Ibadan, particularly Molly Mahood and Axworthy. July was impressed:

> Soyinka is a personable individual whose ideas on African drama make good sense in terms of the development and projection of traditional forms into the present and future. I would think that he makes a potential fellowship case, probably for some kind of study of dramatic forms in other parts of the world, but first he needs to return to Nigeria and establish himself there. At this stage he has had enough contact with Western drama to enable him to have ideas on *how Western and African theatre mix* ... Possibly the best entering point would be through a survey of Nigerian dramatic activities. (Italics mine.)[30]

July's plans and the related Rockefeller archival material demonstrate a conscious strategy on the part of the foundation, executed by July, to promulgate a particular version of the theatrical epistemic community that both July and the foundation considered ideal for Africa. The penultimate sentence in the excerpt above points directly to what later became known as 'syncretic theatre'.[31]

Correspondence between Mahood and July indicates that the aforementioned planning paradigm was in full swing. She opined that Soyinka might want to set up a repertory company, and perhaps lay the foundation for a national theatre in Lagos, the city being part of colonial planning heritage (with ideas on planning from colonial powers going back to the 1950s). At this stage at least, Rockefeller was not planning to build or invest in theatre buildings but in people and in educational and research institutions. Mahood was not in favour of a drama department at the University of Ibadan, arguing that training was best acquired in a professional theatre. In the letter to July she also expressed reservations about the necessity for a school of drama 'when there are so many urgent needs to be met in such fields as medicine and agriculture'. But while she had reservations about the need for a school of drama she energetically supported a grant to Soyinka for a 'survey of the dance drama (and possibly other forms of entertainment) in Yoruba country'.[32]

In July's correspondence with Soyinka he formulated in clear terms his interest, and by extension the interest of the Rockefeller Foundation, in investing in such a survey: 'I am interested to find the gradual emergence of new art forms combining both the traditional African elements and the acquired European types.' He added that it should not be an anthropological or sociological study, but rather an analysis of the 'artistic and aesthetic impulses in Nigerian drama which would be useful to the playwright, producer, the director, and the acting company in direct and specific fashion'.[33]

This vision of a fusion of African and European forms aligned with Soyinka's approach, which he outlined in considerable detail in a letter to July in September 1959. In the letter, Soyinka discussed the question of 'traditional art from the village dweller', which, he argued, continued to be passed down in a creative atmosphere. The problem to be addressed was how 'modern would-be dramatists' could harness these traditions, as the previous output was chiefly European in content and imitative in conception: 'What is needed … is a fusion of the two enthusiasms.' Soyinka excoriated the European tendency to 'freeze' African culture in a discourse of authenticity, adding that anthropological studies actually encouraged 'this process of refrigeration'.[34]

Despite or perhaps because of Soyinka's highly differentiated response, which weighed up the advantages and disadvantages of a 'fusion' approach to Nigerian drama, Soyinka received a grant for the full amount requested, and returned to Nigeria in 1960. Although the Rockefeller Foundation was happy to fund Nigerian and other scholar-practitioners as university faculty, July was not happy with Soyinka taking time off his research to work on practical theatre projects. Soyinka outlined his plans 'to form a semi-professional company … [as a] base for a National Theatre' in the context of what he called 'independence hysteria', and inquired if the foundation would be prepared to fund such an undertaking.[35] July was not amused, and insisted that Soyinka concentrate on the research project for which he had received funding, although ultimately he granted Soyinka unpaid leave from the research project to pursue his playwriting projects. The result was *A Dance of the Forests*, first performed in October 1960 during the Nigerian Independence Day celebrations by the 1960 Masks, the semi-professional company formed by Soyinka. Since Soyinka had sent July two versions of his preliminary research report, it was clear he was both conducting research and writing plays. As *A Dance of the Forests* attests, the two activities were in close symbiosis.

Two years later the Rockefeller Foundation earmarked US$200,000 to establish a school of drama at the University of Ibadan. Final planning for the school was completed in March 1961 when July visited Ibadan again during his annual field trip to Africa. There he met with Soyinka, Beier and the lecturers from the University of Ibadan's English department, including Geoffrey Axworthy and Martin Banham, who would go on to become key staff. The trip included an outing with Beier and Soyinka to Oshogbo via Ife, where they watched a touring student production of a Molière play written partly in pidgin English and directed by Axworthy. They also visited the Mbari Club, founded by Beier and Soyinka, at that time still under construction. July noted prophetically in his diary that 'it could develop into an important literary centre for it will be well directed and is in the middle of the biggest African city in the whole continent'.[36] He also witnessed and was impressed by a performance by the Yoruba travelling theatre troupe of Kola Ogunmola, whom Beier regarded as a 'first-class theatre man who could make a successful full-time business of his troupe were he to get a six-month stake'.[37] The school of drama continued to receive direct annual grants, with additional funds given to individual faculty members, until 1969.

In 1968 July left the Rockefeller Foundation to take up a professorship in history at Hunter College of the City University of New York. By the late 1960s the foundation had discontinued its theatre-related funding to developing nations. There were many, sometimes local, reasons for this. The outbreak of civil war in Nigeria in 1967 was seen as a failure of the plan to train elites at universities to create a bright, democratic future, and student unrest in other countries had dampened the foundation's enthusiasm for cultural development, although it continued its other programmes. The foundation's 1969 annual report does not detail, under the heading cultural development, a single grant outside the US. From a cultural perspective it seemed that the future lay once again in the US.

## The future of the performing arts in Ghana

In 1963 Robert July reviewed the Rockefeller Foundation's support of three seminal figures in the performing arts in Ghana, based at the University of Ghana's new campus in Legon, whom the Rockefeller Foundation had funded in previous years. They were the dramatist Efua Sutherland, the composer Joseph Hanson Kwabena Nketia and the choreographer and dance scholar Albert Opoku. In 1958 the foundation funded J. H. Nketia with a fellowship to the United States, where he attended Columbia University (studying with Henry Cowell), the Juilliard School and Northwestern University, studying musicology and composition.[38] Similar support was extended to Opoku, who studied at the Juilliard School and the Martha Graham School of Contemporary Dance. The latter residency prompted July to remark later, slightly disparagingly: 'Opoku's residence in N.Y. has been helpful in this respect even if it does mean the occasional introduction of a bit of Martha Graham to long-suffering Africa.'[39]

Introducing Martha Graham to 'long-suffering Africa' made sense from a US philanthropic point of view because it meant an extension of the new, 'modern' non-profit model to the developing world.[40] Efua Sutherland was a multiple recipient of Rockefeller funding, most notably for the Ghana Drama Studio,[41] which became, in effect if not in name, Ghana's national theatre.[42]

In 1963 July drew a positive conclusion on the Foundation's institution building in the arts:

> The whole business has gone remarkably well; indeed it is almost a classic case of how foundation help, injected in the right place on behalf of the *right people*, has helped to make some *major changes*, and all for the good. Efua's theatre is now *a fixture with its own repertory and company*, its *own theatre building*, and a *connection with the University* which gives it freedom from government interference – as much as one can ever be assured of such – and a secure institutional base.[43] (Italics mine.)

Rockefeller's goal was institutional support, or more specifically institution building, for the newly independent African nations.

Whatever ulterior motives the foundation might have had (promoting a free market economy over socialism, for example), in the cultural sphere its aim was accelerating indigenous agency, and moving beyond the stranglehold of British expatriate lecturers and their values and norms. Writing on the material needs of Nketia, Opoku and Sutherland, July reports: 'this strikes me as a most promising *indigenous beginning, run by Africans* of taste and ability to the end of *building national institutions in the performing arts*.'[44] (Italics mine.) He also compares favourably the university focus of the artistic undertakings compared to those of the Institute of Culture in downtown Accra: 'the university-based operation is better and likely to remain so with its independence, freedom to experiment, and superior talent and organization'.[45]

From these assessments it is possible to specify further the underlying principles guiding Rockefeller Foundation funding policies in the arts for the newly independent nations in Africa. The first pertains to the fields of theatre, music and dance. These were seen as discrete areas of expertise for which training abroad was required, even if the long-term goal was to foster indigenous African aesthetic preferences and practices. In the case of Ghana, Efua Sutherland's institution-building activities mirrored the US non-profit resident model, as July emphasised when stressing that Sutherland's Ghana Drama Studio was 'a fixture with its own repertory and company, its own theatre building'. The Drama Studio deviated somewhat from the American original, however, in its 'connection with the University', which was not normally the case for equivalent institutions in the US. However, being part of a university – and a flagship one at that – provided the theatre with a secure institutional base and more autonomy than if it had been dependent on government funding.

At the time, both the Rockefeller and Ford foundations were investing considerable sums in exporting the model known in the US as the resident theatre programme to Africa. These theatres were defined by 'their non-profit status and by continuous seasons, of from forty to fifty-two weeks, that include up to a dozen plays. They employ at least a nucleus of their acting companies for the entire season.'[46] In the 1961/62 financial year Ford invested US$3 million in eight such theatres (in New York, San Francisco, Houston, Stratford CT, Milwaukee, Minneapolis, Oklahoma City and Washington DC), and in 1963 it appropriated US$8 million for ballet, 'a medium that only in the last three decades has become an important American art form'.[47] According to this institutional logic, Ghana, with its plans to establish a national dance company and a national theatre, was only three decades behind the US, and if we use the UK as a model there was no time lag, because it was only in the 1950s that the Royal Shakespeare Company and the National Theatre were finally apportioned state subsidies, and the transition to permanent acting companies and continuous seasons began. One could speak of coevality rather than postcolonial catch up.

## Conclusion

The logic of funding – the main business of philanthropy – assumes the existence of established norms, criteria and priorities by which to apportion resources. While mutable and given to change over time, they nevertheless shape the mental map of individuals such as July, who came to Africa bearing promises of fellowships and even institutional funding. It would be too simplistic to suggest that the priorities of the Rockefeller Foundation formed a hidden agenda to promote a fusion model combining Western and African elements. What July's diaries and other archival material make clear, however, is that a notion of theatre, and of the performing arts more generally, preceded 'first contact' between Africans and Europeans. July seems to have had few preconceptions, on a thematic level, of what 'good' works of African dance, drama or music could be; it was Rockefeller's job not to select works but to select people, the 'well-trained men of capacity and character' who would shape the postcolonial nations. Whatever the future held it would certainly not be tied to European works performed by amateurs. African theatre of the future should be professional and syncretic, a mix of the Western and the African. It is clear from the way July supported people such as Wole Soyinka and Efua Sutherland that Rockefeller Foundation support could take an institutional form: institutes of African studies, a university school of drama and in Sutherland's case even a theatre building. The US version of the modern theatre episteme shines through here – the non-profit repertory theatre performing a mixture of classics and indigenous works. This was the progressive institutional model receiving lavish funding in the US from both the Rockefeller and Ford foundations, and that seemed to the foundations' officers to be transferable to most cultural contexts. It was modular and amenable to indigenisation, or so it seemed. It was also the model that writer-directors such as Soyinka and Sutherland aspired to replicate in the early 1960s. If July and the Rockefeller Foundation had a long-term effect on the course of theatre in Africa, then it was by virtue of the conviction that theatre, dance and drama needed to be firmly secured in the university curriculum, whether in a school of drama or in an institute of African studies. In this respect the prognosis was correct.

## Notes

1   July, 1958, 7.
2   Seefried, 2015, 45.
3   Seefried, 2015, 19.
4   Rockefeller Foundation, 1958, 41.
5   Rockefeller Foundation, 1958, 92.
6   Rockefeller Foundation, 1958, 258.
7   Rockefeller Foundation, 1961, 4.
8   Rockefeller Foundation, 1961, 6.
9   Rockefeller Foundation, 1961, 39, 164.
10  Rockefeller Foundation, 1962, 15.
11  Rockefeller Foundation, 1961, 21.
12  Rockefeller Foundation, 1961, 41.
13  Balme, 2019, 7–8.
14  Hess, 2003, 323.
15  Rockefeller Foundation, 1969, 44.
16  Recent research has brought out a wealth of information on 'global socialism': see Mark and Slobodian, 2018; Stanek, 2020; and Mark and Betts, 2022. To the activities of socialist countries should be added non-aligned actors such as Israel, which had an impact in Nigeria, Sierra Leone and Ethiopia. See Levin, 2022.
17  July and Benson, 1982, 17–22.
18  July, 1987, x.
19  July, 1972, 4.
20  On the Ashby Commission report see Livsey, 2017, 131f.
21  For an explication of the term 'culturally matrixed' see Chapter 5, this volume.
22  July, 1958, 4.
23  Table collated from July, 1958.
24  July, 1961, 1.
25  While US foundations such as Ford and Rockefeller were by no means simple extensions of US state policy, their goals were often compatible, and in the cultural field they even acted in close dialogue, as Frances Stonor Saunders has shown in her 1999 study of the Congress for Cultural Freedom (CCF). The foundations were often used to channel funds to recipients without alerting them to the funds' origin. The foundations' function was that of conduit rather than front, although the latter also existed, for example in the case of the Farfield Foundation, which was set up for the sole purpose of channeling CIA money to beneficiaries. There also existed significant social networks linking the big foundations with the CCF and the CIA (Saunders, 1999, 135–6 and 142–5). Research has shown that there was direct CCF involvement in Nigeria through support of journals such as *Transition* and *Black Orpheus* and the establishment and maintenance of the famous Mbari Club in Ibadan. July was probably not aware of the front nature of the CCF or its relationship with the CIA; John Hunt, who joined the CCF in 1956, was of course in the know (see Saunders, 1999, 241–2; see also Benson, 1986.
26  July, 1961, 13.
27  July, 1961, 14.
28  In fact the European expatriate community forced Jackson's resignation because of his attempts to support African performance. See Chapter 5, this volume.
29  July, 1961, 85.
30  July, 1959, 112.
31  See Balme, *Decolonizing the Stage*, 1999.

32   Letter to July, 19 June 1959. Cited in Lindfors, 2008, 102.
33   Letter from July to Soyinka, 2 September 1959. Cited in Lindfors, 2005, 105.
34   Letter from Soyinka to July, September 1959. Cited in Lindfors, 2005, 106.
35   Letter from Soyinka to July, 13 January 1960. Cited in Lindfors, 2005, 114–15.
36   July, 1961, 86.
37   July, 1961, 87.
38   On Nketia's career see https://www.ghanaweb.com/person/J-H-Kwabena-Nketia-168.
39   July, 1963, 70.
40   On the institutionalisation of the non-profit model in the US, see DiMaggio, 'Cultural boundaries and structural change', 1992.
41   Gaines, 2017, 75.
42   Donkor, 2017, 50.
43   July, 1963, 69.
44   July, 1963, 70.
45   July, 1963, 70.
46   Ford Foundation, 1962, 23.
47   Ford Foundation, 1963, 12.

# References

Balme, Christopher. *Decolonizing the Stage: Theatrical syncretism and post-colonial drama*. Oxford: Clarendon Press, 1999.

Balme, Christopher. 'Building theatrical epistemic communities in the Global South: expert networks, philanthropy and theatre studies in Nigeria 1959–1969', *Journal of Global Theatre History* 3 (2) (2019): 3–18. https://doi.org/10.5282/gthj/5119.

Donkor, David Afriye. 'Making space for performance: theatrical-architectural nationalism in postindependence Ghana', *Theatre History Studies* 36 (2017): 29–56. https://doi.org/10.1353/ths.2017.0002.

Ford Foundation. 'Annual Report'. New York: Ford Foundation, 1962.

Ford Foundation. 'Annual Report'. New York: Ford Foundation, 1963.

Gaines, Malik. *Black Performance on the Outskirts of the Left: A history of the impossible*. New York: New York University Press, 2017.

Hess, Gary R. 'Waging the Cold War in the Third World: the foundations and the challenges of development'. In *Charity, Philanthropy and Civility in American History*, edited by L. J. Friedman and M. McGarvie, 319–39. Cambridge: Cambridge University Press, 2003.

July, Robert W. Diary, 1958. Robert W. July collection, New York Public Library. MG748.

July, Robert W. Diary, 1959. Robert W. July collection, New York Public Library. MG748.

July, Robert W. Diary, 1960. Robert W. July collection, New York Public Library. MG748.

July, Robert W. Diary, 1961. Robert W. July collection, New York Public Library. MG748.

July, Robert W. Interviews, 1963–1965. Robert W. July collection, New York Public Library. MG748 b.1 f.8.

July, Robert W. Biographical note, 1972. New York Public Library. MG748 b.1. f. 2.

July, Robert W. *An African Voice: The role of the humanities in African independence*. Durham, NC: Duke University Press, 1987.

July, Robert W. and Benson, Peter Edward. 'African cultural and intellectual leaders and the development of the new African nations'. Rockefeller Foundation, 1982.

Levin, Ayala. *Architecture and Development: Israeli construction in sub-Saharan Africa and the settler colonial imagination, 1958–1973*. Durham, NC: Duke University Press, 2022.

Lindfors, Bernth. *Early Soyinka*. Trenton, NJ: Africa World Press, 2008.

Livsey, Tim. *Nigeria's University Age: Reframing decolonisation and development*. London: Palgrave Macmillan, 2017.

Mark, James and Betts, Paul. *Socialism Goes Global: The Soviet Union and Eastern Europe in the age of decolonisation*. Oxford: Oxford University Press, 2022.

Mark, James and Slobodian, Quinn. 'Eastern Europe in the global history of decolonization'. In *The Oxford Handbook of the Ends of Empire*, edited by Martin Thomas and Andrew S. Thompson, 351–72. Oxford: Oxford University Press, 2018.

Rockefeller Foundation. 'Annual Report'. New York: Rockefeller Foundation, 1958.
Rockefeller Foundation. 'Annual Report'. New York: Rockefeller Foundation, 1959.
Rockefeller Foundation. 'Annual Report'. New York: Rockefeller Foundation, 1960.
Rockefeller Foundation. 'Annual Report'. New York: Rockefeller Foundation, 1962.
Saunders, Frances Stonor. *Who Paid the Piper? The CIA and the cultural Cold War*. London: Granta, 1999.
Seefried, Elke. *Zukünfte: Aufstieg und Krise der Zukunftsforschung 1945–1980*. Berlin: De Gruyter Oldenbourg, 2015.
Stanek, Łukasz. *Architecture in Global Socialism: Eastern Europe, West Africa and the Middle East in the Cold War*. Princeton: Princeton University Press, 2020.

# 14
# Efua Sutherland's Pan-African networks
Abdul Karim Hakib

## Introduction

Efua Sutherland (1924–1996) is arguably the most influential figure in postwar theatre in Ghana. As a dramatist, director, teacher and cultural activist, Sutherland was a seminal figure in the country's theatrical and cultural landscape from the late 1950s until her death. She contributed significantly towards globally popularising Ghanaian theatre and performance from theoretical and practical perspectives. She operated in a network that included W. E. B. Du Bois, Kwame Nkrumah, Wole Soyinka, Chinua Achebe, Langston Hughes, Martin Luther King, Félix Morisseau-Leroy, Es'kia Mphahlele and Ngugi wa Thiong'o, to name only some. Prior to Ghana's independence in 1957, few people wrote plays. Notable exceptions included Kobina Sekyi (*The Blinkards*, 1916), J. B. Danquah (*The Third Woman*, 1935), Mabel Dove (*A Woman in Jade*, 1924) and F. Kwesi Fiawoo (*The Fifth Landing Stage*, 1943), although none of them were dedicated dramatists or playwrights. They had other professions, but used their plays as tools for advancing their political views and sociocultural arguments to the Gold Coast audience.

By contrast, Efua Sutherland was a dedicated dramatist who devoted much of her career to writing, directing, education, research and activism. Born in 1924 in Cape Coast in the central region of the Gold Coast (now Ghana), she was a trained teacher, teaching in several secondary schools, including her alma mater, St. Monica's Secondary School and Training College. After five and half years of teaching, Sutherland undertook further studies in the UK, studying at Homerton College at the University of Cambridge and the School of Oriental and African Studies at the University of London.[1] Upon her return to the Gold

Coast in 1950, she resumed classroom teaching, initially at St. Monica's, then at Fijai Secondary School and, later, at Achimota School. Her teaching experience led to a particular interest in using literature, especially theatre, to educate and inform. These experiences eventually prompted her to use theatre to sustain a vision of a newly independent Ghana, and to create an African identity using its culture, encompassing all its art forms.[2]

This chapter explores Sutherland's international networks, including her connections to the Rockefeller Foundation and the Afro-Asian Writers Conference. It reveals how her involvement with such networks led to the founding of the Ghana Drama Studio, based on the architectural traditions of the Akan people, and the Ghana Experimental Theatre. The chapter will focus on two foundational moments: the establishment of the Drama Studio in the late 1950s, and the Pan-African Historical Theatre Project (PANAFEST), which Sutherland advocated for throughout the 1980s. Finally, the changing nature and composition of transnational networks and support structures from 1960 to 1990 will be elucidated by comparing and contrasting PANAFEST and the Drama Studio.

## Efua Sutherland and the National Theatre Movement (NTM)

The clarion call from African leaders such as Ahmed Sekou Toure, Kwame Nkrumah and Jomo Kenyatta for a cultural renaissance throughout Africa, both during the fight for and after achieving independence, was aimed at tackling what Paulo Freire described as a 'cultural invasion' of the continent.[3] The National Theatre Movement (NTM) in Ghana, founded in 1956 by Kwame Nkrumah, the first president of Ghana, operated explicitly within this context. Nkrumah conceptualised the NTM as a 'project to shatter the colonial mentality and restore the African personality through arts'.[4] The overarching aim was 'to bring into existence a theatre that will derive its vitality and authenticity from roots firmly planted in the true traditions of the people'.[5] The general understanding among leading members of the NTM was that they 'had the mandate to refashion indigenous Ghanaian traditions to suit our modern theatre through creative experimentation'.[6] Furthermore, it was consensus that 'traditional forms of drama should constitute the basis for a Ghana National Theatre'.[7] In effect, the NTM's concept, purpose and plans represented a systematic and practical effort towards achieving cultural decolonisation.[8] In the context of higher education, Kwame Nkrumah expressed his vision for the arts at the formal opening of the University of Ghana's Institute of Africa Studies in 1962:

> I hope also that the institute, in conjunction with the School of Music and Drama will link the University of Ghana closely with the National Theatre Movement in Ghana. In this way the institute can serve the needs of the people by helping to develop new forms of dance and drama, of music and creative writing, that are at the same time closely related to our Ghanaian traditions and express the ideas and aspirations of our people at this critical stage in our history. This should lead to new strides in our cultural development.[9]

This chapter argues that the life, works and creative experiments of Efua Sutherland are located on a critical, creative and historical continuum that segues with the aspirations of the NTM, of which Sutherland was a leading member. Sutherland herself indicates that although she had been interested in theatre from childhood, 'deciding to do it seriously was the outcome of *her* starting the Ghana Writers Society … after independence … in September 1957'[10] (italics mine), by which time the first phase of the NTM was well underway. She believed that 'a newly independent country needed a force of creative writers'. This chimes conspicuously with Nkrumah's vision of a pan-African unity backed by the arts, reflected in his assertion at the opening of the Drama Studio that 'from now on Africa must look inwards … It is only by our own exertions that our … endeavours can bring about the progress, unity and strength of Africa'. Robert W. July, commenting on this statement, writes that 'it was a sentiment that Efua Sutherland might well have echoed, for it was such thoughts that had launched her several years earlier on the course that led to the founding of the Ghana Experimental Theatre and the construction of its building, the Drama Studio'.[11] Sutherland indicates that her work in relation to the Ghana Experimental Theatre and the subsequent founding of the Drama Studio was part of 'a record of experiences and products gained from training schemes, artistic output, and organizational experimentation', adding that 'this record is clearly one of a first-phase development, which, so to speak, has surveyed and cleared the ground … in support of the idea of a National Theatre Movement'.[12] It is important to note, however, that the first phase of the NTM had its challenges. Funds for training programmes were constantly withdrawn, creating a gap between theoretical and practical performance ability in music and dance, and there were limited training opportunities for actors who performed in English, among other issues. It was therefore unsurprising that in Sutherland's assessment of the first phase of the NTM, she claimed: 'of all the factors signifying the end of the first phase of the National Theatre Movement, the most disquieting is the slowdown in output of creative material, particularly dramatic literature'[13] – a point that gives credence to the stance earlier suggested regarding the context in which her creative works and cultural life, and the institutions she founded and helped establish, should be perceived. She was lamenting deficiencies, including a paucity of creative material and the withdrawal of funds for artistic training, and pointing out the urgent actions the NTM needed to undertake to 'achieve the character to which several important statements and actions by the President of Ghana aspire'.[14] To this end, she declared that 'my own work comes into context here, for it was to the objective of a National Theatre Movement that I linked myself. The need for creative experiments is what interests me most and I could see in this pursuit a chance for developing dramatists and playwrights'.[15]

However, the sociocultural and political challenges facing Ghana were enormous. The dynamics of the country as it came out of colonial rule demanded that leaders' rhetoric be directly followed with pragmatic action. A case in point was the debate on language and decolonisation. Sutherland and most of the leading members of the NTM believed that Ghana, a unitary state consisting of many ethnic groups, each with their own traditions, dialects and cultural differences, should not allow the issue of language to be a source of disunity. This was a pertinent issue because cultural and ethnic debates and differences featured in the politics of the first republic of Ghana (1960–6) to the extent that political parties were formed on tribal and ethnic lines. Such events threatened the very existence of the newly independent nation. Consequently, members of the NTM ensured that cultural debates 'focussed attention on the vital issue of cross-cultural communication in a linguistically pluralistic society',[16] and addressed 'how to create an integrated and homogenous national theatre audience'.[17] In an effort to achieve national cohesion, despite cultural and linguistic differences, Nkrumah chose English, the coloniser's language, as Ghana's lingua franca (it has remained so to this day). At the time there were over 100 linguistic and ethnic groups in Ghana,[18] and since language identifies a people, its preservation was held dear by many. Therefore, in the interest of not inflaming passions over the politics of language, the choice of English was prudent. Moreover, it was established as a medium of instruction in educational institutions during the colonial period, and the existence of many different ethnic groups in the major Ghanaian cities made it difficult, if not impossible, to use a single Ghanaian language in schools without disadvantaging certain students. Additionally, the education system could not afford to have more than five different local language teachers per school in the major cities.[19] Finally, the choice of any one local language, whether spoken by a majority of Ghanaians or not, could have fuelled further political tribalism and stalled Nkrumah's efforts to create a united nation.

Just as the issue of language became a conundrum in the political arena, so too was the process of decolonising the country, with regard to Ghana's cultural and academic environment, beset with problems. The NTM was intended as a means to break with colonial cultural legacies through artistic performances and literary works that reflected the aspirations of the audience through language.

The use of English for writing and official business in Africa has been discussed by many scholars in postcolonial and decolonial discourses. While some intellectuals like Ngugi wa Thiong'o preferred to write in their native languages, others like Chinua Achebe and Femi Osofisan focused on the hybridisation of English with local African cultural nuances.[20] Sutherland, in agreement with Nkrumah's position on language, opted to use English, a decision that perhaps signalled the futility of arguing over which language to use to identify the Ghanaian people. Achebe quotes Nkrumah as saying that 'the fact that I speak English does not make me an Englishman'.[21] With this statement, Nkrumah sought to separate language from nationality, and implied that language only functioned as a medium of carrying Ghanaians' culture, traditions and lived experiences because they were used to it. Thus, Sutherland, the members of the NTM and many other Ghanaian writers (including Ama Ata Aidoo, J. C. de Graft and Asiedu Yirenkyi) who favoured English in their writings pursued the course of working in English. They drew on local culture by using literary and dramatic works to create a sense of unity and national identity. The NTM's activities thus birthed a wave of theatrical performances intended to foster national cohesion, encourage people to support the ideologies of the Nkrumah government, and create a performance form that was authentically Ghanaian. Having a space in which to train new performers and writers, and test their creative works on stage, became crucial. Sutherland founded the Ghana Drama Studio to create a sanctuary where new and authentic Ghanaian creative works could be rehearsed and performed.

# Efua Sutherland and the Ghana Drama Studio

In founding the Drama Studio, Efua Sutherland sought to create a symbol, 'something tangible that people could point at and say, "That's the place where African drama, experimental African drama is going on."' Her convictions were summed up in the statement: 'the drama studio as a building is really important, because it helped to make the whole idea gel for the people'.[22] This was a modern theatre rooted in the Ghanaian sociocultural cosmology. When Robert W. July first saw the Drama Studio, it made an impression on him:

> It was a small structure, unpretentious but handsome, traditional in inspiration yet modern in design. The dazzling whitewashed walls with their dark trim resembled a village compound and were meant to. Inside, at one end, a platform stage was covered by an overhanging roof; but the auditorium, with its seats of carved Ghanaian stools, was open to the night sky. It stood in a rough, weedy place approached by dusty footpaths, its simplicity contrasting sharply with the gaudy grandeur of Accra's nearby Ambassador Hotel.[23]

The Ghana Drama Studio was a significant milestone in terms of both Sutherland's creative journey and the aspirations of the NTM. It was made possible with financial support from the Ghanaian government, the Arts Council of Ghana and the Rockefeller Foundation.[24] This complex transnational network helped Sutherland in many ways. Although she had started the Ghana Experimental Theatre sometime prior, it was external funding that allowed her to realise her vision of a performance space attuned to people's cultural sensibilities. As Robert W. July observed, 'the Drama Studio came as a sudden answer to the problem Sutherland had been having' of 'starting the theatre programme'.[25] The Drama Studio served as a place for creative experiments of many kinds, and for networking for both local and international artists and theatre enthusiasts. On the local front, it was a melting pot for artistic creation and creative experimentation, of which Sutherland was a lead expert. Many drama groups from different parts of the country and higher education institutions and government secondary schools experimented and performed at the studio. Sutherland chronicles[26] some of these local artists and groups and their respective performances: Ashanti Agoroma (traditional Ashanti dance); the Theatre Club (*Antigone in Haiti*); Winneba Secondary School (*The King and I*); the Accra Drama Group (*Ama*); the National

Theatre Group (*Afram*); the Odasani Drama Studio Players (*Ananse and the Glue Man*); and the University Drama Studio Players (Jean Anouilh's *Antigone*). The international artists who performed at the Drama Studio during this period include Louis Armstrong, Phillipa Schuyler, Sadi-Knight, Stanislas Niedzielski, Kendall Taylor, the Benthien Quartet of Hamburg, the Congolese Dance Troupe, the Nigerian Opera Troupe, Cozy Cole and a group of Chinese acrobats, to mention but a few.

The vibrant performing-arts activities that took place from 1956 to 1965 in Ghana were the heartbeat of the NTM, and a bedrock from which other theatrical activities expanded. Sutherland's Drama Studio not only served as an incubator for performing artists, but also as a hub for the activities of the NTM. It is worth noting that international artists and groups came to Ghana via a cultural exchange programme under the auspices of the Interim Committee for the Arts Council of the Gold Coast, the Arts Council of Ghana and the Institute of Art and Culture.[27]

These cultural-exchange programmes and performances were strategic in that they strengthened the NTM by offering Ghanaians opportunities to learn from the experiences of artists from across the globe. Furthermore the performances arising from these cultural exchanges served as a motivation to create new Ghanaian performances that synthesised Ghanaian traditional art forms and foreign elements. This was a crucial advantage for the NTM, as exposure to performances from other countries provided a reference for developing new Ghanaian dramatic forms based on local culture. Undoubtedly, these cultural exchanges afforded Sutherland the opportunity to establish and maintain connections with foreign artists, particularly those whose work was relevant to Pan-African activities.

One of the most enduring legacies nurtured by Sutherland at the Drama Studio, within the aims and aspiration of the NTM, was the creation of Anansegoro, a dramatic form rooted in the Akan oral storytelling tradition of Anansesem. Sutherland's quest to champion the aims and aspirations of the NTM, even after it was disbanded, led not only to experimentation with an authentic, functional theatre in Atwia in the central region of Ghana, but also to a desire to create a historical drama festival, which would metamorphose into PANAFEST in the late twentieth century.

## Sutherland and PANAFEST

Sutherland was committed to creating an authentic Ghanaian theatrical form inspired by traditional Ghanaian customs. However, she also believed this form should reflect its time. This quest led to a proposal for a historical drama festival, one located within the purview of the NTM. Kofi Anyidoho and Victor Yankah both acknowledge that PANAFEST grew from Sutherland's idea of a historical drama festival. Professor Esi Sutherland-Addy – Efua Sutherland's daughter – in an interview with the *Contemporary Journal of African Studies*,[28] asserts that the roots of PANAFEST can be found in a memo written by Efua Sutherland in the 1980s. However, Yankah[29] contends that PANAFEST in its current form is a pale reflection of Sutherland's original proposal, having deviated from it in many ways. What is not in contention is that both the historical drama festival and PANAFEST took inspiration from the aims and objectives of the NTM. Therefore, PANAFEST represents a continuation of NTM's efforts to create a theatre that would nurture the creative arts in Ghana and further synergise the creativity of Africans in the diaspora.

PANAFEST is a biennial festival held in Cape Coast, Accra, and other selected cities in Ghana. The first PANAFEST took place in December 1992 under the presidency of Jerry John Rawlings, organised under the auspices of the Ministry of Culture led by Mohammed Ben Abdallah.[30] Broadly, PANAFEST has two major components: an intellectual element and an artistic element. For the intellectual component, often a colloquium is organised around the theme chosen for that particular PANAFEST. This allows academics and others to have a stimulating discourse centred on tourism, Pan-African diasporic connections and indigenous art forms. The artistic component usually draws crowds and tourists to durbars, traditional performances and the castles of Cape Coast and Elmina, and includes tours of the slave routes and slave markets that convey the realities of the transatlantic slave trade.

Arguably, Sutherland's diasporic networks helped shape her thoughts and creative process. Her international experience, pan-African collaborations, and the gaps she identified in the dramatic literature field in both Ghana and Africa played a critical role. They served as inspiration for the historical theatre festival while Sutherland worked at the drama unit of the Institute of African Studies at the University of Ghana.[31] Her Pan-African connections started with her contact with Africans abroad when she undertook further education in the UK. Efua Sutherland and her husband frequently hosted artists and other Pan-Africanists from across the world, and Esi Sutherland-Addy[32] says their 'home became a meeting place for personalities from the African Diaspora. Many repatriated persons of African descent also became family friends … every now and then, courtesy calls were made by freedom fighters who had become leading political figures such as Julius Nyerere'.[33] These relationships demonstrate that the experiences of the African diaspora, as well as Pan-Africanism, were a known reality to Sutherland. Much as Yankah might have reservations about how the festival changed, its expansion reflected Sutherland's lived reality. Sutherland's proposal for the historical theatre festival took into consideration both Pan-African connections, and the need for the festival to give those in the African diaspora an opportunity to reconnect with their roots. This was evident in the approach she proposed for curating the festival. Yankah summarises the measures proposed by Sutherland as follows:

> Orientation workshops were proposed to assist the [participating] writers to produce well-crafted scripts. The second phase asked for a 'call-in of scripts' and the winning dramas were to be produced at the festival. The successful plays would be produced at the festival. To ensure variety other plays would surely be produced alongside these dramas and, in addition, there would be music and dance. Participants would come from not only Ghana, but from other parts of Africa and from the African diaspora.[34]

Sutherland contended that these preparatory workshops should take place one year prior to the festival to ensure a well-structured effort and foster an explosion of artistic works. She had a conscious desire to use the festival as a platform for discovering and training new writers. The end goal was for these writers to produce works that addressed the needs of Ghanaians, Africans living on the continent and Africans in the diaspora. The proposition, which did not differ significantly from the goals of the NTM, eventually became an integral part of the processes that led to at least the initial phase of PANAFEST.

## Conclusion

To confine Efua Sutherland to a single field of expertise would be to do her an injustice. In Ghana, and globally, she embodies the aspirations of theatre experts, cultural activists and creatives. She dared to conduct an experiment that birthed a dramatic form rooted in indigenous African knowledge and art forms, and excelled in a field typically considered a preserve of men. She understood the interrelationship between theory and practice, and the need for a training and performance space for performers. She also recognised the importance of establishing institutions to train artists and artisans. Everything she did was oriented towards decolonising Ghanaian arts and culture, and furthering the aspirations of the NTM.

Sutherland's work established a foundation for the survival of Ghanaian theatre and artistic works. Her ground-breaking experiments led to the creation of an original Ghanaian theatre form, Anansegoro, and her works and creative accomplishments influenced those of other notable Ghanaian writers, including Martin Owusu, Ama Ata Aidoo, Yaw Asare and Kofi Anyidoho. In her bid to see the NTM succeed, she launched initiatives that helped entrench modern theatre in Ghanaian higher education institutions. Her other notable initiatives include founding the Ghana Drama Studio and establishing institutions for the creative training of artists. The credit for PANAFEST's continued existence goes to Sutherland for originally proposing a historical drama festival. Both the festival and Sutherland's work in its totality are geared toward fostering a Pan-African connection, and reflect the continuation of the NTM's aspiration to use the arts to confront the challenges facing post-independence Africa.

From the Afro-Asian Writers Conference in Tashkent to Sutherland's dealings with international philanthropic organisations such as the Rockefeller Foundation, her network spanned both sides of the cultural Cold War, expanded her worldview and facilitated her creative achievements. Although her efforts received support within Ghana, it was not until her transnational network expanded that she started seeing her visions materialise. Therefore, an examination of Sutherland's achievements needs to take account of her relationships with funding agencies and specialist organisations, which assisted in making a significant part of her aspirations a reality. Through the Arts Council of Ghana and the NTM she oversaw a diversified cultural exchange in Ghana featuring performing arts from across the globe. In addition to those performances given above, in 1963 the Nigerian Opera Troupe treated Ghanaian audiences to a performance of the *Palm-Wine Drinkard*, while the Nottingham Playhouse company performed *Twelfth Night*, *Macbeth* and *Arms and the Man*.

Sutherland's performing arts and cultural network cut across international boundaries and continents. She was a global cultural expert, and is a seminal figure in African theatre.

## Notes

1  See Anyidoho, 2000, 78; Adutwumwah, 2020, 43.
2  Agovi, 1990, 15.
3  Freire, 1972, 185.

4  Donkor, 2021, 120.
5  Hammond, 1977, 7.
6  Agovi, 1990, 3.
7  Morisseau-Leroy, 1965, 10.
8  Morisseau-Leroy, 1968, 92.
9  Nkrumah, 1963, 13.
10  July, 2007, 160.
11  July, 1987, 74.
12  Sutherland, 2000, 46.
13  Sutherland, 2000, 46.
14  Sutherland, 2000, 45.
15  Sutherland, 2014, 29.
16  Agovi, 1990, 4.
17  Agovi, 1990, 4.
18  Akramov and Asante, 2009, 20.
19  Tackie-Ofosu et al., 2015, 81.
20  See Achebe, 1989; Thiong'o, 2006.
21  Achebe, 1989, 269.
22  July, 2007, 163.
23  July, 1987, 73.
24  See Donkor, 2017, 29–56; Botwe-Asamoah, 2005, 130–7; July, 1987, 73–4; Gibbs, 2009,
xx.
25  July, 2007, 163.
26  Sutherland, 2000, 55–6.
27  Sutherland, 2000, 55.
28  Ampofo, 2020, 127.
29  Yankah, 2012, 2.
30  Ampofo, 2020, 128. See also Chapter 2 in this volume.
31  Sutherland, 2000, 50–1.
32  Ampofo, 2020, 126.
33  Ampofo, 2020, 127.
34  Yankah, 2012, 7.

# References

Achebe, Chinua. 'The politics of language'. In *The Post-Colonial Studies Reader*, edited by Gareth
Griffiths, Helen Tiffins and Bill Ashcroft, 143–57. London: Routledge, 1989.
Adutwumwah, Doreen Gyimah. 'The continuities within the Ghanaian festival scene: the
performance of nation building and identity formation'. Bard College, 2020. Accessed 29
October 2023. https://digitalcommons.bard.edu/senproj_s2020/195.
Agovi, Kofi E. 'The origin of literary theatre in colonial Ghana, 1920–1957', *Research Reviews* 6 (1)
(1990): 1–23.
Akramov, K. T. and Asante, F. 'Decentralization and local public services in Ghana: do geography
and ethnic diversity matter?' International Food Policy Research Institute discussion paper
00872, Australian Council of State School Organisations, 2009.
Ampofo, Adomako. 'In conversation with Professor Esi Sutherland', *Contemporary Journal of
African Studies* 7 (1) (2020): 126–41.
Anyidoho, Kofi. 'Dr Efua Sutherland: a biographical sketch'. In *FonTomFrom: Contemporary
Ghanaian literature, theatre and film*, edited by Kofi Anyidoho and James Gibbs, 77–82.
Amsterdam: Rodopi, 2000.
Collins, Stephen. 'Playwriting and Postcolonialism: Identifying the key factors in the development
and diminution of playwriting in Ghana 1916–2007'. MPhil(R) thesis. University of Glasgow,
2011.
Djisenu, John K. 'The art of narrative drama in Ghana'. In *FonTomFrom: Contemporary Ghanaian
literature, theatre and film*, edited by Kofi Anyidoho and James Gibbs, 37–44. Amsterdam:
Rodopi, 2000.

Donkor, David Afriyie. 'Toward a new African personality: The National Theatre Movement of Ghana from Nkrumah to Rawlings'. In *Theatre after Empire*, edited by Megan E. Geigner and Harvey Young, 118–32. London and New York: Routledge, 2021.

Freire, Paulo. *Pedagogy of the Oppressed*. New York: Herder and Herder, 1972.

Graham-White, Anthony. 'Drama'. In *European-Language Writing in Sub-Saharan Africa* (Vol. 2), edited by Albert S. Gerard and Gyorgy M. Vajda, 810–19. Amsterdam: John Benjamins Publishing Company, 1986.

Hammond, Albert. 'The moving drama of the arts in Ghana', *Sankofa* 1 (2) and 1 (3) (1997).

July, Robert W. *An African Voice: The role of the humanities in African independence*. Durham, NC: Duke University Press, 1987.

July, Robert W. '"Here, then, is Efua": Sutherland and the Drama Studio'. In *The Legacy of Efua Sutherland: Pan-African cultural activism*, edited by Anne Adams and Esi Sutherland-Addy, 160–5. Banbury: Ayebia Clarke Publishing, 2007.

Morisseau-Leroy, Felix. 'The Ghana Theatre Movement', *Ghana Cultural Review* 1 (1) (1965): 10–14.

Morisseau-Leroy, Felix. 'African national theatre: for whom?', *Okyeame* 4 (1) (1968): 91–4.

Nkrumah, Kwame. 'The African genius' (speech). Accra: Ministry of Information and Broadcasting, 1963.

Okpewho, Isidore. *African Oral Literature: Backgrounds, character and continuity*. Bloomington and Indianapolis: Indiana University Press, 1992.

Sutherland, Efua T. 'The second phase of the National Theatre Movement in Ghana'. In *FonTomFrom: Contemporary Ghanaian literature, theatre and film*, edited by Kofi Anyidoho and James Gibbs, 45–76. Amsterdam: Rodopi, 2000.

Sutherland, Efua T. 'The theatre movement in Ghana and the development of drama'. In *The Performing Arts in Africa: Ghanaian perspectives*, edited by Awo Mana Asiedu, John Collins, Francis Gbormittah and Francis Nii Yartey, 22–31. Banbury, Oxfordshire: Ayebia Clarke Publishing, 2014.

Tackie-Ofosu, Vivian, Mahama, Sheriffa, Vandyck, E. Solomon Tetteh Dosoo, Kumador, David Kwame and Toku, Ama Afriyie. 'Mother tongue usage in Ghanaian pre-schools: perceptions of parents and teachers', *Journal of Education and Practice* 6 (34) (2015): 81–7.

Thiong'o, Ngugi wa. 'The language of African literature'. In *The Post-Colonial Studies Reader*, edited by Gareth Griffiths, Helen Tiffin and Bill Ashcroft, 389–403. London: Routledge, 2006.

Yankah, Victor. 'The Pan-African Historical Theatre Festival (PANAFEST) in Ghana, 1992–2010: the vision and the reality'. In *African Theatre 11: Festivals*, edited by Martin Banham, James Gibbs and Femi Osofisan, 45–55. New York: Boydell & Brewer, 2012.

# Index

References to images are in *italics*; references to notes are indicated by n.

institutions 3–7, 191–3
  and networks 10–11, 12–13
  and Occupied Palestinian
    Territories 67–8
  and Pan-African festivals 38, 44–6
  and the Philippines 159–60
  and Theatre of the Oppressed
    197–200
intellectuals 105–9, 111–12, 114n8
internal enmity 112–13
International Institute for Puppetry
  25, 27–8
international organisations *see* ITI;
  UNIMA
International Union for Puppetry
  Arts *see* UNIMA
IPTA (International Popular Theatre
  Alliance) 59, 60, 126
Iran 22
Iraq 102, 107
Iron Curtain *see* Cold War
Irving, Jules 122
Islamic culture 180, 182–3, 227–8
Israel 67, 71, 72, 74, 113
ITI (International Theatre Institute)
  5, 6–7, 13, 17–23, 28
  and Boal 200
  and costs 208–9
  and CTWT 214, 215, 216
  and India 29n18
  and PETA 205, 210, 211–12
  and Rockefeller Foundation 156–7
  and TfD 52, 53, 60–4
  and workshops 125–6

Jackson, Maxwell 94, 230–1
Jacob, Max 23
Jaji, Tsitsi Ella 39
Japan 23, 29n35, 154, 182
Jedlicki, Jerzy 108, 111–12
Jenin refugee camp 74, 77
*Jesus Christ Superstar* (musical) 133
Johnstone, Keith 101
Jones, Arthur Creech 90–1
Jones, Brooks 210
Jones, Margo: *Theatre-in-the-Round*
  89, 162–3, 166
Jordan, Aniela 143

Joseph, Christopher Odhiambo 71
July, Robert W. 13, 221–2, 225–31,
  236–7
  and Ghana 234–5, 242, 245
  and Ibadan 231–3
Jurkowski, Henryk 19, 25, 27,
  29n33

Kalinangan Ensemble 209, 210
Kamlongera, Christopher 53
Kanan, Meriç Sümen 178
Karadağ, Nurhan 180
Al-Kasaba Theatre (Palestine) 71
Kawadwa, Byron 94
Kawajiri, Taiji 25
Kempny, Marian 107
Kenya 58–9, 85, 86, 95
Kenyatta, Jomo 241
Kerr, David 54, 56
Kidd, Ross 53, 59, 60–1, 126
Kimmel, Anna Jayne 45
King, Martin Luther 13, 240
Kitt, Eartha 122
Kiyingi-Kagwe, Wycliffe: *Gwosussa*
  *Emwani* 94
Klein, William 39
Königsberger, Otto 89
Korsberg, Hanna 17
Kurtz, Maurice 20

Labad, Lutgardo 217
laboratories 119–21, 125
Laedza Batanani project 53–4, 55,
  56
LaMaMa Experimental Theatre Club
  13, 205, 211, 214–15
Lang, Jack 194, 196
Laski, Harold 158
Latin American Theatre Institute
  21
Le Corbusier 89
League of Nations 20
Lebanon 102, 210–11
*Lei Rouanet* (Rouanet Law) 10, 132,
  139, 140–2, 143, 144
Leicester Playhouse 134
Lempel, Joseph 63
Lessing, Gotthold Ephraim 85